HISTORICAL PERSPECTIVES
and the INTERNATIONAL STATUS
of COMPARATIVE PSYCHOLOGY

HISTORICAL PERSPECTIVES
and the INTERNATIONAL STATUS
of COMPARATIVE PSYCHOLOGY

edited by
Ethel Tobach

LEA LAWRENCE ERLBAUM ASSOCIATES, PUBLISHERS
1987   Hillsdale, New Jersey   Hove and London

Lawrence Erlbaum Associates, Inc., Publishers
365 Broadway
Hillsdale, New Jersey 07642

Library of Congress Cataloging-in-Publication Data

Historical perspectives and the international status of comparative psychology.

"Proceedings of the First (Toronto, 1983) and Second (Acapulco, 1984) Conferences of the
International Society for Comparative Psychology"—Pref.
  Bibliography: p.
  Includes index.
  1. Psychology, Comparative—History—Congresses.
2. Psychology, Comparative—History—20th century—Congresses. I. Tobach, Ethel, 1921–
II. International Society for Comparative Psychology. Conference (1st : 1983 : Toronto, Ont.) III.
International Society for Comparative Psychology. Conference (2nd : 1984 : Acapulco, Mexico)
BF671.H57 1987   156   86-24076
ISBN 0-89859-651-3

Printed in the United States of America
10 9 8 7 6 5 4 3 2 1

Contents

List of Contributors

RUBÉN ARDILA, National University of Colombia, Bogota, Colombia

ROBERT A. BOAKES, University of Sussex, Brighton, England

THOMAS C. CADWALLADER, Indiana State University, Terre Haute, Indiana

JACK DEMAREST, Monmouth College, West Long Branch, New Jersey

GRAZIANO FIORITO, Stazione Zoologica, Naples, Italy

LAUREL FURUMOTO, Wellesley College, Wellesley, Massachusetts

GARY GREENBERG, The Wichita State University, Wichita, Kansas

NANCY K. INNIS, The University of Western Ontario, London, Canada

PAUL T. MOUNTJOY, Western Michigan University, Kalamazoo, Michigan

KIYOKO MUROFUSHI, Primate Research Institute, Kyoto University, Inuyama, Japan

ANTHONY NIJSSEN, M.J. VAN RIJSWIJK, University of Amsterdam, Amsterdam, The Netherlands

MAURICIO R. PAPINI, Institute of Biology and Experimental Medicine, Buenos Aires, Argentina

JAMES REED, Rutgers University, New Brunswick, New Jersey

ELIZABETH SCARBOROUGH, State University of New York at Fredonia, Fredonia, New York

CHARLES W. TOLMAN, University of Victoria, Victoria, B.C., Canada

EVERETT J. WYERS, State University of New York at Stony Brook, Stony Brook, New York

Preface

This volume combines the proceedings of the First (Toronto, 1983) and Second (Acapulco, 1984) Conferences of the International Society for Comparative Psychology (ISCP). It reflects the present stage of development of this young organization that was born during a period of proliferation of scientific organizations. Some of the new societies are a response to the increasing specialization in science (e.g., International Society for Developmental Psychobiology); others are an integration of many disciplines under the influence of new technology (e.g., Society for Cognitive Science). The ISCP is a revival of an early subdiscipline in psychology generated by Darwin and Romanes. The Society is integrative rather than specialized and, as in the case of all behavioral sciences, makes use of sophisticated instrumentation and methods. It arose in response to the need for an organization that eschews sectarianism by operationalizing the aim of the earlier comparative psychology, defining it as the study of the evolution and development of behavior. The organization takes pride in the eclectic theoretical representation of its interdisciplinary membership of biologists and psychologists.

In addition to providing a forum for discussion and encouraging the study of behavioral evolution and development, it seeks to promote the training of students in comparative psychology and to bring to the international community of psychologists the special contributions of comparative psychology.

The society also reflects the fact that many present-day comparative psychologists are sensitive to the needs of the people of the world to develop ways to manage their resources so that they can take advantage of technological advances without destroying the ecosystem. They are also aware of the shrinking biosphere in which animals can be observed in environments that have not been modified by people. They are, thus, responsive to the need to promote the exchange of knowledge among the peoples of the world who come together while in the pursuit of the understanding of the evolution and development of behavior.

Ethel Tobach

HISTORICAL PERSPECTIVES

INTRODUCTION I:
Some Historical Perspectives

Ethel Tobach
American Museum of Natural History, New York

Most of the chapters in this volume were presented at sessions organized by the newly formed International Society for Comparative Psychology either before or during the 15th annual meeting of the Cheiron Society at Toronto, Ontario, Canada, 1983. The plan to hold the meeting in conjunction with the Cheiron Society was prompted by the need to form the new organization before the next International Congress of Psychology sponsored by the International Union of Psychological Sciences scheduled to take place in 1984 in Acapulco, Mexico. The timing was essential, because the new organization would have to be presented at that meeting for consideration for affiliate status to the IUPsyS, or else wait 2 or 4 more years for such action, if it were to take place. By having its first international meeting in 1983, the Society could establish itself as having had at least one international meeting, elect officers, regularly publish some type of communication for its members, and in general "be in business" by 1984.

In fact, by the time the 1984 IUPsyS International Congress of Psychology took place, programs had been organized, the Newsletter had appeared fairly regularly, and the Society was able to apply for affiliate status in 1984, which it was unanimously granted by the IUPsyS Assembly.

Meeting with the Cheiron Society was most appropriate, and the theme of History in this first volume of the proceedings of the Society emerges naturally for several reasons. During the last 2 decades, comparative psychologists have become self-conscious about their history because of the developments and strains within the scientific community that studies the evolution and development of behavior (Tobach, Adler, & Adler, 1973). This was a predisposing process that led the comparative psychologists to the Cheiron Society.

Second, the very first meeting of a comparative psychology society took place

3

in Canada. T. W. Mills founded the first such society at the veterinary school of McGill University and published the first journal devoted to comparative psychology as such (Cadwallader, 1984).

Third, as this was the founding meeting of the International Society for Comparative Psychology, the sense of history was preeminent.

This volume is presented in two sections: early history and recent history. In chapter 1, Mountjoy makes a claim for Emperor Frederick to be known as the first comparative psychologist. The analysis by Furumoto and Scarborough (chapter 7) of the history of two women who exemplify different roads by which individuals come to study the behavior of animals, given the constraints of gender discrimination, illuminates another corner of little known history. Chapter 9 by Demarest presents further information about the development of comparative psychology in the United States given the constraints of philosophical and societal pressures.

These three chapters establish an approach to the discipline of comparative psychology that draws strength from the past to enable growth in the future.

REFERENCES

Cadwallader, T. C. (1984). Neglected aspects of the evolution of American comparative and animal psychology. In G. Greenberg & E. Tobach (Eds.), *Behavioral evolution and integrative levels. Proceedings of the First T. C. Schneirla Conference* (pp. 15–56). Hillsdale, NJ: Lawrence Erlbaum Associates.
Tobach, E., Adler, H. E., & L. L. Adler (Eds.). (1973). *Comparative psychology at issue,* Vol. 290 (pp. 197). Annals of the New York Academy of Sciences.

1 The First Systematic Account of Comparative Avian Behavior[1]

Paul T. Mountjoy
Western Michigan University

Comparative psychology is a speciality area that not only greatly contributes to the relationship between psychology and the other sciences but also enables us to understand more fully those continua that unite species in terms of their anatomy, physiology, and behavior (Shaffer, 1983). It does so by study of the behavior of both our close and remote animal relatives and thus provides an intimate link between psychology and general biology—including paleontology. In this sense, comparative psychology is in the forefront of the battle to establish psychology as a natural science among the other natural sciences. Consequently, it behooves us to be familiar with the historical development of comparative psychology as an intellectual discipline, for one would expect indication of the path toward acceptance as a natural science because of the close relationship between it and the science of biology.

The historical development of systematic biology is being explored by historians of science, and one recent work is devoted to ornithology (Farber, 1982). The general development is too well known to be detailed here. To summarize briefly by identification of three major figures in that development: Linnaeus (1707–1778) proposed a system of binomial classification, Cuvier (1769–1832) developed the concept of comparative anatomy, and Darwin (1809–1882) showed that anatomical and behavioral similarities and differences were a matter of relationship in terms of descent.

---

[1]This chapter represents a modified version of a presentation given at the session organized by the International Society for Comparative Psychology at the 15th annual meeting of Cheiron at Toronto, Ontario, Canada, 1983.

EMPEROR FREDERICK II

Less well known are the more remote origins of comparative psychology in the treatise of a man who lived some 700 years past and whom I nominate as the first competent proto-comparative psychologist. (For a complete biography see Kantorowicz, 1931.)

Frederick II (1194–1250),[2] author of the first work to be written in the empirical spirit since classical Antiquity, the Holy Roman Emperor, King of Sicily and Jerusalem, was a true Renaissance man born some centuries before his time. Fluent in six languages, he was greatly influenced by the Moslems who had occupied southern Italy and Sicily until shortly before his birth. He illustrates that flowering of culture which frequently appears when two dissimilar cultures come into contact, and the resulting mixture resembles the hybrid vigor consequent to the crossbreeding of two floral strains.

Called the "Baptized Sultan of Sicily" (p. xxxvii) and a practicing Roman Catholic, he imported Moslem and Hebrew philosophers to his court and, incidently, kept not only a troupe of oriental dancing girls, but also a harem complete with eunuchs in his huge Apulian castle at Lucera. He corresponded with Islamic rulers and oriental scholars concerning religous dogmas, mathematical problems, astronomical puzzles, geography, cartography, and astrological questions. A thoroughgoing rationalist, he frequently and openly stated that the Christian answers to many problems were unsatisfactory. As might be predicted, he was usually in conflict with the current occupant of Saint Peter's throne.

He commissioned Michael Scotus to translate Aristotle's biological works from Greek to Latin, and Giordeno Ruffo to compose the first treatise on veterinary medicine in western Europe. We know the influence of this first translation of Aristotle into Latin, but few of us are aware of the importance of Ruffo's treatise that was translated into various languages and was the standard work for many centuries.

Founder of the University of Naples in 1224 (the first European university to have a charter) he is without doubt the first ruler of relatively modern times to attempt to establish a civilization based entirely on rational principles. Called in his own time *"stupor mundi et immutator mirablis"* (the wonder of the world) (p. xxxvi) Frederick was truly unique. His death at age 56, the fact that his son and successor Manfred was shortly thereafter killed in battle by Charles of Anjou, who then executed Frederick's grandson Conradin on the basis of trumped-up charges, are among the factors responsible for the demise of this plan

---

[2]Unless a specific citation to another publication is given I cite the Wood and Fyfe (1943) translation of Frederick II (ca. 1250) and/or the commentary that accompanies that translation. Arabic page numbers refer to the translation and appended materials, whereas small Roman numerals refer to the translators' commentary.

for rational government. The complete extinction of his descendants is one of the true tragedies of history (see Kantor, 1983).

The Emperor's empirical orientation is unmistakable. He conducted experiments on the artificial incubation of bird eggs (p. 53) and investigated whether vultures found their food by sight or smell through the temporary occlusion of vision by sealing (that is, closing the eyelids by means of a suture) (p. 22). He brought up children in isolation in order to elucidate the process of speech development, and had condemned (and executed) criminals dissected in order to determine the respective effect of sleep and exercise on digestion (Haskins, 1921).

Always the rational empiricist, he denied the truth of the legend, current for many centuries, that "barnacle" (properly "bernicla") geese were generated from either trees or barnacles—stating that this erroneous opinion arose from ignorance—and that the true state of affairs was that the nesting grounds lay far to the north, where people did not venture, and thus the nests, eggs, and immature young had not yet been seen (pp. 51–52). Today we know that this species (*Branta bernicla*—formerly *Branta leucopis*) actually nests in Spitzenbergen, Greenland, and in the north-west of Siberia (Collins, 1981); areas that were unknown to southern Europeans at that time.

A good general zoologist, the Emperor maintained a menagerie, which rivaled that assembled by Ptolemy II, a millenium and a half earlier (Mountjoy, 1980). It contained the first elephant seen in Europe since Roman times, the first giraffe ever imported into Europe, as well as a polar bear, both dromedary and bactrian camels, lions, panthers, leopards, cheetahs, monkeys, and many other species of mammals and birds (pp. xxxvii-xxxviii, xlvii; and Sarton, 1931).

This chapter emphasizes the Emperor's commitment to empirical observation and it is for his major contribution to ornithology that Frederick is worthy of discussion here. Between 1244 and 1250 he either wrote or dictated that wonderful first book (pp. xxxviii–xxxix) to embody the rational and empirical spirit of modern science with reference to which I began this paean to his accomplishments. (For a discussion of the Emperor's personal copy of this work see pp. lxii–lxx and Mountjoy, 1976, which describe different aspects of the Vatican Library, MS. Pal. Lat. 1071.)

The *De Arte Venandi cum Avibus* (literally, *The Art of Hunting with Birds*) is not the general work on ornithology that the Emperor had planned to write if his untimely death had not prevented its execution but is, as its title indicated, largely devoted to the practice of falconry. However, in spite of its emphasis on behavior technology, it contained original observations on comparative anatomy and species-specific behavior as well. The major authority cited is Aristotle's 19 books devoted to animal life: *De Animalibus, De Partibus Animalius,* and *De Generatione Animalium*. It must be pointed out that the Emperor regarded Aristotle as relying far too much on hearsay and tradition, and being deficient in practical experience, especially with raptors (p. xxxix). Frederick was never bashful about criticism of those whom he felt deserved it, and disagreements with Aristotle are frequent and detailed (pp. 3–4, 7, 9, 15, 19, 30, 40, 61, and 108).

Perhaps the most important property of Frederick's treatise is that for the first time in many centuries animal behaviors are presented not as illustrations of the glory of God and representations of salvation and the promise of immortality, but instead as natural occurrences that are of value and worthy of study in their own right. Shortly after the rise of Christianity to dominance in western Europe the tradition of the Medieval bestiary began with the appearance of *Physiologus* that combined the acute naturalistic observations of the ancient world with Neo-Platonic mysticism and Christian gnosticism in a perversion of science. (See White, 1954, for a readily accessible modern translation of a 12th century Latin bestiary and a history of this genre; comparison to the contemporaneous *De Arte* is most instructive.) The earliest works on systematic zoology (e.g., Topsell, 1658) drew in large part from bestiaries rather than actual observations and even retained the convention of listing animals alphabetically!) Indeed, *King Dancus,* one of the oldest extant works on falconry (Mountjoy, 1980) is marred by the drawing of Christian moral lessons from the practice of falconry.

The pursuit of falconry was the Emperor's obsession, even in comparison to other Medieval noblemen who devoted an inordinate amount of time to its practice. The Imperial Register for 1239–1240 actually contains the names of 50 of Frederick's falconers (Haskins, 1921). On one occasion his army was routed during an important siege when he decided to relax from the cares of military command and devote a day to the sport. He imported expert falconers from Syria and Arabia and actually built castles in isolated regions to allow the pursuit of this almost compulsive passion for falconry.

As mentioned previously, it was between 1244 and 1250 that he either wrote or dictated the *De Arte*. It contained the following original anatomical observations: The pneumaticity of the avian skeleton, the form of the avian sternum, the structure of the avian lung, and the avian uropygial, or oil gland (Sarton, 1931).

It is a sad commentary on the current state of scholarship in the history of psychology in general and of comparative psychology in particular—as well as my own ignorance—that I must first establish the Emperor's status as an original scientist by referring to his anatomical contributions. If more were known about the chronology of medieval and prior behavioral observations (Haskins, 1921) we could more readily assign proper priorities of discovery. However, most historians of psychology prefer to devote their time and energies to the explication of the doctrines of those recent historical personages whose theories have hindered the scientific progress of psychology as much if not more than they have furthered its evolution towards the goal of a natural science (Kantor, 1963, 1969). If only historians as a group recognized the importance of empirical observations (as well as theoretical predilections) in science, I would be able to tell you a very different story from the one I now relate here.

Frederick II mentioned or described over 100 genera and/or species of birds (pp. 531–556). Although a few are not identifiable today because they are only given a terse comment in passing, the great majority are readily identified by the modern ornithologist. Remember, this is not the general work on ornithology that he planned. These 100 or so genera and species include a significant number of European, North African (e.g., the ostrich), and western Asian (e.g., pea-fowl) birds. He discussed not just falcons, hawks, vultures, owls, eagles, and other raptors, but also storks, cranes, herons, ducks, geese, pheasants, shore birds, pigeons, passerines, etc.

By contrast, Frederick's contemporary Albertus Magnus (1193–1280) made one contribution to ornithological literature (p.xlviii) that was marred by the inclusion of much unfounded folklore and legend (Harting, 1891). However, Ulysse Aldrovandi (1522–1605), that great pioneer in systematic biology, quoted extensively, and in lauditory fashion, from *De Arte* (p. 562).

DE ARTE VENANDI CUM AVIBUS

I now describe *De Arte* and its unique contributions to ornithology and comparative psychology. The treatise is composed of six books, and the last five of these are almost completely devoted to behavior.

Book I, entitled "The Structure and Habits of Birds," contains 57 chapters and all, save the introductory chapter, contain detailed discussions of taxonomy, anatomy, and behavior.

Taxonomy

Aristotle had divided the class Aves into two major groups: water fowl and land birds (remember how the Hellenes loved dichotomies). Here the Emperor followed Aristotle in part but added a third category: neutral birds (which may at times be on the land and at times on the water). These neutral birds in turn are dived into three subgroups: Those that prefer water to land (e.g., the curlew); those that prefer land to water (e.g., the plover); those that exhibit no preference but divide their time about equally between land and water (e.g., cranes and storks). Thus the Emperor approached a concept resembling that of the modern continuum with major and minor loci and gradual transitions between those loci.

As did Aristotle, Frederick based his groupings on a number of criteria. Among these were sexual relations, parturition, methods of procuring food, residence, and changes in diet. Classifications and criteria (with illustrative and specific examples) are detailed throughout Book I (pp. 7–15, 17, 22–27, 45,

49–52, 62–63, and 79). For example, ducks are subdivided into divers and dabblers (p. 15).

A major division for the Emperor was that between raptors (which feed on the flesh of prey they have killed—never on carrion) and nonraptorial birds, many of which feed partly on grain (e.g., ravens, crows, and magpies) or dead bodies (e.g., vultures) and the "ignoble eagles" (p. 9). The raptorial group includes "eagles, hawks, owls, falcons, and other similar genera" (p. 9). He characterized the raptors as birds that "are strong in flight but walk badly" (p. 9) and any experienced ornithologist is able to verify that observation.

Anatomy

In separate chapters the Emperor described the avian eye, ear, wings, claws, trachea, lungs, esophagus, stomach, liver, kidneys, testes, ovaries, skeleton, etc. Chapter 31 is devoted to that specialized organ found only in avian species, the oil gland, or uropygial gland, located just above the tail on the back of those species that possess it. In this original contribution he accurately described the double-lobed structure of the gland, its duct, and not only the manner of its use but the function of the oil expressed therefrom in protecting the feathers from moisture (p. 31).

As befits the importance of plumage in the only class that possesses feathers, Frederick devoted 10 chapters to a minute description of plumage, its structure and distribution upon the body surface. In addition, chapter 51 elaborated the process of moulting. He pointed out that raptors moult differently than do many nonraptorial birds; that is, many nonraptorials lose all their feathers within a very short period of time (this is especially obvious in the case of ducks and geese) and hence are rendered flightless until the new plumage has grown in. Raptors, and certain other nonraptorial birds, would starve to death under these conditions during moult because flight is an essential aspect of predation and also of reaching feeding grounds for many nonraptorials. Ducks and geese can survive the period of flightlessness because feeding and nesting grounds may be identical for a fairly long time. Also, the marshes in which they nest do serve as a barrier to many predators. However, in raptorial and many nonraptorial species the power of flight is preserved by the successive and symetrical loss of only one pair of flight primaries at a time—one feather from each wing. Not until that pair has been replaced does the next pair drop out. This was most probably an original observation by Frederick.

Behavior

Described here are many behaviors that occupy comparative psychologists today. These include: sleeping, feeding, migration, nesting, mating, coition, egg laying and incubation, the care and feeding of offspring, etc. The originality of his observation, the rejection of hearsay that seemed irrational to him, appears to guarantee his priority. The interpretation of migration as a response to available food supplies as a function of climatic changes has a modern ecological ring and appears to be a considerable advance over the doctrines of his predecessors.

Book II ("Of Falcons Used in Hunting, Their Furniture, Care, and Manning") has been discussed by Mountjoy, Bos, Duncan, and Verplank (1969) with an emphasis on manning (i.e., the basic training of the falcon to tolerate the presence of men and to sit quietly upon the gauntleted fist and eat). Book III ("On the Use of the Lure; on Training Falcons to Fly in a Cast; On Educating Gerfalcons to Fly at Cranes; and On Hounds Used in Falconry") has also been discussed by Mountjoy et al. (1969). Book IV ("Crane Hawking with Gerfalcons and Other Falcons") contains detailed instructions for teaching falcons to attack large and dangerous birds such as cranes, which are never attacked by wild falcons. Book V ("Heron Hawking with Sakers and Other Falcons") continues this discussion. Book VI ("Hawking at the Brook with the Peregrine Falcon") details the procedures to be followed in pursuing water fowl with peregrines. In this case the smaller falcons are utilized in the pursuit of their natural prey (i.e., ducks).

AVIAN BEHAVIORS

I now present a summary, with appropriate page references, of the naturally occurring behaviors observed by the Emperor because these are of special interest to the modern comparative psychologist.

Migration is presented as a relationship between the organism and seasonal changes in its environment (pp. 31–45, and 95). Nonmigratory species are also discussed (pp. 44–45). Calls during migratory flight are regarded as communication rather than involuntary results of the effort of flight as they had been interpreted by Aristotle (p. 34).

Territoriality is touched on in terms of the location of appropriate food supplies and roosting grounds that provide protection from enemies (pp. 15–18, 21–22, and 26–27). Land, neutral, water, and raptorial birds are described, including feeding behaviors.

Care of body surfaces (COBS) is discussed in specific terms of oiling (p. 71, and 192); waterbathing (pp. 8, 157, 170, 190–193, 203, 214, 251, 421, and 426) and sunbathing after waterbathing (pp. 191–193).

Mating (pp. 45–49) includes mention of the sexual function of bird calls (p. 46).

Nesting (pp. 49–52, and 110–112) includes a brief discussion of different types of clutches (see also p. 117).

The pleasure found by all animals in *coitus* (p. 49) is referred to in nearly the same terms as those used by Galen many centuries earlier.

Laying incubating eggs (pp. 52–53), and the Emperor's personal observations of brood parasitism by the cuckoo (pp. 49–50, and 53) are detailed in their presentation.

The care and feeding of the young (pp. 53–56, 117–118, and 130–133) includes a discussion of the fecal sacs of altricial nestlings (p. 55) as well as the behaviors variously called injury feigning or distraction displays. The Emperor did distinguish between precocial and altricial birds.

Development is touched on in the altricial falcon that, if removed from the nest for falconry purposes too early in development, may become a *clamorosus* (in modern falconer's parlance, a ''screamer'') that essentially is useless to the falconer because it calls and gapes for food in the manner of an immature chick rather than attacking prey (p. 616; and Mountjoy et al. 1969).

Bird calls are presented in terms of their functional relationships to food, sexual, and fear behaviors (p. 77) (see migration previously mentioned). The mimicry of human vocalizations by parrots and other species is mentioned (pp. 59, 77).

Offensive and defensive behaviors (pp. 30, 55, 59, 64, 73, 95–96, and 97) include not only distraction displays (see care and feeding of young cited earlier) but also mobbing (p. 30, and 97), the use of spurs (p. 73), and plumage erection (p. 59).

Plumage erection is discussed in terms of its defensive (p. 97) and aggressive (p. 59) and sexual aspects (p. 63). The role of plumage as an indicator of the age of members of a species is considered (p. 113).

Tonic immobility is mentioned as a defensive behavior (i.e., defensive freezing) (p. 97) and as a reaction that the falconer may elicit by placing the newly caught wild falcon into a sock (p. 165). It is noteworthy that modern falconers continue to use this traditional method to control newly trapped falcons.

Sleep is presented (pp. 18–19) with special reference to neutral birds (p. 27).

Raptorial casting (regurgitation of undigestible portions of the diet, i.e., fur, feathers, bones) is elucidated in terms of the specific behavior patterns of individual species during the process of casting pellets (pp. 157–161).

The discussion of robbery of prey by raptors from other raptors (p. 28) did not lead the Emperor to the generalization that falconry itself is a type of prey robbery practiced by man on the falcon. However, I regard falconry as an area in the continuum of robbery that is essentially continuous with the robbing of raptors by raptors themselves. This could be regarded as a failure of generalization by Frederick, but more appropriately it should serve to remind us that despite his prescience the Emperor thought in terms of different categories than do we moderns.

CONCLUSION

By 1250, accurate observations concerning the behaviors of many avian species in their natural environments had been recorded by the Holy Roman Emperor Frederick II. The validity of these observations, even when judged by modern scientific standards, leads me to the conclusion that Frederick was one of the great historical empiricists. He is fully worthy of the title of proto-comparative psychologist. The desirability of additional research to determine a chronology of historical priority for empirical observations of behavior is obvious. It is evident that this area is in need of serious scholarly activity.

ACKNOWLEDGMENTS

I wish to thank Dr. Richard Brewer for his comments upon the ornithological accuracy and Robert Verplank for serving as a consultant on the Medieval falconers.

REFERENCES

Collins, H. H. Jr. (1981). *Harper & Row's complete field guide to north American wildlife*. New York: Harper & Row.

Farber, P. L. (1982). *The emergence of ornithology as a scientific discipline: 1760–1850*. Dordrecht, Holland: D. Reidel.

Frederick II. ca. 1250. (1969). *De arte venandi cum avibus: Fascimile et commentarium*. Graz: Austria.

Harting, J. E. (1891). *Bibliotheca accipitraria*. London: Quaritch.

Haskins, C. H. (1921). The *de arte venandi* of the Emperor Frederick II. *English Historical Review, 13*, 18–27.

Kantor, J. R. (1963, 1969). *The scientific evolution of psychology* (2 vols.) Chicago: Principia Press.

Kantor, J. R. (1983). *Tragedy and the event continuum.* Chicago: Principia Press.

Kantorowicz, E. (1931). *Frederick the Second: 1194–1250.* (E. O. Lorimer, Trans.). New York: R. R. Smith.

Mountjoy, P. T. (1976). The *de arte venandi cum avibus* of Frederick II: A precursor of twentieth century behavioral psychology. *Studies in Medieval Culture, 6* and *7,* 107–115.

Mountjoy, P. T. (1980). An historical approach to comparative psychology. In: M. R. Denny (Ed.), *Comparative psychology: An evolutionary analysis of animal behavior.* New York: Wiley.

Mountjoy, P. T., Bos, J. H., Duncan, M. O., & Verplank R. D. (1969). Falconry: Neglected aspect of the history of psychology. *Journal of the History of the Behavioral Sciences, 5,* 59–67.

Sarton, G. (1931). *Introduction to the history of science* (Vol. II) Washington, DC and Baltimore.

Shaffer, L. C. (1983). Psychological interbehavior as a factor in biological evolution. In N. W. Smith, P. T. Mountjoy, & D. R. Ruben, *Reassessment in psychology: The interbehavioral alternative.* Washington, DC: University Press of America.

Topsell, E. (1658). *The history of four-footed beasts and serpents and insects* (3 vols.) New York: Da Capo Press, 1967.

White, T. H. (1954). *The book of beasts.* New York: Putnam.

Wood, C. A., & Fyfe, F. M. (1943). *The art of falconry; Being the de arte cum avibus of Frederick II of Hohenstaufen.* (C. A. Wood & F. M. Fyfe, Trans. & Eds.). Stanford, CA: Stanford University Press.

2 Theories of Mental Evolution in Comparative Psychology: Darwin to Watson

Charles W. Tolman
University of Victoria, Canada

I have expressed the view elsewhere (Tolman, 1982) that Comparative Psychology's health would be considerably improved if it took its evolutionist foundations more seriously. In its present condition, the discipline displays a puzzling historical irony. Its roots are firmly embedded in evolutionist movement of the mid 19th century—indeed Charles Darwin himself can be claimed as a legitimate parent—yet it has harbored, defended, propogated, succumbed to some of the most antievolutionist thinking of all the biological disciplines. My intention here is to investigate how the founders of our discipline conceived of evolution, in the hope of illuminating our current problems.

The publication of *The Origin of Species* in 1859 marks one of the most significant revolutions in the history of scientific thought. The changes in thinking that Charles Darwin introduced have in the intervening 125 years become sufficiently widespread in acceptance as to become largely taken for granted in much of our current thought. It is therefore useful to remind ourselves of the major features of that revolution.

Although essentialism (the belief that things are only imperfectly patterned on an eternal idea or archetype) had shown distinct signs of losing its hold on scientific thinking already in the 18th century, it was only put conclusively to rest by the acceptance of the evolutionist understanding of nature. This had innumerable consequences on thinking in general, including the shift from an emphasis on types as a goal of scientific investigation and cognition, to an emphasis on individuals in populations, i.e., so-called "population thinking." The acceptance of evolution also forced the move from a static worldview to one that was dynamic. Science could no longer theorize except in terms of change, development, and process: it became self-consciously historical.

These and many other monumental shifts in the scientific worldview were brought forcefully together in Darwin's central idea of the transmutation of species. In contrast to the previously long prevailing view that species, although taxonomically classifiable according to degrees of similarity, represented fundamentally immutable kinds, types, or qualities, the evolutionist asserted the fundamental mutability of species, and therefore also of kinds, types, and qualities. The unity of nature was no longer attributed to an abstract divine Good, but to a concrete process of organic development. Any species now could only be accounted for by the process of its transmutation from another species. The exclusive isolation of all natural categories was relegated to the scrap heap of historical misunderstanding. As Ernst Mayr (1982) has concluded: "A true theory of evolution must postulate a gradual transformation of one species into another and ad infinitum" (p. 352).

Darwin's ideas about mental evolution stand in marked contrast to his theory of the evolution of species. In Darwin's discussion of the evolution of mind any concept even resembling the transmutation of species is conspicuously absent. In brief, by Mayr's criterion for true theories of evolution, Darwin's theory of mind does not qualify.

Darwin's concept of mind was a loose one and included three relatively distinct classes of attributes that he called reflex action, instinct, and intelligence. These three classes of attributes were thought to be hierarchically related, but Darwin was emphatic that they were not sequentially related; that is, instinct did not evolve from reflex action, and intelligence did not evolve from instinct. In even the lowliest animals there exists at least some degree of each. A curious exception is Darwin's concept of "lapsed intelligence" according to which an intelligent act could become transformed into an instinctive one.

What then is imagined to occur in mental evolution? It will be useful to note here that Darwin appears to have been naively Cartesian in his metaphysics (Carter, 1898). He believed that mind and body were two distinct, interacting, interdependent realities. But mind, like body, has survival value and is shaped by natural selection. For example, rats with a higher degree of cunning are more likely to survive and will thus be selected for. The conception of change involved here, however, is not that of transmutation. It is a change not of kind, but of degree. In places, Darwin (1888) was quite explicit about this: "There can be no doubt that the difference between the mind of the lowest man and that of the highest animal is immense. . . . Nevertheless the difference . . . , great as it is, certainly is one of degree and not kind" (p. 127). If Darwin imagined any psychological difference in kind to exist between man and the lower animals— and most of what he wrote suggests that he did not—he failed to provide any theory of how such differences developed. It appears he felt that attributes such as reason had to be there from the beginning in order to be selected for. This is implied by Darwin (1859) in the following: "I have nothing to do with the origin of the mental powers, any more than I have with that of life itself. We are concerned only with the diversities of instinct and of the other mental faculties in animals of the same class'' (p. 207).

It seems odd that a theory that made history by its bold assertion that homoiothermic beings evolved from nonhomoiothermic beings, and that flying creatures evolved from nonflying creatures, could not take the implied next step to assert as well that living and thinking beings evolved from nonliving and nonthinking predecessors. Darwin's metaphysics appears to have contained two fundamentally exclusive categories of qualities, one subject to transmutation and one not. This is disappointingly inconsistent and arbitrary, but it is not surprising in view of his Cartesianism.

Herbert Spencer's position (Spencer, 1899) was virtually the same in this matter as Darwin's:

> in Instinct the (adjustive) correspondence is between inner and outer relations that are very simple or general; in Reason, the correspondence is between inner and outer relations that are complex, or special, or abstract, or infrequent. But the complexity specialty, abstractness, and infrequency of relations, are entirely matters of degree. (p. 453)

It was the monistic materialist John George Romanes, the follower of Darwin and Spencer, who can be credited with the first ''true'' theory of mental evolution. In the words of Carter (1899):

> Romanes had taken upon himself the task of elucidating a theory of mental development in which the genesis of mind is to be traced from non-mental elements, i.e., from instinct and reflex action and, indeed, from physiology itself. This evolutional theory attempted to do for mind what Darwin had done for species, to show a graded series from lower to higher, and a continuity in that series by means of natural inheritance. (p. 115)

Although Romanes adopted Darwin's threefold classification of reflex action, instinct, and intelligence (or reason), these were now understood as forming an evolutionary series, and, equally important, reflex action and instinct were no longer considered as part of the mental, i.e., mind. These two lower categories served as the nonmental from which the mental evolved. According to Romanes, the physiological function underlying this development, was selective excitability or the power of discriminating between different kinds of stimuli.

Romanes's theory of actual transmutation from one level of psychic development to another is not particularly satisfactory. The transition from reflex action to instinct, for example, occurs when into the former ''is imported the element of consciousness'' (quoted in Carter, 1899, p. 110). Reason evolves when instinctual adaptation becomes ''intentional'' (Carter, 1899, p. 110). Presumably the underlying mechanism of change is natural selection, but all in all, the theory remains sketchy, speculative, and weak. It was, however, an important recognition of the need for a theory of mental origins and development.

One further innovative recognition by Romanes should be noted. This was his allusion to the possibility of a qualitative distinction between biological and cultural evolution within a monistic metaphysic. He believed that the "art of writing" formed the basis of this distinction. Romanes (1916) wrote that owing to writing:

> a civilized man inherits mentally, if not physically, the effects of culture for ages past, and this in whatever direction he may choose to profit therefrom. More-over . . . in this unique department of purely intellectual transmission, a kind of non-physical natural selection is perpetually engaged in producing the best results. (p. 33)

The distinction may be crude, but it is a necessary one, and it is one that could only be made because Romanes took seriously the centrality to evolutional thinking of the transmutation of qualities.

Qualitative transformation was central as well to Conwy Lloyd Morgan's thinking on mental evolution. To begin with, mental evolution was placed within the context of a general evolutionary scheme consisting of three qualitatively distinct, yet sequential and continuous, major stages: inorganic, organic, and psychical.

Morgan's version of psychical evolution is complicated by his insistence on a double-aspect form of psychophysical monism. This meant that the conscious aspect of the psychical could not have evolved from the organic substrate. Rather, only the physiological aspect was thought to have so evolved. The conscious aspect could only have developed from something like itself, and thus Morgan postulated an infraconsciousness associated with the organic. Morgan was most insistent, however, that his position was not pan- or even bio-psychistic. Consciousness evolved not from other forms of consciousness, but from some form or other of what he called metakinetics, which accompany, in Spinozist fashion, the kinetics characteristic of all physical matter: Consciousness is a qualitatively novel transmutation of preconscious metakinetics.

Consciousness was understood as having undergone three stages of evolutionary development. The most primitive of these he called "sentience" that was regarded as a "mere accompaniment of organic behavior" (Morgan, 1900, p. 61). The animal behaves primarily instinctively but is in some sense aware of its environment and its own behavior. Morgan's conclusions about this stage (Morgan, 1900) appear to result more from the philosophical considerations mentioned previously than from empirical evidence: "There may be sentience which is merely an accompaniment of organic action without any guiding influence on subsequent modes of behaviour. In that case it is not effective; and whether it is present or not we have no means of ascertaining" (p. 43). From an empirical point of view, then: "we may assume that this sentience is a concomitant of *all* life processes, or only of some. But we have no criterion by which we can hope to determine which of these alternatives is the more probable" (p. 61).

The stages of "effective consciousness" were more subject to verification and investigation. The first of these Morgan called "consentience," sometimes also referred to as the "perceptual" stage because percepts were formed that led to perceptual inference. The common manifestations of this stage were the apparently intelligent actions of the higher animals. Here consciousness guided behavior, but behavior was not under the direct control of consciousness.

The second and highest stage of effective consciousness was called the "ideational" or "conceptual" stage, characterized by conceptual inference or abstraction and by the direct control of behavior by consciousness. This was the stage of "reason," as opposed to mere intelligence, and was exclusively attributed to humans.

Morgan (1900) was less explicit about the actual process of transmutation. With regard to origin, in one place he wrote: "The origin of consciousness, like that of matter or energy, appears to be beyond the pale of scientific discussion" (p. 61). Elsewhere, and obviously in a more speculative mood, Morgan (1890/1891) wrote: "I think that we may fairly believe that some dim form of discrimination is the germ from which the spreading tree of mind shall develop" (p. 338).

He was not much more informative about the interstage transitions once consciousness appears on the scene. He appeared certain, however, that the transition from the perceptual to the conceptual stage is brought about by the introduction of language. In this connection Morgan (1900) indicated how he imagined the problem will be solved:

If we were ever to trace the passage from the instinctive through the indicating stage of communication, and so onwards through the beginnings of description to its higher levels, and thus to the use of language as a medium of explanation; it must be through child study. In every normal human child the passage does actually take place, though, no doubt, in a condensed and abbreviated form as an epitomized recapitulation in individual development, of the steps of evolutional progress. Thus we may obtain a key to the solution of one of the most difficult problems in evolution by continuous process—that of the transition from animal behaviour to human conduct. (p. 337)

The scarcity of details regarding the actual process undoubtedly reflected Morgan's cautious recognition that comparative psychology was yet an infant science. But the general conception of the process was clear. It was a qualitative leap from one distinct stage to another by what in his earlier works he called "selective synthesis" (e.g., Morgan, 1894, chap. 19), and that later became more refined under the rubric of "emergent evolution" (Morgan, 1931).

Quite independent of the particular scientific or philosophical merits of Morgan's comparative psychology, there can be no denying that its intent was evolutionary in the truest sense of the word.

The next figure to be considered in the present account, the mechanistic materialist Jacques Loeb, marks a decided beginning of the end to the evolutional preoccupation among comparative psychologists.

On the one hand, Loeb believed in evolution and was a vigorous opponent of special creation and other mystical accounts of animal origins. He even advanced the idea that what people called conscious or psychic, though it did not exist as such, did exist as associative memory, which was the unique product of increased complexity of the nervous system in higher animals. This hypothesis was further reinforced with a theory of discontinuous emergence similar to that of Morgan (Loeb, 1900, p. 252).

On the other hand, however, Loeb was not a Darwinist and was generally skeptical, if not overtly contemptuous, of the evolutional speculations of his contemporaries. In his 1916 book, *The Organism as a Whole,* he devoted a single chapter of less than three pages to the topic of evolution. His message was simple: He would believe it when some evolutionist could demonstrate an actual transmutation of species—preferably in the laboratory.

Even Loeb's concession to emergence soon broke down. Loeb (1900) stated:

> We, of course, concede that the associative memory shows different degrees of development or perfection in different animals. These different degrees are mainly differences in capacity and resonance. By difference in capacity I mean a difference in the number of associations of which the brain is capable. By difference in the resonance I mean the ease with which associations are produced. (pp. 253–254)

Quality here was reduced to quantity, a manifestation of the intellectual tendency of Loeb's that so clearly distinguished him from Darwin, Romanes, and particularly Morgan. This tendency was reductionism. The psychic was first reduced to association, but only to make it accessible to a more fundamental analysis: "We consider it our aim to work out the dynamics of the processes of association, and find out the physical or chemical conditions which determine the variation in the capacity of memory in the various organisms" (Loeb, 1900, p. 287).

Loeb could not have been anywhere near as disappointed at Herbert Jenning's discovery of associative processes in the most primitive organisms (Jennings, 1906) as Robert Yerkes suggested in 1905.

The reductionist trend continued with Edward Thorndike. He described his comparative psychological task as follows (Thorndike, 1911):

> If we could prove that what we call ideational life and reasoning were not new and unexplainable species of intellectual life but only the natural consequences of an increase in the number, delicacy, and complexity of associations of the general animal sort, we should have made out an evolution of mind comparable to the evolution of living forms. (p. 286)

This reductively quantitative view of development, Thorndike (1911) felt, was born out by the existing evidence of his time. He concluded:

In man this increase reaches such a point that an apparently new type of mind results, which conceals the real continuity of the process. This mental evolution parallels the evolution of the cell structures of the brain from few and simple and gross to many and complex and delicate. (p. 294)

And finally: "[Man's] sense-powers show no new creation. His intellect we have seen to be a simple though extended variation from the general animal sort" (p. 294).

John B. Watson's understanding of evolution is well known. Citing Jennings (1906) in support of his views, Watson (1914) concluded:

No new principle is needed in passing from the unicellular to man. As we pass from the responses of the simple organisms to the more complex one of the higher animals we find (1) a greater number of units, and (2) more complex forms of combinations of these units. (p. 318)

There is for Watson, however, a significant difference between man and "brute," and that is language. But this should not be construed as a difference in principle. Watson (1914) stated:

we will suppose that future analysis will enable us ultimately to show that every word, syllable, and letter, whether spoken or thought, produces a characteristic form of response which, when recorded, must be looked at from the same standpoint which we adopt when looking at habits elsewhere. (p. 328)

With Watson questions of qualitative transformation and of the special status of the human species succumbed completely to the essentially antievolutional program of reductionism.

I close with the following six conclusions and four observations:

1. We have encountered two distinct conceptions of evolution. The first, represented by Romanes and Morgan, emphasized emergence, transmutation, and discontinuity in the evolution process, although not, it seems, at the immediate expense of continuity. The second, represented by Loeb, Thorndike, and Watson, emphasized uniformity of principle and continuity, often at the clear cost of discontinuity.

2. Ernst Mayr (1982, p. 341) reminds us that one of the "great challenges" of evolutionary biology has been to "reconcile continuity and discontinuity," i.e., to overcome the historical tendency to take up one in exclusive opposition to the other. The first understanding, that of Romanes and Morgan appears to have been working toward that end. The second understanding, that of Loeb, Thorndike, and Watson never recognized it, implicitly or explicitly, as a desirable or necessary goal.

3. The first understanding, being emergent in nature, was *prima facie* anti-reductionist. The second was overtly and aggressively reductionist.

4. Curiously, both Loeb and Watson expressed antipathy toward "Darwinian continuity theory," while providing, themselves, the clearest of examples of theory that emphasized continuity over discontinuity.

5. It is true that the emergentist theories had the tendency, despite the best intentions of Morgan's famous canon, to project human traits onto lower animals. This is not a necessary consequence of their emergentism, however. On the other hand, the reductionist theories appear to have been equally guilty of the reciprocal error of projecting the traits of lower animals onto humans, and this *is* a necessary consequence of their reductionism.

6. With respect to mental evolution, Darwin appears not to have been a Darwinian. His views on this were most like those reductionists who pronounced themselves anti-Darwinian, and most unlike those who were called correctly, I believe, Darwinians.

To these conclusions, I add the following observations:

1. The Thorndike–Watson style of reductionist continuity theory appears to have become hegemonic in 20th century comparative psychology.

2. This hegemony successfully absorbed whatever opposition might have come from the functionalists and it has resisted any inroads from antireductionists such as T. C. Schneirla.

3. The result of this hegemony has been a de-emphasis on evolution in comparative psychology, with the development of a consequent vulnerability to reductionist attacks from the ethologists and particularly from sociobiology.

4. I suggest that it is time for comparative psychologists to reexamine their commitment to evolutionary principles and, once again, lend serious attention to the questions of mental evolution with a view to strengthening the philosophical and theoretical basis for their scientific efforts.

REFERENCES

Carter, M. H. (1898). Darwin's idea of mental development. *American Journal of Psychology, 9,* 534–559.

Carter, M. H. (1899). Romanes' idea of mental development. *American Journal of Psychology, 11,* 101–118.

Darwin, C. (1859). *On the origin of species by means of natural selection or the preservation of favored races in the struggle for life.* London: John Murray.

Darwin, C. (1888). *The descent of man.* (Vol. 1, 2nd ed.). New York: A. L. Fowle.

Jennings, H. S. (1906). *Behavior of the lower organisms.* New York: Columbia University Press.

Loeb, J. (1900). *Comparative physiology of the brain and comparative psychology.* New York: G. P. Putnam's Sons.

Loeb, J. (1916). *The organism as a whole.* New York/London: G. P. Putnam's Sons.

Mayr, E. (1982). *The growth of biological thought.* Cambridge and London: Harvard University Press.

Morgan, C. L. (1894). *An introduction to comparative psychology.* London: Walter Scott.

Morgan, C. L. (1900). *Animal behavior.* London: Edward Arnold.

Morgan, C. L. (1931). *Emergent evolution.* New York: Henry Holt.

Morgan, C. L. (1890/1891). *Animal life and intelligence.* London: Edward Arnold.

Romanes, G. J. (1916). *Darwin and after Darwin* (Vol. 2, 4th ed.). Chicago/London: Open Court.

Spencer, H. (1899). *The principles of psychology* (Vol. 1, 4th ed.). London: Williams and Norgate.

Thorndike, E. L. (1911). *Animal intelligence: Experimental studies.* New York: Macmillan.

Tolman, C. W. (1982). The crisis in comparative psychology and the evolutionary concept of levels. In V. J. A. Novak & J. Mlikovsky (Eds.), *Evolution and environment.* Prague: CSAV.

Watson, J. B. (1914). *Behavior: An introduction to comparative psychology.* New York: Henry Holt & Co.

Yerkes, R. M. (1905). Animal psychology and criteria of the psychic. *The Journal of Philosophy, Psychology, and Scientific Method, 11,* 141–149.

3 Behaviorism: On Concerns Relating to its Nexus and Origin[1]

Everett J. Wyers
State University of New York at Stony Brook

> *Varieties have the same general characters as species, for they cannot be distinguished from species.*
>
> *In short, we shall have to treat species in the same manner as those naturalists treat genera, who admit that genera are merely artificial combinations made for convenience.*
>
> —Charles Darwin (1859)

Hindsight can be said to offer the clearest of views. This is true because past events stand out in as many ways as there are modern viewpoints from which to view them.

I am concerned with one question relating to the origin of Behaviorism. I ask out of simple curiosity: Why did J. B. Watson not perceive what Charles Darwin was concerned with in the phenomena of individual variation (i.e., continuous variation)?

I am not an historian. I have not answered the question even to my own satisfaction. Nevertheless, I believe a significant clarification of the origin of Behaviorism has emerged in the effort. It emerges because the question is one seldom considered by a psychologist and because in the nexus of behaviorism's origin the question is a crucial one.

Did Darwin clearly perceive what he meant by individual variation? At times

---

[1] Abridged forms of different portions of this chapter were presented at the Eastern Psychological Association Meeting in Baltimore, Maryland, 1984, and at the 23rd International Congress of Psychology, Acapulco, Mexico, 1984.

he did. He had read Quetelet. He had much data on individual variation before him. He had to assume that at least a portion of the variation was heritable. How it got to be heritable was another question. In effect, Darwin viewed heredity and variation as coextensive (Hogben, 1932; Mayr, 1982). In his fully developed theory of natural selection (Gruben & Barrett, 1974) Darwin said:

> Variations are not necessarily adaptive—some are useful to the organism and favor its chances of survival, others may be useless or harmful, as circumstances dictate. . . . To account for evolutionary progress, variation alone is not enough: it must be coupled with selection. (p. 157)

It is not surprising that Darwin viewed evolution as a continuous process occurring in populations of individuals constrained by the vagaries of environmental (ecological) change. In the final version of his theory a species was seen to be an abstraction. To conceive of a species enduring through countless environmental changes was to speak of populations of varying individuals who live in a kind of dynamic balance, or stasis, with a changeable and variable environment.

Darwin's shift to populational thinking was a slow one (Mayr, 1982). There is no solid evidence that during the writing of *The Origin of Species,* Darwin conceived of species as reproductively isolated populations (Ghiselin, 1969; Mayr, 1982). Nevertheless, in the first edition of the Origin (1859, 24 Nov., p. 52) Darwin (Mayr, 1982) wrote:

> It will be seen that I look at the term species, as one arbitrarily given for the sake of convenience to a *set* of individuals closely resembling each other, and that it does not essentially differ from the term variety, which is given to less distinct and more fluctuating forms. (p. 267)

What is surprising is that Watson (1914) could write; in discussing the "Effect of natural selection upon mutations": "The animal may possess—and often does possess—a host of structural and functional characteristics which have no necessary role in its daily life" (*this is inconceivable on the Darwinian concept of evolution*) (p. 169) (italics: author). Earlier, Watson writes: "On the Darwinian hypothesis natural selection is looked upon as an actual causative agent . . . . that, given fluctuating variations, natural selection would shape the direction of evolution in such a way that, given time, the organism would become perfectly adapted to its habitat." On such an hypothesis *every instinctive act observable in an organism must be looked upon as having adaptive value* (p. 166–67). He goes on to buttress his interpretation by quoting two paragraphs apparently drawn from the sixth edition (1875) of the Origin. Both are on the marvels of adaptation and the species problem. Neither is germane to the conclusion that the existence of nonadaptive and maladaptive characters in living animals is *inconceivable on the Darwinian concept of evolution* (italics: author).

What makes Watson's view surprising is twofold. By 1914 all the major criticisms of Darwinian natural selection had already been effectively answered. In 1914 and later in 1919 and 1924, Watson held a view derived from James (1890) and McDougall (1908) that instinctive behavior is modified, changed, and overridden, by learning (habit) from its earliest occurrence. Watson (1914) stated: "The act must be observed upon its first appearance if it is to be seen pure, i.e., without modification through habit" (p. 107). Such a view has much in common with the Darwinian point of view. What Watson contributed to that view was a concerted effort to conceptualize both instinct and habit in terms of reflexes.

In my view, Watson may have come close to an important point but missed it through his adherence to the conventional wisdom of the time. Variations are preserved through natural selection so as to track environmental change. The variations (underlying mutations) do not occur in a random fashion, but by chance. They occur within physical constraints such that only some are viable (open to preservation by natural selection). There are two forms of constraint: Environmental (ecological) constraints introduce the element of chance; i.e., it is a matter of "chance" in what particular setting a variation appears; physical constraints are deterministic. Some variations (mutations) simply cannot occur. Others do not conform to their internal milieu and therefore are abrogated. (Köhler, 1960, noted the same points in discussing his invariance principle.)

It follows that only structure can evolve (i.e., the opening of new potentialities) (D. Thompson, 1917). Because a potentiality can only be realized if possible: for psychology this means that behavior cannot be "nativistic" (Henle, 1977). Instinct becomes the empirical realization of a possibility. Hence, all instinctive behavior depends on experience in the true sense of Locke's tabula rasa (it builds on structural givens). This was at least implicit in James (1890) and McDougall (1908). It is a shame Watson could only recognize the negative aspect of natural selection. He knew Locke, Hume, and almost certainly Bain (Watson, 1936), and yet he could not make the sort of transition suggested here. Why??

I think the answer can be found in the status of positivism in the science of the time and in Watson's unacknowledged debt to the neorealism appearing in epistemology at the time. The positivistic view encouraged him to overlook the rebuttal of Darwin's critics. And, for Watson, neorealism strongly implied a teleological view (purposiveness), which he could not acknowledge due to his methodological commitment to what he saw as necessary to progress in psychology. He could not see through the hard mind-material dualism imposed by the doctrine of primary and secondary qualities in the natural sciences since Galileo's day.

In 1899 Moulton rebutted Lord Kelvin's doctrine (Thomson, 1865) of loss of the residual heat of both earth and sun as curtailing the time span available for natural selection to work its ways. Moulton suggested that an unknown process could be at work in the sun maintaining both its life and that of the earth. In 1903 Curie and Laborde showed that radium maintained a steady temperature above its immediate surroundings. The discovery did not go unnoticed. The uranium content of rocks showed Kelvin's doctrine to be without significance. Watson did not reference Moulton, or Curie and Laborde, in 1914 or later, but he was aware of the existence of radium and some of its effects (p. 166).

Watson also knew that Mendelian genetics had cut short De Vries' mutant "hopeful monster" theory of evolution (1914, see p. 163, p. 164, and pp. 165–66). Yet he persisted in maintaining macromutationism (discontinuous variation) as of the essence in the course of evolution. He understood the Mendelian genetics of his day (see pp. 152–165) and recognized that similar mutations can occur frequently. Therefore, Fleeming Jenkin's (1867), A. W. Bennett's (1870), and Herbert Spencer's (1893), criticism that individual variants would be "swamped" out by backcrossing is clearly denied (p. 165).

In spite of his knowledge of Mendelian genetics and the facts of mutationism, Watson misunderstood Johannsen's (1903) research results. Those results, for the first time, clearly separated heritable variation (between pure lines) from non-heritable variation (that within pure lines). After reporting Johannsen's results correctly, Watson (1914) stated: "The results of this experimental work . . . prove conclusively that the vast majority of the variations of organisms are not inherited" (p. 161). As Hirsch (1967) put it: "The very observations that, to biology, meant non-inheritance of environmental influences . . . and that variation could be analyzed intelligibly into genetic and environmental components provided psychology, through Watson's *mis*interpretation, with the procrustean frame that was to trap us in typological thinking for another half century" (p. 419).

One other criticism of natural selection, that artificial selection over many generations eventuates in stabilization of mean values for selected traits (also anticipated by Jenkin) need not concern us in view of Johannsen's results. That criticism and those noted earlier represent all the major criticism of Darwinian natural selection within the scientific community at the time save one. That one criticism was that "Darwin had failed to provide proof for his theory of evolution by natural selection" (Hull, 1973).

With the years, a debate over the proper role of induction and deduction (a debate concerned with the logic of discovery and the logic of proof) continued to be a focus of attention in both the science of the times and its philosophy. The hypothetical-deductive method had yet to gain ascendency (Ghiselin, 1969). One consequence was a division between those developing relativistic views regarding the problem of verification (those tending to acceptance of probabilistic inference) and those hewing to what amounted to traditional essentialistic views (the acceptance of the deterministic Newtonian model) (Mayr, 1982). With the development and increasing accessibility of necessary technical skills and methods, many scientists turned from strict adherence to the comparative method and its logical pitfalls, to straightforward descriptive and analytical laboratory research (Oppenheim, 1982). Experimentation became the touchstone of reality in the biological sciences and the emerging science of psychology.

Watson was not immune. For him science had to be hands-on experimentation with resultant "touchable" recordings of events that produce hard data. Simple verbalisms would not do. His science was reductionistic and sought the mechanistic essences of the phenomena he chose to investigate. It is no wonder he could not accept the probabilistic inferences Darwin was forced to accept in treatment of the individual variation he was confronted with. It is no wonder he misinterpreted Johannsen's results. He also misinterpreted the current embryological findings of his time in a similar manner, i.e., as indicating in essence a form of preformationism (see Oppenheim, 1982).

Although the debate over what constituted proper science continued and those concerned with the doing of science turned to laying their hands on what could be done, a number of philosopher/scientists concerned with epistemology and psychology attempted to bridge over the developing gap between the essentialists and the new relativists. They were not concerned with the modern rule of probabilistic inference as the criterion of verification in science. Rather, they were concerned with an issue that cut across relativist and essentialist concerns to an issue that had inhibited the development of the psychological sciences for many generations and, in effect, prevented any serious concern with probabilistic inference and maturation of the hypothetical deductive method during that time. Boring (1950) concluded:

> The Greeks were quite thoroughly objective. Man is concerned first with the external world and discovers himself last. He can take his ego for granted but not the objective world—not if he is to survive. Aristotle's dualism of matter and form was an objective dualism, since both matter and form were regarded as inherent in objects. (p. 632)

Smith (1983) stated that:

> The New Realists held that the world is *presented* to an observer rather than being *represented* by 'invisible pawns' in the perceiver's private sphere, a dualist fiction regarded as 'concretely intolerable' for psychology. To the neorealists, materialism was an equally fallacious doctrine primarily because it erred in 'denying the *facts*, as well as the theory, of consciousness.' Materialism's assignment of mental events to the realm of epiphenomena collided with the New Realists' insistence that the things of thought be given the same ontological status as physical entities. (p. 154)

Neorealism was an active movement during the first few decades of the present century. It held forth a nondualistic realism, a form of realism closely related to pragmatism. As such, it was heavily indebted to James (Murphy, 1949; O'Neil, 1968). In "Does Consciousness Exist?" (1904), James says that the world we know consists only of the things we perceive. Mind does not "know" the things we perceive but consists in (comprises) the very same entities. He separates the mental and the physical through the order in which events are perceived. That order depends on both events in time and space and on the life of the organism. He concluded (in Murphy, 1949) that: " 'Consciousness,' as an 'entity,' does not exist. It is only a name, encompassing the fact that 'events are related not only to time and space but to the life of the experiencing organism' " (p. 206).

Much in the doctrines of Neorealisism fit well with the program of Behaviorism. Watson, at least in his early formulations, tacitly accepted the Neorealist form of psychophysical monism. It rejected mind (consciousness) as a realm of secondary qualities, although incorporating such aspects of perceptual experience into the physical (natural) sciences realm of the primary qualities.

Following on the progress seen in the natural sciences (and Biology and Psychology) during the last half of the 19th century, the Neorealist movement provided an impetus to reduce (expiate) the phenomena of the mind (the secondary qualities of Galileo and Locke) to rules of measurement consistent with those of the primary qualities (i.e., realism) of the natural sciences. In addition, it insisted on the need to objectify the phenomena of error in perception (illusion, hallucination, etc.), as well as events related to the experience of feeling, emotion, and voliion, which apparently do not, on occurrence, seem to correspond with contextual physical events (see Holt, 1914, 1915; Perry, 1912).

Uncritical acceptance of neorealism by Watson is indicated, as Tolman (1932) put it, by his lack of consistency in definition of response and stimulus. Reflexes were to be basic. They were to be both the ultimate units of analysis and the fundamental elements of explanation. However, in fact, molar acts implying both purpose and goal orientation (e.g., building a house) were from the beginning incorporated in the analysis under the response rubric.

Positivism implied strict adherence to the data of physicalistic objective measurement in specifying both the stimulus and the response. In using a physicalistic pointer reading as an index of some property or characteristic of an act (e.g., number of bricks laid per unit time as a measure of efficency of house building), description is confused with measurement.

In describing behavior, one observes its sequence in time, while simultaneously comparing what one has seen to the moment with various classes of activity. In the course of time a decision is reached, and the behavior assigned to a category is meaningful within the experience of the obsever (e.g., "Aha, he's building a house"). The concept "house," as James Mill would say, involves a great many meanings. Juxtaposing it to the concept "building" restricts those meanings to a particular subset. The behavior is thus described and a specific set of meanings is conveyed.

In the preface to *Psychology from the Standpoint of a Behaviorist* (1919) Watson states that objectivists, such as Beer, Bethe, and von Uexkull, "are perfectly orthodox parallelists.'' Behaviorism, in Watson's view, is a strict monistic materialism. Thought *is* physical movement composed solely of chains of reflexes; in actuality, complexes of simultaneously occurring reflexes. Because such a strongly positivistic stance is taken, confusion results. Emphasis goes to a reductionist strategy and elementistic physiological, anatomical, and embryological data become critical in measurement methodology. This forces a form of realism similar to that of the British Empirical philosophers, but one, I should add, excluding Locke's secondary qualities: Color *is* a wavelength of light, or composite thereof.

This is not to say that the neorealists did not make use of reductionistic dicta when occasion demanded. Evidence for their views was seen in reflexological considerations. For both the underlying basis of emotion and speech (thinking), Watson's views were presaged (see Holt, 1914; Perry, 1912). In fact, the basis of Watson's views on "thinking" (the reflexological and motor nature of thought) is given extensive consideration in Holt (1914). The ideas and contributions to Watson's manifesto (1913) and *Comparative Psychology* (1914), are evident in more of the literature of the times than the writings of the neorealists. The ideas and the information was there. It remained only for one person of concern to collate and expound them in crisp and clear methodological terms. For the time, Watson was the master of this and he deserved to be, considering his concern with, and devotion to objective methodology in all his work (at least through 1919).

Unfortunately, this zealousness for objectivity and methodology, already evident in his *Animal Education* (1903), his *Comparative Psychology* (1914), and in his presidential address to the APA in 1915 (Watson, 1916) led him to a serious neglect of the epistemological basis of his approach to reality. All had to be seen in terms of the primary qualities of Galileo and Locke and in terms of physically measureable events of extent, duration, etc.: recordable and exhibitable to public view on paper. There was no better way to do this than through the achievements of the physiological sciences of the past century. Unwittingly (perhaps) he became, in effect, a student of the Russian reflexologist, Sechenov.

It is difficult, but not improbable, to believe that an editor of the Psychological Review and the Journal of Experimental Psychology, who became president of the APA, and in the course of going about the quite deliberate revolutionizing of psychology, was not thoroughly familiar with the basic scientific literature of his time. Perry, and others of the neorealist movement, published in the Psychological Review. The "Popular Science Monthly" and "Science" published reports on science in general. The results and conclusions of the work of Planck, Rutherford, and Bohr (not to mention Einstein, and others) was in evidence. Watson must have been (should have been, or at least, could have been) well aware of what was going on in the natural sciences and what the neorealists were saying. An epistemological revolution based on developments in both the biological and physical sciences was in progress.

He neglected not only the epistemological basis of his soon to be christened Behaviorism, but many of the methods of objective description of mental phenomena, that, in fact, gave rise to the neorealist effort to breakthrough the time-honored distinction between the primary and secondary qualities. In short, the "Manifesto," "Comparative Psychology," and "Psychology as the Behaviorist sees it," to say the least, represent a conservatively minded effort to hold to what was given by the past.

One looks in vain for reference to Ebbinghaus in 1914. The method of introspection is rejected; the imageless thought controversy is disparaged, but little or no attention is given to the objective aspects of behavioral measurement in any of the structualists camps (Adler, 1977; Blumenthal, 1977). The measurement methods generated in the last half of the last century, which tended to undercut the physicists refuge in Galileo's distinction of "mind" versus "reality," are almost totally ignored in Watson's early writings. Watson may be regarded as a revolutionary in psychology, but there is little evidence that he played such a role in revolutionizing science. In that aspect of his life he was strictly conservative.

Watson seems to have had an ardent wish to be plain spoken—as we would say, relevant to the student of psychology. He does this remarkably well. His 1919 book is still a delight to read from this standpoint; however, his success in this gets him into epistemological trouble. He adopts (adapts?) a neorealist stance in writing about and interpreting behavior in terms of S's and R's. As Tolman (1932) might have said: purpose and goal orientation are "immanent" in his descriptions of both stimuli and responses as components of behavior.

He rejects Thorndike's trial and error learning—and emphasizes contiguity through recency and frequency—even though Thorndike provides an acceptable positivistic definition of his principle of reinforcement (the law of effect).

It is a truism that the present helps determine our view of the past. It is evident to us that the conception of "scientific method" broadened enormously during the last half of the last century. By the turn of the century confidence in science was widespread. A rigorous and exact science of human nature could be seen as resulting from application of those methods, so fruitful in the development of the natural sciences to the human condition. Confidence in this belief stemmed from Darwin's inclusion of humankind with the rest of nature and the positivist character of science at the time (Mackenzie, 1976, 1977).

The positivism of the day was based on three ostensibly firm convictions regarding scientific method: (a) avoidance of dependence on metaphysical principles, (b) collection and emphasis of facts, and (c) the necessity and sufficiency for science to do so. These beliefs regarding scientific method represented a culmination of the influence of Baconian empiricism in the philosophy of science (Clifford, 1973; Hull, 1973).

The positivism of 1900–1910 consisted in the faith that the methods, concepts, and theories, of the physical sciences provide "the key to complete knowledge of the world'' (Mackenzie & Mackenzie, 1974). The secondary qualities of Galileo and Locke were to be reduced to the concepts of space, time, motion, matter, distance, position, force, and so on. This was so because such concepts were about what ''reality'' *really* is. In fact, however, the distinction between fundamental and derived properties of events does not cut across the phenomena of perception, i.e., of mind and consciousness.

By 1910 it was becoming evident, and by 1925 it was clearly the case, that what one observed (and measured) depended on one's vantage point. Even so elemental a concept as ''the electron'' could be seen as both particle and wave. It is a pity Watson could not ''see,'' accept, and develop within psychology the relativistic view of truth implicit in Darwinism.

EPILOGUE

Watson denied introspection but not consciousness. Mentalistic concepts were to be reduced to the concepts of the natural (i.e., physical) sciences. This was to be done in terms of the measurement procedures of the natural sciences, that is, in terms of the primary qualities.

The possibility of developing direct measures of the secondary qualities, the phenomena of mind, was ignored, even though structuralist methodology had made considerable progress in this regard. A central problem here was Watson's bias against describing and analyzing behavior at an adequate level of complexity (his reflexological curse).

Watson was an essentialist at heart. All was to be reduced to a set of fundamental laws in the Newtonian sense. Thus, he was confused by the need to ''see'' individual differences as ''error deviation'' (a la Quetelet) rather than as indicative of the uniqueness of each of the fundamental units in biological science.

REFERENCES

Adler, H. E. (1977). The vicissittudes of Fechnerian psychophysics in America. In R. W. Rieber & K. Salzinger (Eds.), *The roots of American psychology: Historical influences and implications for the future* (Vol. 291, pp. 21–32). New York: Annals of the New York Academy of Sciences.

Bennett, A. W. (1870). The theory of selection from a mathematical point of view. *Nature, 3*, 30–31.

Blumenthal, A. L. (1977). Wilhelm Wundt and early american psychology: A clash of two cultures. In R. W. Rieber & K. Salzinger (Eds.), *The roots of american psychology: Historical influences and implications for the future* (Vol. 291, pp. 13–20). New York: Annals of the New York Academy of Sciences.

Boring, E. G. (1950). *A history of experimental psychology.* New York: Appleton–Century.

Clifford, G. J. (1973). E. L. Thorndike: The psychologist as professional man of science. In M.

Henle, J. Jaynes, & J. J. Sullivan (Eds.), *Historical conceptions of psychology* (pp. 230–248). New York: Springer.

Curie, P., & Laborde (1903). Cited in A. C. Clifford (1932). The origin of the solar system. *Scientia, 52,* 141–156.

Darwin, C. (1859: 24 Nov.). *On the origin of species by means of natural selection or the preservation of favored races in the struggle for life.* London: Murray.

Ghiselin, M. T. (1969). *The triumph of the Darwinian method.* Berkeley: University of California Press.

Gruber, H. E., & Barrett, P. H. (1974). *Darwin on man: A psychological study of scientific creativity.* New York: Dutton.

Henle, M. (1977). The influence of gestalt psychology in America. In R. W. Rieber & K. Salzinger (Eds.), *The roots of american psychology: Historical influences and implications for the future* (Vol. 291, pp. 3–12). New York: Annals of the New York Academy of Sciences.

Hirsch, J. (1967). Behavior-genetic analysis. In J. Hirsch (Ed.), *Behavior-genetic analysis* (p. 419). New York: McGraw–Hill.

Hogben, L. (1932). *Genetic principles in medicine and social science.* New York: Knopf.

Holt, E. B. (1914). *The Concept of consciousness.* New York: Macmillan.

Holt, E. B. (1915). *The Freudian wish and its place in ethics.* New York: Holt.

Hull, D. L. (1973). *Darwin and his critics.* Cambridge: Harvard University Press.

James, W. (1890). *The principles of psychology.* New York: Holt.

James, W. (1904). Does consciousness exist. *The Journal of Philosophy, Psychology, and Scientific Method, 1,* 477–491.

Jenkin, F. (1867). The origin of species. *North British Review. 46,* 149–171.

Johannsen, W. (1903). *Ueber erblichkeit in populationen und in reinen linien.* Jena: Gustav Fischer.

Köhler, W. (1960). The mind–body problem. In S. Hook (Ed.), *Dimensions of mind* (pp. 3–23). New York: New York University Press.

Mackenzie, B. (1976). Darwinism and positivism as methodological influences on the development of psychology. *Journal of the History of the Behavioral Sciences, 12,* 330–337.

Mackenzie, B. D. (1977). *Behaviorism and the limits of scientific method.* London: Routledge & Kegan Paul.

Mackenzie, B. D., & Mackenzie, S. L. (1974). The case for a revised systematic approach to the history of psychology. *Journal of the History of the Behavioral Sciences, 10,* 324–347.

Mayr, E. (1982). *The growth of biological thought: Diversity, evolution, and inheritance.* Cambridge: Harvard University Press.

McDougall, W. (1908). *Introduction to social psychology.* London: Methuen.

Moulton, F. R. (1899). Cited in: A. C. Clifford (1932). The origin of the solar system. *Scientia, 52,* 141–156.

Murphy, G. (1949). *Historical introduction to modern psychology.* New York: Harcourt Brace.

O'Neil, W. M. (1968). Realism and behaviorism. *Journal of the History of the Behavioral Sciences, 4,* 152–160.

Oppenheim, R. W. (1982). Preformation and epigenesis in the origins of the nervous system and behavior: Issues, concepts, and their history. In P. P. G. Bateson & P. H. Klopfer (Eds.), *Perspectives in ethology* (pp. 1–100). New York: Plenum.

Perry, R. B. (1912). *Present philosophical tendencies.* New York: Longmans.

Smith, L. D. (1983). Purpose and cognition: The limits of neorealist influence on Tolman's psychology. *Behaviorism, 11,* 151–163.

Spencer, H. (1893). The inadequacy of natural selection. *Popular Science Monthly, 42,* 807.

Thompson, D. W. (1917). *On growth and form.* (Abridged ed., 1961, J. T. Bonner, Ed.). Cambridge: Cambridge University Press.

Thomson, W., Lord Kelvin. (1865). The doctrine of uniformity in geology briefly refuted. *Pro-*

ceedings, *Royal Society of Edinburgh, 5,* 512. (Reprinted in: *Popular lectures and addresses by Sir William Thomson,* 1894, (Vol. 2, pp. 6–9). London: MacMillan.

Tolman, E. C. (1932). *Purposive behavior in animals and men.* New York: Century.

Watson, J. B. (1903). *Animal education.* Chicago: University of Chicago Press.

Watson, J. B. (1913). Psychology as a behaviorist views it. *Psychological Review, 20,* 158–177.

Watson, J. B. (1914). *Behavior: An introduction to comparative psychology.* New York: Holt.

Watson, J. B. (1916). The place of the conditioned-reflex in psychology. *Psychological Review, 23,* 89–116.

Watson, J. B. (1919). *Psychology from the standpoint of a behaviorist.* Philadelphia: Lippincott.

Watson, J. B. (1924). *Psychology from the standpoint of a behaviorist* (2nd ed.). Philadelphia: Lippincott.

Watson, J. B. (1936). Autobiography. In C. Murchison (Ed.), *A history of psychology in autobiography* (Vol. 3, pp. 271–281). Worchester, MA.: Clark University Press.

4

Early Zoological Input to Comparative and Animal Psychology at the University of Chicago

Thomas C. Cadwallader
Indiana State University

It is generally held that comparative and animal psychology in America got its impetus from the 1895–1896 visit to the United States by the great English comparative psychologist Conwy Lloyd Morgan (1852–1936). Morgan, whose *Introduction to Comparative Psychology* had been published in 1894, came primarily to deliver (in Boston) the Lowell Lectures, which were published later in 1896 under the title *Habit and Instinct*. (On this trip to America, Morgan also gave a lecture at the University of Chicago. It was given on February 7, 1896 to the Biological Club on the subject "The question of the transmission of acquired characteristics"; University of Chicago *Annual Register*, 1895–1896, p. 177.) It should be noted that Morgan had been trained as a geologist and zoologist.

Dewsbury has suggested that 1894 should be taken as "the beginning of American comparative psychology" (1984, p. 44) largely on the dual bases of the publication dates of Morgan's *Introduction* and of the English translation of Wundt's *Lectures on Human and Animal Psychology*.

Although there are several variations on the story (e.g., Jonçich, 1968, pp. 131–133; Murphy & Kovach, 1972, p. 314), they basically say that during Morgan's visit to the United States, a Harvard student came in contact with him, became inspired, and the result was the birth of American comparative and animal psychology. The Harvard student was Edward Lee Thorndike (1874–1949). Although this may have been Thorndike's entrance into comparative and animal psychology, it is not how comparative or animal psychology came to America.

Part of the earlier story has been told in a previous publication (Cadwallader, 1984a). The early and much neglected pioneers of American comparative and animal psychology all seem to have been zoologists. One of the earliest was

David F. Weinland (1829–1915) who in 1858 published a paper entitled "A method of comparative animal psychology." Another was Thomas Wesley Mills (1847–1915) who in 1885 founded "The Society for the Study of Comparative Psychology" in Montreal (see, e.g., Mills, 1887).

Although it has been recognized that some of the zoologists at the University of Chicago were involved in early comparative and animal psychology, the extent of that involvement has not been adequately appreciated. This statement holds not only for the extent of the of the known individuals' involvement, but also to the extent of the numbers of zoologists involved. In the present article, the term *zoologist* is meant in the broad sense to include any biologist working with (subhuman) animals. One of the Chicago zoologists, Horatio H. Newman (1875–1957), has written a history of the Department (Newman, 1948) but mentions little of the subject of the present chapter.

Some background is necessary before starting the present story. There had been what later came to be called "The Old University of Chicago." It had been founded in 1857 by a group of Chicago Baptists, but after a rocky existence it was forced to shut its doors in 1886 due to a mortgage foreclosure (for details, see Goodspeed, 1916/1972). Efforts for a "new" university began almost immediately when it became apparent that the "old" university could not be resuscitated.

The impetus again came from Chicago Baptists who persuaded a prominent eastern Baptist layman and multimillionaire, John D. Rockefeller (1839–1937) to be a benefactor. From the beginning, the choice for a president by all concerned was William Rainey Harper (1856–1906). Harper at one time had been associated with the "old" university but was then Professor of Semitic Languages and of Bible Literature at Yale University and was one of the country's most popular lecturers. Harper was elected President of the University in September of 1890. Although the University did not begin instruction until the fall of 1892, Harper began almost immediately to select a faculty.

Applications and recommendations for the faculty poured in. One recommendation (Cheney, 1890) was for a young man then Professor of Natural History and Geology at the University of Cincinnati, Clarence Luther Herrick (1858–1904; he should not be confused with his younger brother, Charles Judson Herrick, 1866–1960, who later was Professor of Neurology at the University of Chicago). Clarence Luther Herrick was then one of a rather limited number of prominent Baptist scientists in the country. Herrick had been among the first Americans (in the narrow sense) to be involved in comparative psychology as recounted earlier (Cadwallader, 1984a). In brief, he had included behavioral observations as early as his 1882 paper, had translated (1885) *Outlines of Psychology* by Hermann Lotze (1817–1881), and had included comparative psychology in one of his Zoology courses at Denison University from 1885 until he went to Cincinnati in 1889. While at Cincinnati, in 1891 Herrick founded *The Journal of Comparative Neurology* (which today ranks as one of the leading publications in the neurosciences). Herrick soon announced that the journal's scope included comparative psychology (C. L. Herrick, 1891). Later Herrick (1903) changed the journal's title to *The Journal of Comparative Neurology and Psychology*.

After extended correspondence, Harper offered Herrick a professorship with the title to be decided on later. There was a clear understanding that all future arrangements would safeguard Herrick's interests. This correspondence also makes it very clear that Herrick's intentions were to inaugurate an integrated Ph.D. program including comparative psychology, comparative neurology, and physiological psychology—areas today included under the term "the neurosciences" (on Herrick as a pioneer American neuroscientist, see Windle, 1979).

Herrick resigned his position at Cincinnati and went to Europe (at his own expense—a common practice among Harper's appointees) to visit laboratories and to acquire laboratory equipment that Harper indicated (without a formal commitment) would be reimbursed by the University.

While in Europe, Herrick learned that Harper was negotiating with a number of individuals to cover the areas already promised to him. (Many of these individuals were involved in the infamous faculty mutiny at Clark University against the psychologist-president, G. Stanley Hall (1844–1924) [for a summary, see Cadwallader, 1984a].) Herrick returned to the United States and after failure to resolve the matter, resigned his position prior to the opening of the University. (For details of this unhappy matter and the tragic consequences for Herrick, see Cadwallader, 1984a.) One consequence of Herrick's resignation from the University of Chicago was a delay in the appearance of comparative psychology in the University's curriculum.

For the following account, note that information concerning University of Chicago course offerings was taken from two sources. One was *The Quarterly Calendar*, which was published only during the University's first 4 years, 1892–1896. The other was the continuing *Annual Register*. The announcements appearing in *The Quarterly Calendar*, by virtue of its quarterly publication, could be close in time to the courses described. In contrast, the *Annual Register*, published near the close of the academic year and containing announcements for the ensuing year, might be, in the extreme, almost a year in advance of the courses for the following spring quarter. It should be remembered that announcements in the *Annual Register* were prospective; it is quite possible that some of the announced courses were not offered.

The University of Chicago began instruction in the fall of 1892. Had Herrick been involved, presumably the curriculum would have included an integrated program in which comparative and animal psychology would have played a central role. In contrast, nothing involving comparative psychology, and only one course definitely involving animal psychology, can be found in the *Annual Registers* or *The Quarterly Calendars;* a second course possibly concerned animal psychology.

This situation held, first of all, for the Department of Philosophy, where the sole psychologist was Charles A. Strong (1862–1940; he was a son-in-law of John D. Rockefeller and one of the individuals with whose hiring Harper violated the agreement with Herrick—in this case with respect to physiological psychology). In Philosophy there was nothing involving either comparative or animal psychology. Although this chapter focuses on the contributions of the zoological sciences at Chicago to comparative and animal psychology, it is of interest that it was not until 1894–1895 that a course in comparative psychology was offered in the Department of Philosophy (*Annual Register*, 1893–1894, p. 44). Although by the fall of 1894 there were two psychologists in the Department of Philosophy (Strong and James R. Angell, 1869–1949), the course in comparative psychology was taught by an Assistant Professor of Philosophy, George Herbert Mead (1863–1931), who is generally regarded as a philosopher importantly involved with social psychology. (For Mead's intellectual biography, see Miller, 1973.)

It was in the Department of Biology where both a course definitely involving animal psychology and one possibly involving it were offered. The following account centers on courses for which either the title or description (or both) indicate a concern with matters relating to comparative and/or animal psychology—which here is taken to include animal behavior. As is seen, there is considerable material. Because of the extent of the story, a departmental approach is taken. Following the description of the two 1892–1893 courses definitely or possibly containing psychological material, the approach here is to follow each of the post-1892 zoological departments' involvements.

Because this departmental approach obscures either a chronological or a cross-sectional view of what was going on at any one time, a table has been appended (Appendix 1) giving a year-by-year listing of courses, instructors, and the psychological terminology involved. Also, by the end of the 1905–1906 year, only the Department of Zoology, among any of the zoological departments at Chicago (excluding, of course, Philosophy/Psychology), continued to offer courses involving comparative- and/or animal-psychological concerns. Because the vast majority of individuals who taught such courses were members of the Department of Zoology, and because it is difficult to keep such individuals in any kind of historical perspective, Appendix 2 lists Zoology Department members and their titles year-by-year.

There may have been course-content pertaining to comparative or animal psychology in courses for which the catalog description provides no clue. Only extant course notes or course examinations or mention of such course content in correspondence can provide information in cases where catalog descriptions fail to mention it; the author hopes to explore for such material in the future. As a consequence, what follows should be regarded as a minimal account of the involvement of the zoological scientists at Chicago in comparative and animal psychology.

Henry H. Donaldson (1857–1938) was one of the Clark University emigrees who had joined Chicago's Biology Department as Professor of Neurology (a title that Harper had clearly promised to Herrick). Donaldson was responsible both for the course definitely involving animal psychology and for the one possibly involving animal psychology during the University's first year of instruction. Biology 142 was the course definitely involving animal psychology. It was offered during the winter quarter and was entitled "Physical Character of the Brain as Related to Intelligence" (*The Quarterly Calendar*, Graduate School and College Edition, No. 2, September 1892, p. 44; No. 3, December 1892, p. 43; No. 4, April 1893, p. 43.). The *Annual Register* (1892–1893) described this course in the announcements for 1893–1894 as follows: "The attempt has been so often made to correlate the Physical characters of the Brain with intelligence, that it has seemed desirable to give one term to the statements of the facts and arguments bearing on this question" (p. 95). This course was offered at least once each year until Donaldson left in 1906.

The course offered by Donaldson that possibly may have involved animal psychology was Biology 139, "Doctrine of localization of function in the cerebral cortex." It was described in the *Annual Register* for 1893–1894: "It is of course understood, that the anatomical conditions found in the Cerebral Cortex are but a special example of a law of arrangement, applying to the entire Nervous System, and the subject will be discussed from this point of view" (p. 131). This course was also offered in 1895–1896 and 1896–1897 (*Annual Register*, 1894–1895, p. 173; 1895–1896, p. 182).

In April of 1893, i.e., late in the University's first year of instruction, the Department of Biology was divided into five departments: Zoology and Palaeontology (which became separate departments in 1894–1895), Neurology, Physiology, Anatomy, and Botany (*The Quarterly Calendar*, 1893–1894, 2(1), p. 22; *Annual Register*, 1892–1893, p. 91; no instruction was offered in Botany during 1893–1894, *Annual Register*, 1892–1893, p. 90).

Because animal psychology was first taught at the University of Chicago by the neurologist H. H. Donaldson, the present account continues with the offerings of the Department of Neurology. During the 1893–1894 year, subsequent to the splitting of the Department of Biology into the five departments, Donaldson constituted the entire faculty of the Department of Neurology. In September of 1893 Donaldson became Dean of the Ogden (Graduate) School of Science (University of Chicago Trustees, 1890–1896, pp. 122, 129). He subsequently became Head Professor of Neurology in 1895. (Because of widespread inaccuracies concerning the date of Donaldson's appointment as Dean of the Ogden School of Science, the following is included to set the record straight. Every secondary source on Donaldson seen by the present writer, including those based on information supplied by Donaldson, i.e., *American Men of Science, Who's Who in America*, and *Psychological Registers* [Murchison, 1929, 1932], give 1892 as the date he became Dean of the Ogden [Graduate] School of Science. However, the record is absolutely clear. In addition to the action of the Board of

Trustees just cited, there is the following: (a) The Trustees, at their meeting of June 26, 1893 [p. 115], had appointed Donaldson *Acting* Dean of the Ogden Graduate School of Science; (b) all issues of the 1892–1893 *Quarterly Calender* list President William R. Harper as Acting Dean of the Graduate School [all four "numbers" on p. 3]. Donaldson is simply listed as "Professor of Neurology" [all four "numbers" on p. 5]; (c) *The Quarterly Calendar* for November 1893 [Vol. 2(3) p. 13] notes that "Professor Henry H. Donaldson has been appointed to the Deanship of" the Ogden [Graduate] School of Science. The action of the Board in this regard is subsequently cited on p. 16, and the new title for Donaldson is again noted on p. 17.)

For 1893–1894 Donaldson's course involving animal psychology was listed as "Physical Characters of the Brain as Related to Intelligence" (*Annual Register*, 1892–1893, p. 95). With the exception of 1893–1894 when it was announced (*Annual Register*, 1892–1893, p. 95) but subsequently listed as "not given" (*The Quarterly Calendar*, 1893–1894, 2[3], p. 54), Donaldson continued to offer this course through the 1905–1906 year when he left the University of Chicago. In 1894–1895, the course was renamed "The Growth of the Brain and its Physical Characters as Related to Intelligence" (*Annual Register*, 1893–1894, p. 131). On two occasions this course was taught during the summer quarter by a departmental "Fellow." During the summers of 1897 (*Annual Register*, 1896–1897, p. 307) and 1898 (*Annual Register*, 1897–1898, p. 317) the course was taught by Irving Hardesty (1866–1944).

Donaldson left for Philadelphia at the end of the 1905–1906 year to become Professor of Neurology and Director of Research at the Wistar Institute of Anatomy and Biology.

Both before and after his Chicago years, Donaldson was importantly involved with psychology, e.g., his 1888 paper, "On the Relation of Neurology to Psychology." Another manifestation of this involvement was his joining the American Psychological Association in 1894 (which had been founded by G. Stanley Hall in 1892—very possibly to take attention away from the loss of many of his Clark University faculty to the University of Chicago as a consequence of the mutiny). Donaldson remained an APA member until 1937, just 2 years before his death (Cadwallader, 1979, 1980). For more on Donaldson's involvement in psychology, see, e.g., his entries in *The Psychological Registers* (Murchison, 1929, 1932) or his biography (Conklin, 1939).

Following Donaldson's departure from Chicago, the Department of Neurology was disbanded and incorporated into the Department of Anatomy. For 1906–1907, immediately following Donaldson's departure, the only member of the Department of Anatomy staff with a title in Neurology was Elizabeth H. Dunn (1867–1929), M.D., who was an Assistant (*Annual Register*, 1905–1906, p. 267). It is rather ironic that for the following year (*Annual Register*, 1906–1907, p. 262), the individual appointed as Professor of Neurology was Charles J. Herrick (1866–1960), the younger brother of, by then, the late Clarence L.

Herrick. (C. J. Herrick [1955a] credited his elder brother with drawing him into neurology.)

Another of the original members of the Department of Biology who was involved with comparative and animal psychology was Jacques Loeb (1859–1924). Following the division of the Department of Biology in 1893, Loeb became the senior member of the Department of Physiology (as an Assistant Professor). The Department also had an Assistant, David J. Lingle (1863–1936). Loeb subsequently advanced up the academic ranks and became Professor in 1900 and Head in 1901.

Despite the fact that Loeb had been publishing on tropisms since 1888, he did not include anything on tropisms in course descriptions until 1897–1898 when they were included in his course on "General Physiology" (*Annual Register, 1896–1897, p. 306*). Two years later (1899–1900) that course's description was changed to exclude any reference to tropisms, but "Advanced Physiology" included "laboratory work on animal tropisms" (*Annual Register, 1898–1899, p. 321*). The following year the situation remained the same. However in 1901–1902, "Advanced Physiology" was not offered, but a new course, "Physiology of Space Sensation," was offered (*Annual Register, 1900–1901, p. 293*). This course was also scheduled for 1902–1903 (*Annual Register, 1901–1902, p. 317*), but Loeb departed before the start of the 1902–1903 year.

The extent of Loeb's involvement with comparative and animal psychology while he was at Chicago, can be seen from the fact that in 1899 he published the German version of what in the following year became his important book, *Comparative Physiology of the Brain and Comparative Psychology*. This book, dedicated to Ernst Mach (1838–1916), the Austrian physicist and positivistic philosopher of science, was extremely positivistic. For example, Loeb (1900) argued that:

> The aim of modern biology is no longer word-discussions, but the control of life-phenomena. Accordingly we do not raise and discuss the question as to whether or not animals possess intelligence, but we consider it our aim to work out the dynamics of the processes of association, and find out the physical or chemical conditions which determine the variation in the capacity of memory in the various organisms. (p. 287)

It is perhaps not coincidental that John B. Watson (1878–1958), the founder of "Behaviorism," noted in his autobiography (1936) that Loeb was one of the three Chicago faculty to whom he owed the greatest intellectual debt (the other two were James R. Angell, the psychologist, and H. H. Donaldson, the neurologist) and that it was in his Chicago days that his behavioristic views began to be formulated.

In 1902 Loeb left Chicago for the University of California. (For more on Loeb see Hirsch, 1973.)

After Loeb's departure, only during the 1902–1903 year (the schedule for which was prepared while Loeb was Department Head) was there a course in the Department of Physiology for which the description suggested content bearing on comparative or animal psychology. The course was "Special Physiology of Mammals" and included the study of "localization." Elias P. Lyon (1867–1937) and Martin H. Fischer (1879–1962) were the instructors (*Annual Register*, 1901–1902, p. 317).

Another of the ex-Clark faculty at Chicago was Charles O. Whitman (1842–1910). At Clark he had been Chairman of the Department of Biology. He was also the Director of the Marine Biological Laboratory at Woods Holl (now called Woods Hole), Massachusetts from 1888–1908. At Chicago, Whitman first held the title of Head of the Department of Biology, then Head of the Department of Zoology and Palaeontology, and finally, after Palaeontology became a separate department in 1894, Head of the Department of Zoology. Whitman held the latter position until his death in 1910.

Whitman's interest in animal behavior can be traced to 1880 when he published "Do Flying Fish Fly?" This paper described observations he made on a 23-day trip from San Francisco to Yokohama (Whitman was Professor of Zoology at the Imperial University of Japan, 1879–1881). In contrast to the negative answer given in a paper (1878) by the German zoologist, Karl August Mobius (1825–1908) to the question posed in the title of Whitman's paper, Whitman's answer was affirmative. He reported clear and frequent observation of pectoral fin flapping and occasional changes in direction of flight (cf. Mobius, 1889). It is interesting to note that Whitman called attention to Mobius's laying to "historical and psycological [sic] grounds" what Mobius considered as the false notion that flying fish actually fly (Whitman, 1880, p. 649).

At Chicago Whitman published a number of papers involving animal psychology and/or animal behavior. For example, in 1898 he published a paper entitled "Animal Behavior" in the *Marine Biological Laboratory Biological Lectures;* this was a 53-page, wide-ranging article including instinct, intelligence, and habit. Another was the 1899 article "Myths in Animal Psychology"; it referred to "the coming science of comparative psychology" (1899, p. 525; cf. p. 537).

In 1902 Whitman proposed "A biological farm for the experimental investigation of heredity, variations and evolution, and for the study of life histories, habits, instincts and intelligence." While a "biological farm" was not forthcoming, a number of zoologists and a few psychologists carried out behavioral research at the Marine Biological Laboratory; but that is another story for another paper.

In addition to his administrative responsibilities as department head at Chicago and as Director at Woods Holl, Whitman had many other important scientific responsibilities. Among these, for example, was the editorship of *Biological Bulletin, Journal of Morphology,* and *Marine Biological Laboratory Biological Lectures.*

Despite a very heavy research involvement, Whitman published relatively little. Undoubtedly his heavy administrative responsibilities contributed to his limited publication, but another factor was his insistence that his publications "be as perfect as he could make [them]," i.e., he was a perfectionist (Newman, 1948, p. 218).

At his death in 1910, Whitman left an enormous accumulation of data. This led to the posthumous publication in 1919 of three volumes of Whitman's unpublished research. Volume III, edited by the University of Chicago psychologist, Harvey Carr (1873–1954), was entitled *The Behavior of Pigeons* (a title B. F. Skinner must surely covet). As in the papers mentioned earlier, it covered a wide gambit of behavior; in this case, it ranged from sleep to intelligent behavior.

Finally, Whitman's interest in psychological questions was great enough that in 1906 he joined the American Psychological Association. He was a member of the association at the time of his death in 1910 (Cadwallader, 1979, 1980).

In the foregoing review of Whitman's involvement with comparative and animal psychology there has been no mention of any course taught by Whitman. He was associated with only one course for which the description included material on comparative or animal psychology, and in that course he was one of several faculty involved; this course is noted later.

Although the virtual absence of subjects bearing on comparative or animal psychology may have occurred in the descriptions of courses taught by the Head of the Department of Zoology, there was no such absence in courses taught by some of the other members of the department.

Charles M. Child (1869–1954) was the first member of the Department of Zoology to offer a course for which the description indicated a concern with psychological issues. Child received a PhB in 1890 and an M.S. in 1892 from Wesleyan University. It seems likely that it was at Wesleyan that Child developed his interest in psychology, for in 1892 he published a questionnaire study, "Statistics of 'Unconscious Cerebration'," in *The American Journal of Psychology*. Wesleyan was given as his institutional affiliation. In 1892 Child went to Leipzig where he was inclined to experimental psychology—until he worked for a semester in Wundt's laboratory (Hyman, 1957). He then shifted to the zoological laboratory of Rudolph Leuckart (1822–1898) and received a PhD in 1894. After working at the Naples Zoological Station, Child went to the University of Chicago in 1894–1895 as an "Honorary Fellow" (but with a stipend of $200, (University of Chicago Trustees, [1890–1896], p. 216 [May 29, 1894]; *Annual Register,* 1893–1894, p. 20). The 1894 date is also given in the *Annual Register,* 1894–1895, p. 168 and in all following *Annual Registers*. (All secondary accounts read by the present writer say—or imply—that Child went to Chicago in 1895.) He subsequently moved through the academic ranks (see Appendix 2) and became Professor in 1916. Child succeeded Lillie as Chairman of the Department in 1931; he held the position until 1934 when he became Professor Emeritus.

Throughout the remainder of his career, Child showed a strong interest in behavioral subjects as is seen from his courses. His interest in behavioral subjects also manifested itself in many behavioral papers (see Child, 1926, 1928, for example), and especially in his 1924 book, *Physiological Foundations of Behavior*.

Starting in 1897–1898, the Department of Zoology revised its curriculum and offered a three-quarter sequence "Elementary Zoology" ("Zoology 1, 2, 3"). The first two courses were taught by Child, the third by William M. Wheeler (1865–1937), then Assistant Professor of Embryology in the Department of Zoology. The description for "Zoology 1" read: "Classification, structure, development, geographical distribution, habits, and instincts of Protozoa [and other lower organisms]" (*Annual Register*, 1896–1897, p. 302). The course descriptions for courses 2 and 3 simply read "(continued)" and listed the species studied; the species advanced phylogenetically with the higher courses. Wheeler, who left Chicago in 1899 for the University of Texas, was importantly involved in the study of animal behavior throughout his career, e.g., his 1900 and 1908 papers (q.q.v.), his 1910 book, *Ants, Their Structure, Development, and Behavior*, and his membership in the American Psychological Association from 1904 until the year before his death in 1937 (Cadwallader, 1979, 1980).

In the following year (1898–1899), Child was involved with several new courses, which were concerned with psychological topics. One, "Zoology 4," was added for the summer quarter. Its description included the study of "habits and instincts" also. Two courses in "Field Zoology" (Zoology 46 and 47) were also offered, one in the spring and one in the summer. "Habits" were included among the subjects for study (*Annual Register*, 1897–1898, pp. 310–312). Child also had been promoted to Instructor (p. 23, p. 310).

In 1899–1900, the Department offered a new course, "General Biology," which was "open to all University students" but, in contrast to the "Elementary Zoology" courses, had no laboratory. The course description included "habit and instinct." Most members of the departmental faculty including Child, Wheeler, and Whitman, were involved with the course (*Annual Register*, 1898–1899, p. 316).

For the following year (1900–1901), this course was turned over to a new member of the Department, Assistant Professor Charles B. Davenport (1866–1944). Throughout his stay at Chicago, Davenport taught the course (changed to "General Zoology" for 1902–1903), for which the description continued to include both habit and instinct, (*Annual Register*, 1899–1900, p. 293; 1902–1903, p. 339).

Before coming to Chicago, while he was still at Harvard, Davenport had published two studies involving what today would be called behavior (Davenport & Cannon, 1897; Davenport & Perkins, 1897). Later he became a leader in the eugenics movement and published a large number of papers and books on this and related subjects (for Davenport's extensive bibliography, see Riddle, 1949). Davenport left Chicago in 1904 to become the Director of the new "Station for Experimental Evolution" at Cold Spring Harbor, New York.

From this point onward to the end of the period under review, it was common for general courses in the Department to mention ''habit'' and/or ''instinct''; for a complete list, see Appendix 1. An individual teaching some of these courses but not otherwise mentioned in conjunction with other courses was H. H. Newman (who wrote the departmental history referred to earlier). He taught ''General Zoology (I), (II), and (III)'' during the 1911–1912 year. ''Habits'' was included in the course descriptions. Newman wrote at least two papers concerned with behavior (1906a & b).

It was not only just in descriptions of individual courses that the zoological sciences noted a concern with psychology. This concern may be found in both the departmental narratives preceding the course descriptions and in the narrative for the group of the biological sciences as a whole. The 1892–1893 *Annual Register* entries (for the 1893–1894 year) for both the Departments of Physiology and Neurology contained statements concerning their relevance for psychology. The statement for the Department of Physiology noted that one class of courses was for ''beginners and advanced students of Physiology and of those sciences for which the knowledge of Physiology is fundamental or desirable, namely, Medicine, Psychology, Zoology, and Sociology'' (p. 93). The statement for Neurology was similar (p. 94).

There was not a statement concerning the Biological Departments en masse until the 1894–1895 *Annual Register*. It then drew attention to ''a few of the more important lines of work'' (p. 165) and mentioned ''habits'' and ''instincts.'' Such a statement continued until the 1896–1897 *Annual Register* when the opening statement was greatly revised to feature a description of the gift to the University that permitted the construction of the Hull Biological Laboratories. As is seen, there were later references to psychological matters included in the introductory materials for the Department of Zoology.

During the summer when some of the faculty went to marine laboratories, e.g., Woods Holl, Cold Spring Harbor, or Pacific Grove, Assistants and other junior members of the Department would teach courses for which the description involved matters concerning comparative or animal psychology. Thus, during the summer quarters of 1902, 1903, and 1904, ''Invertebrate Zoology'' was taught by Eugene H. Harper (1867–1953), Edwin G. Kirk (1880–1926), and Ruben M. Strong (1872–1964), respectively. All three were Assistants (*Annual Register*, 1901–1902, p. 309 & p. 310; 1902–1903, p. 340; 1903–1904, p. 346). Similarly, ''Field Zoology'' was taught in the summer of 1902 by Charles C. Adams (1873–1955), and ''Vertebrate Zoology'' was taught in the summer of 1905 by Henry H. Lane (1878–1965). Both Adams and Lane were also Assistants (*Annual Register*, 1901–1902, p. 309; 1904–1905, p. 303). ''General Zoology of Vertebrates'' was taught in the summer of 1904 by William L. Tower (1872–19??) who was then an Instructor (*Annual Register*, 1903–1904, p. 345).

Among these six junior members of the Department, Harper went on to publish at least three behaviorally oriented papers (e.g., Harper, 1905, 1907, 1909). Adams published at least one (1918). Lane published at least one study involving behavioral description (of a single armadillo; 1916), and his *Animal Biology* (1929) contained considerable material concerning behavior. For example, chapter 11 is entitled "Psychology," and chapter 14, "The Social Life of Animals." Tower published at least two papers concerned with behavior (1910a, b). Strong is met shortly.

The first specialized course that incorporated a behavioral subject in its description was entitled "Studies of Birds" ("Zoology 14"). It was added in the spring of 1906 (*Annual Register, 1904–1905*, p. 305) with R. M. Strong as the instructor. "Habits" were among the subjects of study. The course continued thru 1913–1914 after which it became Ornithology (*Annual Register, 1913–1914*, p. 277). The course, however, did not survive the departure of Strong, who was the sole instructor for the entire period. While at the University of Chicago, R. M. Strong published at least two behavioral papers (1911, 1914). He left for the University of Mississippi in 1914.

A course in "Animal Ecology" (Zoology 16) was first taught in 1908–1909. It involved the study of "breeding habits" and was taught by Victor E. Shelford (1877–1968) then an Associate in Zoology.

Shortly after the turn of the century, the word "behavior" began to appear in Department of Zoology doctoral dissertation titles. Among such dissertations was that of Charles Henry Turner (1867–1923) entitled "The Homing of Ants: An Experimental Study of Ant Behavior" (1907). (Turner had been a student of Herrick's at the University of Cincinnati; his paper, "Psychological Notes Upon The Gallery Spider" [1892], makes him by almost 30 years, the first black American psychologist. For a history of black psychologists—but not including Turner—see Guthrie, 1976. For more on Turner, see Cadwallader, 1984a).

There is a related matter of some interest to the history of comparative and animal psychology. Turner (1906) published an article entitled "A Preliminary Note on Ant Behavior" based on what would become his dissertation. This article was reviewed by John B. Watson in the *Psychological Bulletin* (1907). Watson's use of the word "behavior" in this review was, I believe, his first use of the word "behavior" in print. Watson's current biographer Cedric Larson has told me, however, that Watson did use the word "behavior" in an earlier Carnegie Foundation grant application (personal communication, May 25, 1978). Whether Watson's adoption of the word "behavior" can be traced to its use in the Department of Zoology, remains a question for further research; but it is certainly a viable hypothesis. (As noted earlier, Whitman had used "behavior" as early as his 1898 paper. T. W. Mills, however, had used the word behavior in a paper as early as 1887; see Cadwallader, 1984a.)

Although the word "behavior" first appeared in a dissertation in 1902, it did not appear in a course description until that for the 1909–1910 year (*Annual Register, 1908–1909*, p. 368). The course was "Animal Ecology" (Zoology 16) and was offered in the spring quarter. A "similar" course, "Zoology 17," with the same title was offered in the summer quarter (p. 369). The instructor was V. E. Shelford.

For the following year, the "Introductory" to the Departmental offerings was revised. The previous year's "Introductory" entry for "Ecology" had included "the study of *living* animals, habits, instincts, and modes of life" (*Annual Register,* 1908–1909, p. 367). For 1910–1911, however, the section was entitled "Behavior and Ecology." It noted that "Course 17 is devoted to analytical study of behavior; [*sic*] and supplements the work in the Department of Psychology. Courses 18 and 19 deal with behavior in nature and its relation to local and geographic distribution" (*Annual Register,* 1909–1910, p. 367).

Course 17 was "Animal Behavior." Its description in the *Annual Register* (1909–1910) read: "A general course dealing with the facts, principles, theories, and methods of analysis of behavior, with particular reference to the lower animals. Lectures and conferences, 2 hours a week; laboratory and field work, 6 hours a week" (p. 369).

Although Zoology 18 ("Animal Ecology"), referred to in the "Introductory," did list behavior among its subjects of study, Zoology 19 ("Geographic Zoology") did not. Shelford was the instructor of all three courses and also of three others, which included the study of behavior, two courses in "Field Zoology" (Zoology 3 and 4) and "Studies in Animal Ecology" (Zoology 34).

Shelford remained at the University of Chicago through the 1913–1914 year. During this time he continued to offer courses in which the title and/or description used the word "behavior" (see Appendix 1). He also wrote a number of papers involving behavior (Shelford, 1914a,b; Shelford & Allee, 1914; Shelford & Powers, 1915).

After Shelford left Chicago for the University of Illinois, the behavioral courses at Chicago were reduced to two. These two were the courses in "Ornithology," taught by R. M. Strong, and "Invertebrate Zoology," taught by Child. The behavioral subjects of study were feeding habits, and habits, respectively.

R. M. Strong left Chicago at the end of the 1914–1915 year, only a year after Shelford's departure. This combination of departures suggests that there was a policy change to disfavor behavioral study in the Department. One might suspect that with the death of Whitman (in 1910), who obviously was interested in behavioral subjects, there was to be a shift away from matters relating to comparative and animal psychology.

Whitman's successor as Department Chair was Frank R. Lillie (1870–1947) who had received a Ph.D. from the Department in 1894, taught at Michigan and Vassar, and returned to Chicago in 1900 as an Assistant Professor. He advanced rapidly and became Professor in 1907 and Chairman in 1910 following Whitman's death. Lillie had never taught a course for which the description involved any behavioral terminology and only one paper to that date, "Breeding Habits of the Heteronereis Form of Nereis Limbata at Woods Hole, Massachusetts," showed any interest in behavior. However, the paper (Lillie & Just, 1913, p. 147) makes clear that the behavioral observations were carried out by the junior author, the early and important black zoologist, E. E. Just (1883–1941; for Just's biography, see Manning, 1983). Nevertheless, this paper suggests that Lillie was not opposed to behavioral studies.

On the other hand, the nearly simultaneous departure of the two nontenured members among the three faculty with interests in behavioral matters (both Shelford and Strong were Instructors; Child was an Associate Professor) might perhaps have been due to a policy instituted by Lillie to reduce the amount of interest in this area.

The course listings for 1915–1916, immediately after R. M. Strong's departure, however, show that there was no lack of behavioral subjects. In addition to Child's course in "Invertebrate Zoology" (Zoology 15), which involved the study of "habits," three other courses were concerned with behavioral subjects. Two of these also involved "habits," "Elementary Field Zoology" (Zoology 7) and "Entomology" (Zoology 28). The third course was "Animal Behavior and Ecology" (Zoology 26). The instructor in all three of these courses was Morris M. Wells (1885–1930), who had just received his Ph.D. from Chicago and was then a newly appointed Instructor.

That the 1915–1916 set of behaviorally oriented courses was not the last year of such courses can be seen from the courses in a latter year chosen haphazardly (but without foreknowledge of its content), 1930–1931. There were two courses that contained the word "behavior" in their title: "Animal Behavior" (Zoology 305) and "Problems in Animal Behavior and Ecology" (Zoology 360) and two other courses the titles for which suggest behavioral content: "Animal Ecology" (Zoology 305) and "Animal Aggregations" (Zoology 411). Unfortunately, course descriptions were not included in the 1929–1930 *Annual Register* (p. 218). The instructor for all of these courses was Warder C. Allee (1885–1955) who was then Professor (on Allee, see Banks, 1985, which appeared after the present chapter was submitted; reading Bank's paper suggests that Allee's course "Animal Aggregations" would have included behavior).

As might be expected, there was an interchange between the zoological departments and the Department of Philosophy/Psychology. Graduate students in psychology sometimes minored in one or another of the zoological sciences. John B. Watson (PhD, 1903), for example, minored in Neurology. The reverse was, of course, also true; Turner (PhD, 1907), for example, minored in Psychology.

At the end point of this account, 1915, the study of behavior at the national level was increasing at a rapid pace. Only 2 years earlier, the paper, which came to be known as the "Behavioristic Manifesto," was published by a 1903 recipient of a Chicago PhD in psychology. This paper was, of course, "Psychology as the Behaviorist Views It," by John B. Watson (1913), who, as the present chapter has noted, had been importantly influenced by Chicago zoologists. Only 1 year earlier than our end point, Watson (1914) had published *Behavior: An Introduction to Comparative Psychology*. (Watson had left Chicago for Johns Hopkins in 1908—and in the process jumped from what would have been an

Assistant Professorship had he remained at Chicago [University of Chicago Trustees, (1907–1909), p. 166 (February 18, 1908)] to a Professorship of Experimental and Comparative Psychology [Johns Hopkins Trustees, (1907–1916), p. 12 (March 2, 1908)]).

By 1915 there were two specialized journals, *Behavior Monographs* and *The Journal of Animal Behavior,* both founded in 1911. Moreover, another important journal was to be established in the not-too-distant future (February of 1921), *The Journal of Comparative Psychology.* Prior to the establishment of these specialized journals, there had been, of course, *The Journal of Comparative Neurology and Psychology.*

The heavy involvement of zoologists in general and University of Chicago-related zoologists in particular with comparative and animal psychology can be seen from their involvement in these early publications. The earliest of the journals specializing—or in this case semispecializing—in comparative and animal psychology was *The Journal of Comparative Neurology and Psychology.* (It should be remembered that Clarence Luther Herrick had added *Psychology* to the title starting in 1904, not long before his death on September 15th of that year.)

Because *The Journal of Comparative Neurology and Psychology* was concerned with both comparative neurology and psychology, it is perhaps impossible to say which of the Chicago-related zoologists on the editorial board should be considered as being involved with the comparative and/or animal psychology aspects of the journal. All that can be done is to note the kinds of psychological involvement by the zoologists concerned.

To begin with, the 1904 title page listed three editors; Clarence Luther Herrick's name was listed above the other two. One of the other two was the younger Herrick, Charles Judson, who was listed as "Manager" and who was then at Denison University but who was to move to the University of Chicago in 1907 as Professor of Neurology. C. J. Herrick, like his older brother, was heavily involved in the study of behavior. C. J. Herrick published on behavior at least as early as 1902 and included the word "behavior" in a paper at least as early as 1905 (Herrick, 1902, 1905). He wrote "Comparative Psychology" in 1907, "Introspection as a Biological Method" in 1915(a), a review of J. B. Watson's *Behavior* that same year (1915b), *Neurological Foundations of Behavior* in 1924, *The Thinking Machine* in 1929, "Psychology From a Biologist's Point of View" in 1955(b), and, finally, *The Evolution of Human Nature* in 1956, among many involved with psychology. Although C. J. Herrick never joined the American Psychological Association (Cadwallader, 1979, 1980), his involvement in psychological matters was recognized by his inclusion in Murchison's 1932 *Psychological Register.* (On C. J. Herrick, see Bartelmez, 1973, and Roofe, 1960).

The third editor was the Harvard comparative psychologist, Robert M. Yerkes (1876–1956).

These three editors were associated with two zoologists, O. S. Strong (1864–

1951) of Columbia University and H. S. Jennings (1868–1947) of Johns Hopkins. Incomplete research has not yet revealed any behavioral work by O. S. Strong. Jennings was importantly involved in behavioral work with lower organisms, e.g., "The Psychology of a Protozoan" (1899) and *Behavior of the Lower Organisms* (1906). Later he wrote *The Biological Basis of Human Nature* (1930). He was included in Murchison's (1932) *Psychological Register*. An obituary was published in *The American Journal of Psychology* (Schneirla, 1947; see also Jensen, 1962, and Sonneborn, 1975). It is interesting to note that although Jennings was never formally affiliated with the University of Chicago, he had been voted a Fellowship with a stipend of $200 for the 1894–1895 year (Chicago Trustees, [1890–1896], p. 218 [May 29, 1894]). However Jennings declined it (Chicago Trustees, 1890–1896, p. 226 [June 26, 1894]). In the spring of 1894 Jennings had been an Assistant in Vertebrate Morphology at Michigan (University of Michigan *Calendar*, 1893–94, p. 17). He then went to Harvard on an assistantship (Harvard University *Catalogue*, 1894–95, p. 301) with a stipend of $225 (Sonneborn, 1975, p. 159), although it appears that it was the prestige of Harvard that drew him there (Sonneborn, 1975, p. 156).

Of the other 44 individuals ("Collaborators") listed on the title page, 10 were psychologists: J. M. Baldwin (1861–1934), W. H. Davis (1877–1933), S. I. Franz (1874–1933), T. H. Haines (1871–1951), E. B. Holt (1873–1946), Joseph Jastrow (1863–1944), C. L. Morgan (1852–1936), Hugo Münsterberg (1863–1916), E. L. Thorndike (1874–1949), and the Chicago-trained and by then, junior member of the Department of Philosophy (Psychology) Department at Chicago, J. B. Watson. Two others were psychologists secondarily. H. H. Bawden (1871–1954) was primarily a philosopher, but also a psychologist; T. W. Mills (1847–1915) was the early zoologist-comparative psychologist referred to earlier.

Of the 34 other "Collaborators," seven were located in Europe (as was C. L. Morgan) or Africa: Albrecht Bethe (1872–1954) of Strassburg, Frank J. Cole (1872–1959) of Liverpool, Ludwig Edinger (1855–1918) of Frankfurt a-M., A. van Gehuchten (1861–1914) of Louvain, W. A. Nagel (1871–1911) of Berlin, C. S. Sherrington (1856–1952) of Liverpool (who was, in 1932, to win the Nobel Prize in Physiology), and G. Elliot Smith (1871–1937) of Cairo. (Mills was located in Canada.)

Excluding from the total of 49 names on the title page the 9 living outside the United states and the 11 U.S. psychologists (including Bawden), there are 29 names remaining. All were zoologists or had been affiliated with zoology. Of them, 10 were then, or previously, affiliated with a zoological department at the University of Chicago. Eight have already been encountered in the present article: the two Herricks, C. B. Davenport, H. H. Donaldson, J. Loeb, E. P. Lyon, W. M. Wheeler, and C. O. Whitman. A ninth was S. J. Holmes (1868–1964) who had been a Fellow in 1895–1896 and 1896–1897 (PhD, 1897) and who became heavily involved in the study of behavior. He wrote *The Evolution of Animal Intelligence* (1911) and *Studies in Animal Behavior* (1916) and was a member of the American Psychological Association from 1911 to 1935 (Cadwallader, 1979, 1980). The tenth was Adolf Meyer (1866–1950) who had been an Honorary Fellow or Docent in Neurology at Chicago, 1892–1895. (He was also Pathologist at the Eastern Hospital for the Insane at nearby Kankakee, Illinois, 1893–1895.) Meyer was later to be regarded as the most influential psychiatrist of his day. He was a member of the American Psychological Association from 1905 to his death (Cadwallader, 1979, 1980).

Five of the 10 Chicago-related nonpsychologists listed on the title page were members of the American Psychological Association (Donaldson, Holmes, Meyer, Wheeler, and Whitman). In contrast only one (Jennings) of the 19 non-Chicago zoologists located in the U.S. was an APA member (Cadwallader, 1979, 1980). Although a number of these zoologists were importantly involved in work in comparative and animal psychology, their involvement is beyond the scope of the present chapter.

The establishment of the two specialized journals in 1911 was simultaneously the occasion for *The Journal of Comparative Neurology and Psychology* to revert to its original title of *The Journal of Comparative Neurology*. An ''Editorial Announcement'' at the end of 1910 (Vol. 20, p. 625) called attention to the ''reorganization'' to be caused by the prospective establishment of *The Journal of Animal Behavior*.

Just as Chicago zoologists were involved with *The Journal of Comparative Neurology and Psychology,* so too were they involved with the specialized journals.

The Journal of Animal Behavior, first published in 1911, had as its editor the psychologist Robert M. Yerkes. On its editorial board were eight individuals of whom five were psychologists; two were Chicago related: John B. Watson and Harvey A. Carr—previously encountered as the editor of Whitman's *The Behavior of Pigeons*—and who was both Chicago trained and a University of Chicago faculty member. (The other psychologists were Madison Bentley [1870–1955] then at Cornell; Edward L. Thondike of Columbia University; and Margaret F. Washburn [1871–1939], of Vassar College, who served as ''Editor of Reviews.'') The other three editorial board members were zoologists; two were former members of the Department of Zoology at Chicago: S. J. Holmes and W. M. Wheeler. The third zoologist was H. S. Jennings.

The other 1911-established journal was *Behavior Monographs*. Its editor initially was J. B. Watson. He edited the first three volumes plus the first three monographs (each dated 1919) of volume four. The final two monographs, both dated 1922, were edited by the Chicago-trained psychologist, Walter S. Hunter (1889–1954). None of the *Behavior Monographs* that I have been able to examine have contained the listing of an editorial board. However its successor,

Comparative Psychology Monographs, which began publication during 1922, the same year as the final *Behavior Monograph,* did have an editorial board.

The editor of *Comparative Psychology Monographs* was also Hunter (both *Monographs* were published by the Williams & Wilkins Company of Baltimore). On its editorial board was the Chicago psychologist, H. A. Carr; the Harvard psychologist, R. M. Yerkes; the Chicago-trained zoologist, S. J. Holmes; and an individual universally considered a psychologist (as he considered himself) but who was trained as a zoologist, Karl S. Lashley (1890–1958), then at the University of Minnesota, but later (1929–1935) at Chicago (Lashley's A. B. From West Virginia was in zoology, his M.S. from Pittsburgh was in bacteriology, and his Ph.D. from Johns Hopkins was in genetics).

As noted earlier, *The Journal of Comparative Psychology* began publication in 1921. The psychologists Knight Dunlap (1875–1949) and Yerkes were the Editors. Initially its masthead noted that it "Continu[ed] *Psychobiology* and the *The Journal of Animal Behavior.*" The 14-member editorial board included five Chicago-related individuals. Three were psychologists: Carr, Hunter, and Watson; two were zoologists: Holmes and Wheeler. Others on the editorial board were five psychologists: Bentley, Franz, Thorndike, and Washburn, all previously encountered, and a newcomer, Raymond Dodge (1871–1942), then at Wesleyan. There were four others, Jennings and three newcomers, the physiologist Walter B. Cannon (1871–1945), the psychiatrist-primatologist Gilbert V. T. Hamilton (1877–1943), and the zoologist George H. Parker (1864–1955). All these individuals except Parker were members of the American Psychological Association and had been prior to their involvement with *The Journal of Comparative Psychology* (Cadwallader, 1979, 1980).

Although the story of the involvement of University of Chicago zoologists in comparative and animal psychology is certainly not complete, even the present limited account shows that this contribution was substantial during the period here covered and beyond. The story warrants completion. Certainly the titles of dissertations and the publications that were concerned with comparative and animal psychology and that were produced by members of the zoological departments at Chicago should be compiled. All the Chicago-related individuals (at the very least) mentioned in the present chapter (including those whose names appear only in Appendix 2) warrant having their contributions to the field more fully described. At least the story has been started; it deserves to be finished.

But so too does the larger account of the input of zoologists to comparative and animal psychology in general. Indeed, the whole history of comparative and animal psychology similarly deserves greater attention (as indeed does the whole of American psychology; Cadwallader, 1984b, 1986). Fortunately there are signs that the field is coming under renewed historical scrutiny. The present volume is a case in point as is Dewsbury's recent book (1984). Let us hope the trend continues.

ACKNOWLEDGMENTS

I wish to thank the Indiana State University Research Committee for grants that supported, in part, the research on which this article is based. To the many individuals and institutions who provided materials and/or assistance, I am greatly indebted. High among this category are Professors Paul G. Roofe and William F. Windle who shared their Herrick scholarship with me. So also are two former graduate students: Dr. Michael G. Luxenberg, who served as my graduate assistant during much of the period when library materials used in this article were being gathered, and Dr. Christopher Joyce, who gathered much material concerning C. H. Turner, and also my present graduate assistant, Daniel M. Williams. I especially wish to thank the following and their staffs for the considerable assistance and many personal courtesies, as well as many materials, provided me when I visited their institutions: Mr. Robert Rosenthal, Department of Special Collections, Regenstein Library, University of Chicago; Ms. Maxine Klapp and Ms. Penelope Krosch, University Archives, Walter Library, University of Minnesota; the staff of the Department of Special Collections, Central Library, University of Cincinnati. I also thank Mr. Stuart W. Campbell of the University Archives, Goddard Library, Clark University, who has been sending documents to me for many years. And, finally, though not by any means least in their importance, I would like to acknowledge my thanks to Mr. Gene Norman and his staff of the Reference Department, to the staff of the Inter-Library Loan Department, and, indeed, to the entire staff of the Cunningham Memorial Library of Indiana State University; their assistance over the years has been very great.

REFERENCES

Banks, E. M. (1985). Warder Clyde Allee and the Chicago school of animal behavior. *Journal of the History of the Behavioral Sciences, 21*, 345–353.

Bartelmez, G. W. (1973). Charles Judson Herrick. *Biographical Memoirs of the National Academy of Sciences, 43*, 78–108.

Cadwallader, T. C. (1979, September). *A cumulative membership list for the American Psychological Association's first fifty years, 1892–1941, with follow-up thru 1979.* Paper presented at the meeting of the American Psychological Association, New York.

Cadwallader, T. C. (1980, October). *Other-scientist-members of the American Psychological Association, 1892–1941: Interdisciplinary involvement.* Paper presented at the meeting of the History of Science Society, Toronto.

Cadwallader, T. C. (1984a). Neglected aspects of the evolution of American comparative and animal psychology. In G. Greenberg & E. Tobach, (Eds.), *Behavioral evolution and integrative levels.* Hillsdale, NJ: Lawrence Erlbaum Associates.

Cadwallader, T. C. (1984b, April). *Towards demythologizing psychology's history: Harvard,*

Hopkins, James, and other matters. Invited address presented at the meeting of the Eastern Psychological Association, Baltimore.

Cadwallader, T. C. (1986, August). *Towards demythologizing the history of American psychology: Beyond Harvard and Hopkins.* Presidential address, Division of the History of Psychology, American Psychological Association, presented at the meeting of the American Psychological Association, Washington, DC.

Cheney, J. L. (1890). *Letter to Rev. Dr. [Alonzo K.] Parker, Sept. 3, 1890. William Rainey Harper Papers,* Box XV, Folder 17. Department of Special Collections, Regenstein Library, University of Chicago.

Child, C. M. (1892). Statistics of "unconscious cerebration." *The American Journal of Psychology, 5,* 249–259.

Child, C. M. (1901). The habits and natural history of *Stichostemma. American Naturalist, 35,* 975–1006.

Child, C. M. (1924). *Physiological foundations of behavior.* New York: Holt.

Child, C. M. (1926). Behavior origins from a physiologic point of view. *Archives of Neurology and Psychiatry, 15,* 173–184.

Child, C. M. (1928). Biological foundations of social integration. *Publications of the American Sociological Society, 22,* 26–42.

Conklin, E. G. (1939). Henry Herbert Donaldson. *Biographical Memoirs of the National Academy of Sciences, 29,* 229–243.

Davenport, C. B., & Cannon, W. B. (1897). On the determination of the direction and rate of movement of organisms by light. *Journal of Physiology, 21,* 22–32.

Davenport, C. B., & Perkins, H. (1897). A contribution to the study of geotaxis in the higher animals. *Journal of Physiology, 22,* 99–110.

Dewsbury, D. A. (1984). *Comparative psychology in the twentieth century.* Stroudsburg, PA: Hutchinson Ross.

Donaldson, H. H. (1888). On the relation of neurology to psychology. *The American Journal of Psychology, 1,* 209–221.

Goodspeed, T. W. (1916). *A history of the University of Chicago.* Chicago: University of Chicago Press. (Reprinted, 1972).

Guthrie, R. V. (1976). *Even the rat was white.* New York: Harper & Row.

Harper, E. H. (1905). Reactions to light and mechanical stimuli in the earthworm Perichaeta Bermudensis (Beddard). *Biological Bulletin, 10,* 17–34.

Harper, E. H. (1907). The behavior of the phantom larvae of Corethra plumicornis Fabricius. *The Journal of Comparative Neurology and Psychology, 19,* 435–456.

Harper, E. H. (1909). Tropic and shock reactions in Perichaeta and Lumbricus. *The Journal of Comparative Neurology and Psychology, 19,* 569–588.

Herrick, C. J. (1902). The feeding habits of fishes. *School Science, 2,* 324–327.

Herrick, C. J. (1905). A functional view of nature as seen by a biologist. *Journal of Philosophy, Psychology, and Scientific Method, 2,* 428–438.

Herrick, C. J. (1907). Comparative psychology. *Popular Science Monthly, 70,* 76–78.

Herrick, C. J. (1915a). Introspection as a biological method. *Journal of Philosophy, Psychology, and Scientific Method, 12,* 543–551.

Herrick, C. J. (1915b). Watson's "Behavior." *The Journal of Animal Behavior, 5,* 467–470.

Herrick, C. J. (1924). *Neurological foundations of animal behavior.* New York: Holt.

Herrick, C. J. (1929). *The thinking machine.* Chicago: University of Chicago Press.

Herrick, C. J. (1955a). Clarence Luther Herrick: Pioneer naturalist, teacher, and psychobiologist. *Transactions of the American Philosophical Society,* N.S. 45 (Part 1).

Herrick, C. J. (1955b). Psychology from a biologist's point of view. *Psychological Review, 62,* 333–340.

Herrick, C. J. (1945). *The evolution of human nature.* Austin: University of Texas Press.

Herrick, C. L. (1882). Habits of fresh-water Crustacea. *American Naturalist, 16,* 813–816.

Herrick, C. L. (1891). Editor's announcement. *The Journal of Comparative Neurology, 1,* 358.

Herrick, C. L. (1903). Editorial announcement. *The Journal of Comparative Neurology, 13,* 335–336.

Hirsch, J. (1973). Introduction to the Dover edition of J. Loeb, *Forced movements, tropisms, & animal conduct.* New York: Dover. (Originally published in 1918 by Lippencott.)

Holmes, S. J. (1911). *The evolution of animal intelligence.* New York: Holt.

Holmes, S. J. (1916). *Studies in animal behavior.* Boston: Badger.

Hyman, L. H. (1957). Charles Manning Child. *Biographical Memoirs of the National Academy of Sciences, 30,* 73–103.

Jennings, H. S. (1899). The psychology of a protozoan. *The American Journal of Psychology, 10,* 503–515.

Jennings, H. S. (1906). *Behavior of the lower organisms.* New York: Columbia University Press. (Republished: Bloomington, IN: Indiana University Press, 1962, 1976.)

Jennings, H. S. (1930). *The biological basis of human nature.* New York: Norton.

Jensen, D. D. (1962). Foreword to the 1962 and 1976 editions of Jennings, H. S. (1906). *Behavior of the lower organisms.* New York: Columbia University Press. (Republished: Bloomington, IN: Indiana University Press, 1962, 1976.)

Johns Hopkins University Board of Trustees. (1907–1916). *Minutes, November 4, 1907–May 8, 1916,* (Vol. 3). Ferdinand Hamburger, Jr. Archives, Johns Hopkins University.

Jonçich, G. (1968). *The sane positivist: A biography of Edward L. Thorndike.* Middletown, CT: Wesleyan University Press.

Lane, H. H. (1916). Some observations on the habits and placentation of Tatu Novemcinctum. *The State University of Oklahoma Research Bulletin.* No. 1.

Lane, H. H. (1929). *Animal biology.* Philadelphia: Blakiston.

Lillie, F. R., & Just, E. E. (1913). Breeding habits of the heteronereis form of *Nereis limbata* at Woods Hole, Massachusetts. *Biological Bulletin, 24,* 147–168.

Loeb, J. (1900). *Comparative physiology of the brain and comparative psychology.* New York: Putnam.

Lotze, H. (1885). *Outlines of psychology: Dictations from lectures.* Translated from the German with the addition of a chapter on the brain by C. L. Herrick. Minneapolis: Williams. (Original work published 1881)

Manning, K. R. (1983). *Black Appolo of science: The life of Ernest Everett Just.* New York: Oxford University Press.

Miller, D. L. (1973). *George Herbert Mead: Self, language, and the world.* Austin: University of Texas Press.

Mills, T. W. (1887). Comparative psychology: Its objects and problems. *The Popular Science Monthly, 30,* 651–660.

Mobius, K. A. (1878). Die Bewegungen der Fliegenden Fische Durch die Luft. *Zeitschrift für Wissenschaftlich Zoologie, 30* (Supplement), 343–382.

Mobius, K. A. (1889). Ueber die bewegung der fliegenden fisch durch die Luft. *Archiv für Anatomie und Physiologie (Physiologische Abtheilung), [13],* 348–349.

Morgan, C. L. (1894). *An introduction to comparative psychology.* London: Scott.

Morgan, C. L. (1896). *Habit and instinct.* New York: Arnold.

Murchison, C. (Ed.). (1929). *The psychological register* (2nd ed.). Worchester: Clark University Press.

Murchison, C. (Ed.). (1932). *The psychological register* (3rd ed.). Worcester: Clark University Press.

Murphy, G., & Kovach, J. K. (1972). *Historical introduction to modern psychology* (3rd ed.). New York: Harcourt Brace Jovanovich.

Newman, H. H. (1906a). The habits of certain tortoises. *The Journal of Comparative Neurology and Psychology, 16,* 126–152.

Newman, H. H. (1906b). Spawning behavior and sexual dimorphism in Fundulus heteroclitus and allied fish. *Biological Bulletin, 12,* 314–348.

Newman, H. H. (1948). History of the Department of Zoology in the University of Chicago. *Bios, 19,* 215–239.

Riddle, O. (1949). Charles Benedict Davenport. *Biographical Memoirs of the National Academy of Sciences, 25,* 75–110.

Roofe, P. G. (1960). Charles Judson Herrick: 1868–1960. *Anatomical Record, 137,* 162–164.

Schneirla, T. C. (1947). Herbert Spencer Jennings: 1867–1947. *American Journal of Psychology, 60,* 447–450.

Shelford, V. E. (1914a). An experimental study of the behavior agreement among the animals of an animal community. *Biological Bulletin, 26,* 294–316.

Shelford, V. E. (1914b). Modification of the behavior of land animals by contact with air of high evaporating power. *The Journal of Animal Behavior, 4,* 31–49.

Shelford, V. E., & Allee, W. C. (1914). Rapid modification of the behavior of fishes by contact with modified water. *The Journal of Animal Behavior, 4,* 1–30.

Shelford, V. E., & Powers, E. B. (1915). An experimental study of the movements of herring and other marine fishes. *Biological Bulletin, 28,* 315–334.

Sonneborn, T. M. (1975). Herbert Spencer Jennings. *Biographical Memoirs of the National Academy of Sciences, 47,* 143–223.

Strong, R. M. (1911). On the olfactory organs and the sense of smell in birds. *Journal of Morphology, 22,* 619–662.

Strong, R. M. (1914). On the habits and behavior of the herring gull. *The Auk, 31,* 22–49, 178–199.

Tower, W. L. (1910a). The determination of dominance and the modification of behavior in alternative (Mendelian) inheritance, by conditions surrounding or incident upon the germ cells at fertilization. *Biological Bulletin, 18,* 285–353.

Tower, W. L. (1910b). The determination of dominance and the modification of behavior in alternative (Mendelian) inheritance, by conditions surrounding or incident upon the germ cells at fertilization. *Biological Bulletin, 20,* 67–70.

Turner, C. H. (1892). Psychological notes upon the gallery spider—Illustration of intelligent variations in the construction of the web. *The Journal of Comparative Neurology, 2,* 95–110.

Turner, C. H. (1906). A preliminary note on ant behavior. *Biological Bulletin, 12,* 31–36.

Turner, C. H. (1907). The homing of ants: An experimental study of ant behavior. *The Journal of Comparative Neurology and Psychology, 17,* 367–434.

University of Chicago Board of Trustees. (1890–1896). *Minutes.* (Vol. 1). Department of Special Collections, Regenstein Library, University of Chicago.

University of Chicago Board of Trustees. (1907–1909). *Minutes* (Vol. 6). Department of Special Collections, Regenstein Library, University of Chicago.

Watson, J. B. (1907). [Review of Turner, C. H. (1906). A preliminary note on ant behavior. *Biological Bulletin, 12,* 31–36]. *Psychological Bulletin, 4,* 296–297.

Watson, J. B. (1913). Psychology as the behaviorist views it. *Psychological Review, 20,* 158–177.

Watson, J. B. (1914). *Behavior: An introduction to comparative psychology.* New York: Holt.

Watson, J. B. (1936). John Broadus Watson. In C. Murchison (Ed.), *History of psychology in autobiography* (Vol. 3, pp. 271–282). Worcester, Ma.: Clark University Press.

Weinland, D. F. (1858). A method of comparative animal psychology. *Proceedings of the American Association for the Advancement of Science, 12,* 256–266.

Wheeler, W. M. (1900). The habits of Ponera and Stigmatomma. *Biological Bulletin, 2,* 43–69.

Wheeler, W. M. (1908). Vestigial instincts in insects and other animals. *The American Journal of Psychology, 19,* 1–13.

Whitman, C. O. (1880). Do flying fish fly? *American Naturalist, 14,* 641–653; *Zoologist, 4,* 471–481.

Whitman, C. O. (1898). Animal behavior. *Marine Biological Laboratory Biological Lectures,* 285–338.

Whitman, C. O. (1899). Myths in animal psychology. *The Monist, 9,* 524–537.

Whitman, C. O. (1902). A biological farm for the experimental investigation of heredity, variations and evolution, and for the study of life histories, habits, instincts and intelligence. *Biological Bulletin, 3,* 214–224. Also, *Science, 16,* 504–510.

Whitman, C. O. (1919). *The behavior of pigeons: Posthumous works of Charles Otis Whitman* (Vol. 3). (Ed. by H. A. Carr). Washington: The Carnegie Institution.

Windle, W. F. (1979). *The pioneering role of Clarence Luther Herrick in American neuroscience.* New York: Exposition.

Wundt, W. (1894). *Lectures on human and animal psychology* (J. E. Creighton & E. B. Titchener, Trans.). New York: Macmillan. (Based on the second German edition of 1892).

PSYCHOLOGICAL TERMINOLOGY IN ZOOLOGICAL COURSES,

APPENDIX 1   1892–1914

Year	Course	Course Title	Instructor	Terminology[a]
1892–93[b]	Biology-142 (Winter)	Physical Character of the Brain as Related to Intelligence	Donaldson	
	Biology-139 (Spring)	The Doctrine of Localization of Function in the Cerebral Cortex	Donaldson	
1893–94	Neurology-3	Physical Characters of the Brain as Related to Intelligence	Donaldson	the intelligence
1894–95	Neurology-3	The Growth of the Brain and its Physical Characters as Related to Intelligence	Donaldson	intelligence
	Neurology-4	Doctrine of Localization of Function in the Cerebral Cortex	Donaldson	
1895–96	"Introductory"	[Remarks]		habits, instincts
	Neurology-3	The Growth of the Brain and	Donaldson	intelligence

(*continued*)

APPENDIX 1 *(Continued)*

Year	Course	Course Title	Instructor	Terminology[a]
		its Physical Characters as Related to Intelligence		
	Neurology-4	Doctrine of Localization of Function in the Cerebral Cortex	Donaldson	
1896–97	"Introductory"	[Remarks]		habits, instincts
	Neurology-2	The Growth of the Brain and its Physical Characters as Related to Intelligence	Donaldson	intelligence
	Neurology-4	Doctrine of Localization of Function in the Cerebral Cortex	Donaldson	
1897–98	Zoology-1	Elementary Zoology	Child	habits, instincts
	Zoology-2	Elementary Zoology (cont.)	Child	habits, instincts
	Zoology-3	Elementary Zoology (cont.)	Wheeler	habits, instincts
	Physiology-2	General Physiology	Loeb	galvanotropism, heliotropism, chemotropism, geotropism
	Physiology-3	Laboratory Work in General Physiology	Loeb	heliotropism, galvanotropism, etc.
	Neurology-2	The Growth of the Brain and its Physical Characters as Related to Intelligence	Donaldson	intelligence
	Neurology-5	Growth of the Brain (Course 2 repeated) (Su)	Hardesty	intelligence
1898–99	Zoology-1	Elementary Zoology	Child	habits, instincts
	Zoology-2	Elementary Zoology (cont.)	Wheeler & Child	habits, instincts

APPENDIX 1   (*Continued*)

Year	Course	Course Title	Instructor	Terminology[a]
	Zoology-3	Elementary Zoology (cont.)	Wheeler	habits, instincts
	Zoology-4	Elementary Zoology (Su; less)[c]	Child	habits, instincts
	Zoology-46	Field Zoology	Child	habits
	Zoology-47	Field Zoology (Su; less)[c]	Child	habits
	Physiology-2	General Physiology	Loeb	galvanotropism, heliotropism, chemotropism, geotropism
	Neurology-2	The Growth of the Brain and its Physical Characters as Related to Intelligence	Donaldson	intelligence
	Neurology-5	Growth of the Brain (cont.) (Su)	Hardesty	intelligence
1899–00	Zoology-1	Elementary Zoology	Child	habits, instincts
	Zoology-2	Elementary Zoology (cont.)	Wheeler & Child	habits, instincts
	Zoology-3	Elementary Zoology (cont.)	Wheeler	habits, instincts
	Zoology-4	Elementary Zoology (same as Zool. 1) (Su)	Child	habits, instincts
	Zoology-5	General Biology	Whitman, Wheeler, Watase, Jordan, Elliot, Child	habit, instinct
	Zoology-46	Field Zoology	Child	habits
	Zoology-47	Field Zoology (Su; less)[c]	Child	habits
	Physiology-10	Advanced Physiology	Loeb	tropisms
	Neurology-2	The Growth of the Brain and its Physical Characters as	Donaldson	

(*continued*)

APPENDIX 1 (*Continued*)

Year	Course	Course Title	Instructor	Terminology[a]
		Related to Intelligence		
1900–01	Zoology-1	General Morphology	Child	habits
	Zoology-2	General Morphology (cont.)	Child	habits
	Zoology-3	General Morphology (cont.)	Child	habits
	Zoology-4	General Zoology (Su)	Child	habits
	Zoology-5	General Biology	Davenport	habit, instinct
	Zoology-46	Field Zoology (Au)	Child	habits
	Zoology-47	Field Zoology (Sp)	Child	habits
	Zoology-48	Field Zoology (Su; less)[c]	Child	habits
	Physiology-10	Advanced Physiology	Loeb	tropisms
	Neurology-2	The Growth of the Brain and its Physical Characters as Related to Intelligence	Donaldson	
1901–02	Zoology-1	Elementary Zoology	Child	habits
	Zoology-2	Elementary Zoology (cont.)	Child	habits
	Zoology-3	Elementary Zoology (cont.)	Child	habits
	Zoology-4	Field Zoology (Su; less)[c]	Child	habits
	Zoology-5	General Biology	Davenport	habit and instinct
	Zoology-46	Field Zoology (I)	Child	habits
	Physiology-32	Physiology of space sensations	Loeb	
	Neurology-2	The Growth of the Brain and its Physical Characters as Related to Intelligence	Donaldson	
1902–03	Zoology-1	General Zoology	Davenport	habit and instinct
	Zoology-3	Field Zoology	Child	habits

APPENDIX 1   (*Continued*)

Year	Course	Course Title	Instructor	Terminology[a]
	Zoology-4	Field Zoology (Su; less)[c]	Adams	habits
	Zoology-5	Invertebrate Zoology (I)	Child	habits
	"Not to be given in 1902–3"			
	Zoology-6	Invertebrate Zoology (II)	Child	habits
	"Not to be given in 1902–03"			
	Zoology-7	Invertebrate Zoology (Su)	Harper	habits
	Physiology-32	Physiology of space sensations	Loeb	space sensations
	Neurology-2	The Growth of the Brain and its Physical Characters as Related to Intelligence	Donaldson	
1903–04	Biology-1	General Zoology	Davenport	habit and instinct
	Zoology-3	Field Zoology	Child	habits
	Zoology-4	Field Zoology (Su; less)[c]	Child	habits
	Zoology-5	Invertebrate Zoology (I)	Child	habits
	Zoology-6	Invertebrate Zoology (II)	Child	habits
	Zoology-7	Invertebrate Zoology (Su; less)[c]	Kirk	habits
	Neurology-2	The Growth of the Brain and its Physical Characters as Related to Intelligence	Donaldson	
1904–05	Zoology-3	Field Zoology	Child	habits
	Zoology-4	Field Zoology (Su; less)[c]	Child	habits
	Zoology-5	Invertebrate Zoology (I)	Child	habits
	Zoology-6	Invertebrate Zoology (II)	Child	habits
	Zoology-7	Invertebrate Zoology (Su; less)[c]	Strong	habits
	Zoology-9	General Zoology of Vertebrates (Su)	Tower	habits

(*continued*)

APPENDIX 1   (*Continued*)

Year	Course	Course Title	Instructor	Terminology[a]
	Neurology-2	The Growth of the Brain and its Physical Characters as Related to Intelligence	Donaldson	
1905–06	Zoology-3	Field Zoology	Child	habits
	(Zoology-3)[d]	(Field Zoology) (Su; less)[c]	Child	habits
	Zoology-5	Invertebrate Zoology (I)	Child	habits
	Zoology-6	Invertebrate Zoology (II)	Child	habits
	Zoology-7	Invertebrate Zoology (Su; less)[c]	Child	habits
	Zoology-9	Vertebrate Zoology (Su)	Lane	habits
	Zoology-14	Studies of Birds	Strong	habits
	(Zoology-14)[d]	(Studies of Birds) (Su; less)[c]	Strong	habits
	Neurology-2	The Growth of the Brain and its Physical Characters as Related to Intelligence	Donaldson	
1906–07	Zoology-3	Field Zoology (Spring and Summer)	Child	habits
	Zoology-5	Invertebrate Zoology (I)	(Child)	habits
	Zoology-6	Invertebrate Zoology (II)	Child	habits
	Zoology-9	Vertebrate Zoology	Riddle	habits
	Zoology-14	Studies of Birds	Strong	habits
1907–08	Zoology-3	Field Zoology	Shelford	habits
	Zoology-5	Invertebrate Zoology (I) "Not to be given in 1907–08"	Child	habits
	Zoology-6	Invertebrate Zoology (II) "Not to be given in 1907–08"	Child	habits
	Zoology-7	Invertebrate Zoology (Su; less)[c] "Not to be given in 1907"	Child	habits

APPENDIX 1   (*Continued*)

Year	Course	Course Title	Instructor	Terminology[a]
	Zoology-9	Vertebrate Zoology (Su)	Riddle	habits
	Zoology-14	Studies of birds	Strong	habits
1908–09	Zoology-3	Field Zoology	Shelford	breeding habits
	Zoology-4	Field Zoology (Su; less)[c]	Shelford	breeding habits
	Zoology-9	Vertebrate Zoology (Su)	Riddle	habits
	Zoology-10	Invertebrate Zoology (I)	Child	habits
	Zoology-11	Invertebrate Zoology (II)	Child	habits
	Zoology-16	Animal Ecology	Shelford	breeding habits
	"Not given in 1909"			
	Zoology-18	Studies of Birds	Strong	feeding habits, habits
1909–10	"Introductory [Remarks]"			habits, instincts
	Zoology-5	Field Zoology	Shelford	breeding habits
	Zoology-6	Field Zoology (Su; less)[c]	Shelford	breeding habits
	Zoology-10	Invertebrate Zoology (I)	Child	habits
	Zoology-11	Invertebrate Zoology (II)	Child	habits
	Zoology-15	Studies of Birds	Strong	feeding habits
	Zoology-16	Animal Ecology	Shelford	behavior
	Zoology-17	Animal Ecology (Su; less)[c]	Shelford	behavior
1910–11	"Introductory [Remarks] II. Behavior and Ecology"			analytic study of behavior, behavior
	Zoology-3	Field Zoology	Shelford	behavior, breeding habits
	Zoology-4	Field Zoology (Su; less)[c]	Shelford	behavior
	Zoology-10	Invertebrate Zoology (I)	Child	habits
	Zoology-11A	Invertebrate Zoology (II)	Child	habits
	(Winter Quarter, 1911)			
	Zoology-11B	Invertebrate Zoology (II)	Child	habits
	(Winter Quarter, 1912)			
	Zoology-16	Studies of Birds	Strong	feeding habits, habits

(*continued*)

APPENDIX 1   (*Continued*)

Year	Course	Course Title	Instructor	Terminology[a]
	Zoology-17	Animal Behavior	Shelford	behavior
	Zoology-18	Animal Ecology	Shelford	behavior
	"Not given in 1911"			
	Zoology-34	Studies in Animal Ecology	Shelford	behavior
	"Spring and Summer"			
1911–12	Zoology-7	Field Zoology (Su)	Shelford	behavior
	"[Not given after 1911. See Course 26]"			
	Zoology-9	Bird Studies	Strong	habits
	Zoology-15	General Zoology (I)	Newman	habits
	Zoology-16	General Zoology (II)	Newman	habits
	Zoology-17	General Zoology (III)	Newman	habits
	Zoology-26	Ecology and Behavior	Shelford	methods of analysis of behavior
	"Note.—This course combines the subject-matter of former courses in Field Zoology and Animal Behavior."			
	Zoology-27	Animal Behavior	Shelford	methods of analysis of behavior
	"[Not given after 1911. See course 26]"			
	Zoology-29	Animal Ecology	Shelford	behavior
	Zoology-75-78	Master's Theses. Behavior and Ecology	Shelford	
	"Each Quarter"			
1912–13	Zoology-4	Animal Activities and Relationships	Shelford	
	Zoology-9	Studies of Birds (Su)	Strong	feeding habits
	Zoology-15	Invertebrate Zoology	Child	habits
	Zoology-26	Ecology and Behavior	Shelford	methods of analysis of behavior
	Zoology-27	Animal Responses	Shelford	theories of animal behavior
	"[Not given in 1912–13]"			
	Zoology-28	Animal Geography	Shelford	animal behavior

APPENDIX 1 (Continued)

Year	Course	Course Title	Instructor	Terminology[a]
	Zoology-29	Physiographic Animal Ecology (Su)	Shelford	behavior
	Zoology-52	Topics in Ecology "Spring and Summer"	Shelford	behavior
	Zoology-75-78	Master's Theses. Behavior and Ecology "Each Quarter"	Shelford	
1913–14	Zoology-9	Studies of Birds	Strong	feeding habits
	Zoology-15	Invertebrate Zoology	Child	habits
	Zoology-26	Experimental Behavior and Ecology "Summer and Autumn"	Shelford	methods of analysis of behavior
	Zoology-28	Animal Geography "Summer and Winter"	Shelford	behavior
	Zoology-29	Physiographic Animal Ecology	Shelford	behavior, breeding relations
	Zoology-52	Topics in Behavior and Ecology "Each Quarter"	Shelford	behavior (x2)
	Zoology-75-78	Master's Theses. Behavior and Ecology "Each Quarter"	Shelford	
1914–15	Zoology-9	Ornithology	Strong	feeding habits
	Zoology-15	Invertebrate Zoology	Child	habits
1915–16	Zoology-7	Elementary Field Zoology	Wells	habits
	Zoology-15	Invertebrate Zoology	Child	habits
	Zoology-26	Animal Behavior and Ecology	Wells	behavior
	Zoology-28	Entomology	Wells	habits

Note: Information is generally taken from the departmental entry in the University of Chicago Annual Register. Because a given year's Annual Register contains "Announcements" for the following year, Biology Department members and titles for 1892–1893, are taken from "Officers of Government and Instruction," Quarterly Calendar, 1892–1893 (April, 1893), 4–12. A second consequence of the Annual Register's

(continued)

APPENDIX 1   *(Continued)*

date and the "Announcement's" date, is that to find additional information about events for any given year in Appendix 1 (or 2), one must consult the *Annual Register* for the year preceeding the date in Appendix 1 (or 2).

[a]For some courses, the only psychological terminology is that contained in the title.

[b]During the 1892–1893 year, courses were numbered consecutively across all departments each quarter. This practice was common in American academic institutions during the 19th century *after* courses began to be numbered. Prior to the second half of the 19th century, because of the few courses available, it was the practice to refer to courses as, e.g., "the junior required course in X," and "the junior elective course in X." And, of course, *elective* courses were a new phenomenon in the 19th century.

[c]"Less" means the summer description contains less information than did the description for the non-summer course.

[d]When a course was to be offered during the summer, the material shown in parentheses here was not repeated; the remainder of the material, e.g., time, instructor, credit, all appear.

ZOOLOGY DEPARTMENT[a]
MEMBERS AND TITLES,
APPENDIX 2 **1892–1916**

Year	Name	Title[b]
1892–1893	Whitman, Charles O. PhD	Head Professor of Biology and Professor of Animal Morphology
	Donaldson, Herbert H., PhD	Professor of Neurology
	Mall, Franklin P., M.D.	Professor of Anatomy
	Baur, George, PhD	Assistant Professor of Comparative Osteology and Palaeontology
	Loeb, Jacques, M.D.	Assistant Professor of Experimental Biology and Physiology
	Wheeler, William M., PhD	Instructor in Embryology
	Jordan, Edwin O., PhD	Tutor in Anatomy
	Watase, S., PhD	Reader in Cellular Biology
	Lingle, David J., PhD	Reader in Biology
	Bristol, Charles L., M.S.	Fellow
	Russell, Harry L., PhD	Fellow
	Johnson, Herbert P., A.M.	Fellow
	Mead, A. D., A.M.	Fellow
	Eycleshymer, Albert C., B.S.	Fellow
	Lillie, Frank R., A.B.	Fellow
	Locy, William A., M.S.	Honorary Fellow
	Platt, Julia A., Ph.B.	Honorary Fellow
	Treadwell, Arron L., M.S.	Honorary Fellow
	Meyer, Adolph, M.D.	Honrary Fellow in Neurology

(*continued*)

APPENDIX 2   (*Continued*)

Year	Name	Title[b]
1893–1894[c]	Whitman	Head Professor of Zoology
	Baur	
	Wheeler	
	Jordan	Instructor in Zoology
	Watase	Instructor in Cellular Biology
	Lillie, F. R.	Reader in Embryology
	Bristol	
	Munson, John P., S.M.	Fellow
	Mead	
	Farr, Marcus S., S.M.	Fellow
	Hay, Oliver Perry, PhD	Honorary Fellow
	Boyer, Emanuel R., A.M.	Honorary Fellow
	Locy	
	Treadwell	
	Clapp, Cornelia M., PhD	Honorary Fellow in Biology
1894–1895	Whitman, LL. D.	
	Wheeler	
	Jordan	Instructor in Biology
	Watase	
	Lillie, F. R., PhD	
	Boyer	
	Child, Charles M., PhD	Honorary Fellow
	Locy	
	Merrill, Harriet B., A.M.	Honorary Fellow
	Treadwell	
	Brode, Howard S.	Fellow
	Clapp	Fellow
	Mead	
	Munson	
	McCaskill, Virgil E.	Graduate Scholar
1895–1896	Whitman	
	Wheeler	Assistant Professor in Embryology
	Jordan	Assistant Professor in Zoology
	Watase	Assistant Professor in Cellular Biology
	Elliot, D. G., F.R.S.E.	Lecturer in Zoology
	Wyld, Norman	Docent in Zoology
	Boyer	
	Child	
	Holmes, Samuel J., M.S.	Fellow
	Treadwell	
	Brode	
	Clapp	
	Munson	

APPENDIX 2   (*Continued*)

Year	Name	Title[b]
	McCaskill	
1896–1897	Whitman	
	Wheeler	
	Jordan	
	Watase	
	Elliot	
	Wyld	
	Fling, Harry R., A.B.	Fellow in Biology
	Holmes	
	Munson	
	Packard, Wales H., S.B.	Fellow
	Sturges, Mary M., S.B.	Fellow
1897–1898	Whitman	
	Wheeler	
	Jordan	
	Watase	
	Child	Associate in Zoology
	Davies, Howell E., A.B.	Fellow
	Gregory, Emily R., A.M.	Fellow
	Guyer, Michael F., A.M.	Fellow
	Hunter, George W., A.M.	Fellow
	Charles, Fred L., S.M.	Fellow
	Packard	
1898	Smith, A. L., PhD	Lecturer in Bacteriology
Summer		
1898–1899	Whitman	
	Wheeler	
	Watase	
	Jordan	
	Child	Instructor in Zoology
	Davies	
	Gregory	
	Guyer	
	Lillie, Ralph S., A.B.	Fellow
	Newman, Horatio H., A.B.	Fellow
	Packard	
1899	Smith	
Summer		
1899–1900	Whitman	Professor and Head of the Department
	Wheeler	
	Watase	
	Jordan	
	Child	
	Davies	

(*continued*)

APPENDIX 2   (*Continued*)

Year	Name	Title[b]
	Hefferan, Mary, A.B.	Fellow
	Newman	
	Guyer	
	Lillie, R. S.	
	Moore, Anne	Vassar Fellow
1900	Smith	
Summer		
1900–1901	Whitman	
	Jordan	Associate Professor of Bacteriology
	Davenport, Charles B., PhD	Assistant Professor of Zoology
	Lillie, Frank R., PhD	Assistant Professor of Zoology
	Child	
	Davies, PhD	Assistant in Bacteriology
	Adams, Charles, C.S.M.	Fellow
	Newman	
	Downing, Elliot R., S.M.	Fellow
	Entemann, Minnie M., S.B.	Fellow
	Harper, Eugene H., A.M.	Fellow
	Moenkhaus, William J., A.M.	Fellow
	Lillie, Ralph S., A.B.	Fellow
1901	Cole, Aaron H.	Lecturer in Biology
Summer		
	Downing	Assistant in Zoology
	Harper	Assistant in Zoology
1901–1902	Whitman	
	Davenport	Associate Professor of Zoology and Embryology
	Lillie, F. R.	Assistant Professor of Zoology and Embryology
	Child	
	Adams	
	Hubbard, Marion E., S.B.	Fellow
	Allen, Bennett M., PhB	Fellow
1902	Adams	Assistant in Zoology
Summer		
	Harper, PhD	Assistant in Zoology
1902–1903	Whitman	Professor and Head of the Department; Curator of the Zoological Museum
	Davenport	Associate Professor of Zoology and Embryology; Assistant Curator of the Zoological Museum
	Lillie, F. R.	Associate Professor of Embryology; Assistant

APPENDIX 2 (*Continued*)

Year	Name	Title[b]
		Curator of the Zoological Museum
	Child	
	Tower, William L.	Assistant in Embryology
	Craig, Wallace, S.M.	Assistant in Zoology
	Gates, Dana Lewis	Assistant in Zoology
	Kirk, Edwin G., S.B.	Assistant in Zoology
	Adams	
	Hubbard	
	Allen, B. M.	
	Baumgartner, William J., A. M.	Fellow
	Melander, Axel L., S.B.	Fellow
1903	Large, Thomas, S.B.	Assistant in Zoology
Summer		
	Melander	Assistant in Zoology
1903–1904	Whitman	
	Davenport	
	Lillie, F. R.	
	Child	
	Tower, S. B.	Associate in Embryology
	Lutz, Frank E., A.M.	Assistant in Zoology
	Craig, S.B.	
	Kirk	
	Abbott, James F., A.B.	Fellow
	Melander	
	Baumgartner	
	Scott, John W., A.M.	Fellow
	Zeleny, Charles, S.M.	Fellow
1904	Strong, Reuben M., PhD	Assistant in Zoology
Summer		
	Scott	Laboratory Assistant in Zoology
	Baumgartner	Laboratory Assistant in Zoology
	Abbott	Laboratory Assistant in Zoology
1904–1905	Whitman	
	Lillie, F. R.	
	——	Assistant Professor of Zoology
	Child	
	Tower	Instructor in Embryology
	Lane, Henry H., S.B.	Laboratory Assistant in Zoology
	Shelford, Victor E., S.B.	Laboratory Assistant in Zoology

(*continued*)

APPENDIX 2 *(Continued)*

Year	Name	Title[b]
	Riddle, Oscar, S.B.	Laboratory Assistant in Zoology
	Baumgartner	
	Jones, Lynds, S.M.	Fellow
	Newman	
	Stephens, Thomas C., A.B.	Fellow
1905 Summer	Transeau, Edgar N., PhD	Instructor in Biology
1905–1906	Whitman	
	Lillie, F. R.	
	Child	Assistant Professor of Zoology
	Tower	
	Strong	Associate in Zoology
	Lane	
	Shelford	
	Hegner, Robert W., S.M.	Laboratory Assistant in Zoology
	Blount, Mary, S.B.	Fellow
	Shull, Charles A., S.B.	Fellow
	Stephens	
1906 Summer	Tyler, John M., PhD	Instructor in Biology
1906–1907	Whitman	
	Lillie, F. R.	
	Child	
	Tower	
	Strong	
	Shelford	
	Hegner	
	Patterson, John T., S.B.	Laboratory Assistant in Zoology
	Riddle	
	Blount	
	Shull	
	Stephens	
1907–1908	Whitman	
	Lillie, F. R.	Professor of Embryology; Assistant Curator of the Zoological Museum
	Child	Assistant Professor of Zoology
	Tower	
	Strong	
	Shelford, PhD	Associate in Zoology
	Patterson	
	Bartelmez, George W., S.B.	Fellow
	Shorey, Marian L., A.M.	Fellow

APPENDIX 2   (*Continued*)

Year	Name	Title[b]
	Takahashi, Katashi, ScD	Fellow
1908	Riddle, PhD	Instructor in Embryology
Summer		
1908–1909	Whitman	
	Lillie, F. R.	
	Child	
	Tower	
	Strong	
	Allen, George D.., A.B.	Fellow
	Shorey	
	Takahashi	
1909–1910	Whitman	
	Lillie, F. R.	
	Child	Associate Professor of Zoology
	Tower	
	Strong	
	Shelford	Instructor in Zoology
	Riddle	Instructor in Zoology
	Blount, PhD	Assistant in Zoology
	Stephenson, Joseph C., S.B.	Assistant in Zoology
	Slye, Maud, A.B.	Laboratory Assistant
	Bartelmez, George W., S.B.	Fellow
1910	Blount	
Summer		
1910–1911	Whitman	
	Lillie, F. R.	
	Child	
	Tower	
	Strong	
	Riddle	
	Shelford	
	Stephenson	Laboratory Assistant (Resigned)
	Visher, Stephen S., S.M.	Laboratory Assistant
	Allee, Warder C., S.B.	Laboratory Assistant
	Allyn, Harriet M., A.B.	Fellow
	Kite, George L., S.B.	Fellow
	Slye	Fellow
1911	Riddle	
Summer	Blount	Instructor in Zoology
	Lane, PhD	Instructor in Zoology
1911–1912	Lillie, F. R.	Professor of Embryology and Chairman of the Department
	Child	
	Tower	Associate Professor of Zoology

(*continued*)

APPENDIX 2   (*Continued*)

Year	Name	Title[b]
	Newman, PhD	Associate Professor of Zoology
	Strong	
	Shelford	
	Allee	
	Allyn	
	Kite	
	Slye	
1912	Bartelmez, PhD	Instructor
Summer		
1912–1913	Stephenson	Assistant
	Allee	Assistant
	Lillie, F. R.	
	Child	
	Tower	
	Newman	
	Strong	
	Shelford	
	Brown, W. L., A.B.	Laboratory Assistant
	Douthitt, Herman, A.M.	Laboratory Assistant
	MacArthur, John W., S.B.	Laboratory Assistant
	Wells, Morris M., S.B.	Laboratory Assistant
	Breitenbecher, Joseph K., S.B.	Fellow
	Green, Wyman R., S.M.	Fellow
	Hill, Homer A., S.M.	Fellow
	Hyman, Libbie H., S.B.	Fellow
	Sinclair, John G., S.B.	Fellow
1913	Zeleny, Charles, PhD	Associate Professor
Summer		
1913–1914	Lillie, F. R.	
	Child	
	Tower	
	Newman	
	Strong	
	Shelford	
	Brown	
	Heilbrunn, V. L.	Laboratory Assistant
	——	Laboratory Assistant
	——	Laboratory Assistant
	Green	
	Hyman	
	MacArthur	Fellow
	Wells	Fellow
1914–1915	Lillie, F. R.	
	Child	
	Tower	

APPENDIX 2 (*Continued*)

Year	Name	Title[b]
	Newman	
	Strong	
	Shelford (Resigned)	
	Heilbrunn	Associate
	MacArthur	Laboratory Assistant
	Hyman	Laboratory Assistant
	Becker, Wesley C., S.B.	Laboratory Assistant
	Martin, Bertha, A.B.	Fellow
	Moore, Carl R., S.B.	Fellow
	Wells	
1915–1916	Lillie, F. R.	
	Child	
	Tower	
	Newman	
	Wells, PhD	Instructor
	Heilbrunn, PhD	
	MacArthur	Associate
	Hyman, PhD	
	Becker	
	Moore, A.M.	Assistant
	Sinclair	Assistant
	Buchanan, James William	Fellow
	Chapin, Catharine Lines	Fellow

Note: Information is generally taken from the departmental entry in the University of Chicago *Annual Register.* Because a given year's *Annual Register* contains "Announcements" for the following year, Biology Department members and titles for 1892–1893, are taken from "Officers of Government and Instruction," *Quarterly Calendar,* 1892–1893 (April, 1893), 4–12. A second consequence of the *Annual Register's* date and the "Announcement's" date, is that to find additional information about events for any given year in Appendix 2 (or 1), one must consult the *Annual Register* for the year preceeding the date in Appendix 2 (or 1). For the years 1893–1894 and 1896–1897, information concerning Fellows and other lower ranking positions is taken from the *Annual Register* section labeled "Fellows Appointed for [ensuing year]" near the end of "Officers of Government and Instruction" (or a similar title) near the beginning of the *Annual Register* for 1892–1893 and 1895–1896 respectively. For 1894–1895 and 1895–1896 this information is taken from the Departmental entries in the 1894–1985 and 1895–1896 *Annual Registers* respectively. Starting with the 1896–1896 *Annual Register,* the listing of Fellows and other lower ranking positions for the ensuing year, like that for the higher ranking positions, is included in the Departmental entry.

[a]The designation "Department of Zoology," did not come about until the 1894–1895 year. Originally the designation was Department of Biology. In April of 1893 (*The Quarterly Calendar,* 1893–1894, 2(1), p. 22; *Annual Register,* 1892–1893, p. 91), the Department of Biology was divided into five departments: Zoology and Paleontology (which divided the following year), Anatomy and Histology, Physiology, Neurology, and Botany (for which no instruction was offered in 1893–1894, *Annual Register,* 1892–1893, p. 90).

[b]Only changes in titles or additional degrees are noted. Although this procedure is awkward in some respects, it facilitates location of title changes.

[c]In 1893–1894 the Department's designation was Zoology and Palaeontology.

5 Historical Review of the Use of Captive Animals in Comparative Psychology[1]

Gary Greenberg
Wichita State University Wichita, Kansas

The eventual adoption of animal behavior as a scientific area of investigation in psychology is traceable to the fact that students of prominent men began to use animals as subjects for dissertation research. The academic zoologists of the same period were just as slow to make animal behavior an academic discipline, and when they did integrate ethology they did so partially on the excuse that behavior could be used as a taxanomic indicator. Actually, both psychologists and zoologists borrowed problems and techniques from the amateurs who were the major contributors to the science. (Gray, 1968, p. 372)

In his review of the early history of the study of animal behavior Gray traced the path to the development of comparative psychology by Darwin and his followers. It is sufficient that this has already been done. The focus of the present chapter is comparative psychology's use of animals in captive settings, that is, in laboratories, zoos, and field stations. Although it is recognized that theoretical progress in comparative psychology is greatly enhanced by research in both laboratory and natural settings (Schneirla, 1950), this was not always the case.

Comparative psychology, which we define as the study of the evolution and development of behavior, owes its origins as a distinct natural science discipline to Darwin himself who attempted to demonstrate in his work that threat, courtship, and other types of behavior were products of natural selection. Comparative psychology was immersed in the evolution revolution right from its inception. Following Darwin, many well-known biologists were attracted to the study of the evolution of behavior although they tended to focus on evolutionary

---

[1]Presented at Second International Conference, Acapulco, 1984

classifications of mental processes in animals and man. Among them were George Romanes (1895) who compared intelligence among animals, Herbert Spencer (1886) who developed a theory of animal ethics, and Lloyd Morgan (1899) who discussed mental evolution.

Although it was recognized from the earliest point in the history of our discipline that the development of generalizable principles of behavior required the comparison of the behaviors of many species of animals, the practitioners of the young science had not yet established the tradition of maintaining animal collections for observational purposes. They therefore depended on observations and procedures in field settings that were typically not experimentally rigorous. The anecdotal method of Romanes was initially *the* method of comparative psychology, although it was quickly criticized. There were exceptions to this loose approach to the study of animal behavior. The naturalistic experiments conducted by Audubon (Ford, 1967), for example, are still exemplars of the value of the experimental method in field settings. I believe it is fair to characterize these earliest approaches to the study of the evolution of behavior as unsystematic and loose. This is clear from Romanes' (1895) proscription for the methodology of the new science, which included the following set of principles:

> First, never to accept an alleged fact without the authority of some name.

> Second, in the case of the name being unknown, and the alleged fact of sufficient importance to be entertained, carefully to consider whether, from all the circumstances of the case as recorded, there was any considerable opportunity for malobservation. . . .

> Third, to tabulate all important observations recorded by unknown observers, with the view of ascertaining whether they have ever been corroborated by similar or analogous observations made by other and independent observers. (p. viii)

Similarly, the anecdotal method lacked the experimental rigor necessary to succeed as a scientific method. Again, some examples from Romanes make this point rather clearly:

> A dog has always been accustomed to eat a piece of meat when his organism requires nourishment, and when his olfactory nerves respond to the particular stimulus occasioned by the proximity of the food. So far, it may be said, there is no evidence of mind. . . . But now suppose . . . the dog has been taught not to eat the meat when he is hungry until he received a certain verbal signal: [the success of this procedure can be taken as evidence of the existence of a mind in the dog]. (p. 7)

Romanes also said:

> That is to say, if we observe an ant or a bee apparently exhibiting sympathy or rage,

we must either conclude that some psychological state resembling that of sympathy or rage is present, or else refuse to think about the subject at all. (p. 9)

It is no wonder that the anecdotal method was short lived, although it did flourish for some 3 decades following Darwin. Warden, 1927 stated:

[The anecdotalists] set themselves the task of showing that mental continuity was a indubitable fact. . . . [They tried to prove] that the higher animals possessed a rudimentary reason from which the intellectual life of man might conceivably have evolved. (p. 146)

Under the leadership of Darwin, Romanes, and others, the anecdotal school confined their efforts to collecting stories about the behavior of animals which were often of dubious value and veracity. Such stories emphasized the display of human characteristics such as emotion and ethical conduct of many animals, particularly the higher vertebrates. Warden (1927) asserted:

The anthropomorphic and teleological approach of the anecdotalists coupled with the technique of collecting stories rather than depending on controlled observation and the experimental method stood in the way of the normal development of comparative psychology until the end of the 19th century. To this point, comparative psychology had still not developed a tradition of maintaining animals in captivity for experimental study. Indeed, there were until Thorndike, virtually no laboratory studies in comparative psychology. (p. 158)

From Warden's and the other historical reports cited earlier we learn that Lubbock was among the first to use a constructed device or apparatus to study insect behavior; Morgan and Loeb employed experimental methods; and Galton used experimental techniques and devices to study the auditory range of various animals in the London Zoo as early as 1883. All these represent very early use of experimental and laboratory approaches to the study of comparative psychology. However, animals were still missing from laboratories and although occasional observations were made on captive animals in zoos, this was still not a routine practice.

Hobhouse, whose work has been neglected until recently (Gottlieb, 1979), was among the first to recognize the importance of animal collections for comparative psychological study. His own words are revealing. Hobhouse (1901) commented:

In the hope of deciding whether animals can learn by perception of results . . . I made a number of experiments on a variety of animals. . . . My experiments were begun with my own dog and cat. They were afterward, by the courtesy of Messrs. Jennison, extended to several animals in their great collection at the Belle Vue Gardens, Manchester, including monkeys of several species, a young female elephant, and an otter. It seemed to me that interesting analogies and contrasts might be drawn by confronting different animals with the same or different problems. (p. 152)

These experiments required animals to acquire novel behaviors (string pulling, lever pulling), which resulted in the securing of a food reinforcement. Hobhouse seems to have been responsible for a research methodology that became the mainstay of much research into learning in the early and middle parts of this century. He also seems to have invented the procedure of motivating research subjects by food depriving them, by realizing that "It was of course necessary that the experiments should be tried before the animal's ordinary meal" (p. 153).

Although we can attribute the regular use of animals in laboratory preparations to Thorndike, it was really Jacques Loeb and C. Lloyd Morgan who began the experimental tradition beginning around 1860. Both were stridently opposed to the anthropomorphic approach of the anecdotalists. Loeb's importance for comparative psychology does not involve the validity of his theoretical outlook. Rather, as Warden (1927) has put it, "[Loeb's] bold attempt to analyze the behavior of animals experimentally, and explain it objectively . . . was little short of heroic" (p. 152).

We must recognize the significance of the experimental methodology employed by Jennings (1904) who introduced the trial and error method into psychology. And, Pavlov was certainly an experimental scientist, although not a comparative psychologist. Interestingly, the move into the laboratory was not without opposition in comparative psychology. Indeed, Wesley Mills (1899) was in fact contemptuous of those who failed to make detailed and careful studies of their animals under reasonably normal, i.e., natural, conditions.

Mills (1899) was particularly critical of the laboratory approach adopted by Thorndike, claiming that the artificial nature of his puzzle boxes interfered with the natural behavior of the organism. This is reflected in the following statement: "As well enclose a living man in a coffin, lower him, against his will, into the earth, and attempt to deduce normal psychology from his conduct" (p. 266).

Considering the influence that Mills wielded in his day, it is surprising that comparative psychology developed in the successful direction that it eventually did. Mills (1899) went so far as to suggest that the experimental method not only interfered with the natural behavior of animals, it was a dangerous technique to the success of science because it blinded experimenters to the truth. Again, his own words are telling: "one cannot but marvel at the degree to which that magic word of modern science 'experiment' can blind the mind to facts thick as the leaves of the forest" (p. 267). It is fortunate for science in general that such criticisms did not prevent experimental approaches from becoming popular. Where would we be if Kepler or Newton had used such reasoning.

I do not want to leave the impression that Mill's impact on comparative psychology was all negative. He did recognize the importance of observation in natural settings; he did suggest that the developmental study of behavior was of great significance to comparative psychology; he did see the importance of large collections of animals such as are housed in zoos.

Despite criticisms as those raised by Mills, the move to the laboratory was rapid following Thorndike's lead. It was he who pioneered the comparative study of various animals species in laboratory settings in his now classic puzzle box experiments (Thorndike, 1898). Although recognizing the significance and the importance of this move, researchers were still cautious lest it replace observation in natural settings. For example, writing in 1902, Kinnaman warned that "Probably no other method suffers so great limitations. The caged animal often ceases to be himself. . . . The method is only semi-scientific" (p. 101).

Nevertheless, Kinnaman was essentially providing a rationale for the continued use of the experimental method in laboratory settings in this influential paper of the period, pointing out that such procedures had the great virtue of permitting replication of research from laboratory to laboratory. On this point Kinnaman (1902) says, "Therefore the work done by one investigator may be repeated and verified or modified by another. No personal factor is present" (p. 102).

This paper appears to be one of the earliest reports utilizing rhesus monkeys in comparative psychology laboratory settings. In it Kinnaman attempted to respond to the criticisms such as those raised earlier by Mills with regard to the unnaturalness of behavior under such conditions. In explaining the use of food deprivation as a motivating procedure, Kinnaman (1902) said: "It can hardly be maintained that [the monkeys] were subjected by this to unnatural conditions, since in their wild state, it is no uncommon thing for them to become ravenously hungry" (p. 110–111).

Again, responding to criticisms such as those raised by Mills regarding the unnaturalness of the procedures used in the experimental method, Kinnaman (1902) said:

[In the natural environment the monkey spends] much of his time searching for food. . . . Bark must be pulled away to get a fallen nut or to catch an insect. Fallen limbs and sticks must be removed in order to procure a nut or a root. These acts are not entirely unlike moving a bolt, button or hook, or pulling a string or plug. (p. 111)

The eventual widespread study of rat behavior in mazes began by recognizing that a rat's typical runs are similar in appearance to the pathways in a maze. This was discovered by chance as Kline lifted the steps to his home beneath which some rats had taken up residence (Miles, 1930). The history of psychology's romance with the rat has been told by Lockard (1968) and so is not necessary to repeat here.

The die had been cast. Comparative psychologists discovered the laboratory in the earliest days of the 20th century. The first organized laboratories were opened in 1899 at Clark and Harvard universities. The University of Chicago ran a close second, organizing its laboratory in 1903. Then followed the University of Texas and Johns Hopkins University in 1908, and Cornell and Michigan in 1909. By 1927 there were some 23 comparative psychology laboratories in the United States (Warden & Warner, 1927). The typical laboratory was modest, being staffed by one or two comparative psychologists, their students, and associated staff.

An examination of the use of large collections of animals by comparative psychologists is discussed next. I have already indicated that several early researchers recognized the research value of zoo collections, among them Romanes and Hobhouse. We must realize that by the end of the 19th century, a number of fine zoos (from the perspective of the day) had developed in Europe. Although we can trace the history of zoos back many hundreds of years (Fiedler, 1968; Fisher, 1966; Gersh, 1971; Livingston, 1967) the modern zoo was established by Louis XIV of France who built the Menagerie du Parc at Versailles. The French Revolution put an end to many traditions begun by the royalty, and the zoo was no exception. The Jardin des Plantes in Paris was the successor of the Versailles zoo and subsequently became the first public zoo, although the oldest zoos in continuous existence were at Vienna (opened in 1765) and Madrid. In 1826 the London Zoological Society was established and it, in turn, established a 5-acre zoological garden. European naturalists then had animal collections available for study for quite a long time. The earliest zoos in the United States were the Central Park Zoo in New York (1864), followed by Buffalo, Chicago's Lincoln Park, and Philadelphia in 1874. The San Diego Zoo was established in 1916.

It must, however, be pointed out that although comparative psychologists recognized the value of zoo collections for research purposes, zoo directors were not necessarily easily persuaded that research was an appropriate activity for them to support. Although it is difficult to discover what the attitudes of directors were in the earliest days of comparative psychology's history, Hediger painted a bleak picture as recently as 1969:

For instance, on 9 September 1961 a gorilla was born in the United States National Zoo in Washington, D. C. This was a most unusual event, namely the fourth gorilla to be born in the history of zoological gardens, the second in the New World. . . . In view of the fact that insufficient data are available on the onset of sexual maturity and the development of the gorilla, exact weight measurements on the growth of the parents of the [newborn gorilla] would have been of exceptional interest. . . . [However,] the National Zoo in Washington unfortunately possessed no suitable weighing machine. (pp. 47–48)

Comparative psychologists have put these limited facilities to good use as evidenced by their continued dependence on zoos since the turn of the century. This is particularly true of the past 25 years, especially in the United States. In addition to the organized research programs of the major zoos in the United States, including the National Zoo, the Bronx Zoo, the San Diego Zoo, the Brookfield Zoo in Chicago, and the Philadelphia Zoo, a number of smaller zoos have also recognized their potential contribution to comparative psychology and accordingly support research programs. Included in this group are the Portland Zoo, The Washington Park Zoo in Seattle, the Milwaukee Zoo, the Sedgwick County Zoo in Wichita, the Los Angeles Zoo, and the San Francisco Zoo.

It is now possible to find comparative psychologists maintaining relatively formal associations with zoos (e.g., Erwin, Maple, & Mitchell, 1979; American Association of Zoological Parks and Aquariums, 1975). The reciprocal value of such relationships is shown in the work of Hal Markowitz (1982) who is perhaps singularly responsible for the introduction of behavioral engineering into the design of zoo exhibits. In this way zoo exhibits incorporate important aspects of an animal's normal behavioral repertoire. Exhibits of this type are found in the Brookfield Zoo, the Bronx Zoo, the San Diego Zoo, and the San Francisco Zoo, among others. These contemporary uses of zoo collections can be traced to the suggestions by the very earliest comparative psychologists that research be conducted in zoo settings.

I focus finally on the development of experimental field stations because a great many comparative psychologists currently conduct research in such settings. They have the advantage of being naturalistic because many of them are located in the same environment in which a species is typically found. Comparative psychologists recognized early that something more natural than a laboratory, yet less open than free ranging conditions, was essential for their research preparations. Thus was born the experimental station.

Among the earliest to call for the creation of such a facility was John Watson. In an article he wrote in 1906 Watson pointed out that few psychology laboratories in the United States had adequate space for maintaining mammals. With the possible exception of Harvard University, the various comparative psychology labs referred to previously amounted to little more than a single room. At the University of Chicago the laboratory was a single large room in the basement. Psychology labs have been in the basement ever since. Watson called for a large, well-lighted, heated facility with lots of room, on the order of acres, to accommodate studies of homing and migration in birds.

Following Watson, Yerkes in 1916 proposed a similar experimental station for the study of primates. This facility would provide for the maintenance, the breeding, and rearing of primates; for the systematic and continuous observation of primate behavior under reasonably natural conditions; and for the profitable cooperation with existing biological institutes and departments. Yerkes proposed that such a research station should be equipped to study problems of behavior, mind, physiology, genetics, development, and anatomy and should accordingly be staffed by a comparative psychologist, a comparative physiologist, a geneticist and experimental zoologist, an anatomist and embryologist, someone specialized in experimental medicine, a neurologist and corresponding support staff. Few were quick to heed these calls, I imagine because of the costs associated with them. We do know, however, that Yerkes' was eventually successful because an elaborate set of regional primate centers was established in the United States in the 1960s. The Yerkes Regional Primate Center at Emory University In Atlanta, Georgia bears witness to the success Yerkes had in convincing science of the need for such facilities (Bourne, 1973; Shannon, 1971). Today there are a number of research stations of the type called for by Watson and Yerkes.

This historical review has been concerned with overall trends in comparative psychology at large. I have tried to show that almost from its inception comparative psychology turned to large collections in zoos; that when they finally adopted the tradition of maintaining animals in captivity in laboratory settings, comparative psychologists still recognized the importance of moving between natural conditions and artificial laboratory conditions; and that it was recognized very early that laboratories could not provide all the facilities necessary for the study of behavior, the proposal being made to establish large and elaborately staffed research stations.

REFERENCES

American Association of Zoological Parks and Aquariums. (1975). *Research in zoos and aquariums*. Washington, DC: National Academy of Sciences.

Bourne, G. H. (1973). The primate research center program of the National Institutes of Health. In G. H. Bourne (Ed.), *Nonhuman primates and medical research* (pp. 487–513). New York: Academic Press.

Erwin, J., Maple, T. L., & Mitchell, G. (Eds.). (1979). *Captivity and behavior: Primates in breeding colonies, laboratories, and zoos*. New York: Van Nostrand.

Fiedler, W. (1968). The oldest zoo in the world. In R. Kirchshofer (Ed.), *The world of zoos* (pp. 204–214). New York: Viking.

Fisher, J. (1966). *Zoos of the world*. London: Aldus Books.

Ford, A. (1967). *The 1826 journal of John James Audubon*. Norman, OK: University of Oklahoma Press.

Gersh, H. (1971). *The animals next door: A guide to the zoos and aquariums of the Americas*. New York: Fleet Academic Editions.

Gottlieb, G. (1979). Comparative psychology and ethology. In E. Hearst (Ed.), *The first century of experimental psychology*, (pp. 147–176). Hillsdale, NJ: Lawrence Erlbaum Associates.

Gray, P. H. (1968). The early animal behaviorists: Prolegomena to ethology. *Isis, 59*, 372–383.

Hediger, H. (1969). *Man and animal in the zoo: Zoo biology*. New York: Delacorte Press.

Hobhouse, L. T. (1901). *Mind in evolution*. London: Macmillan.

Jennings, H. S. (1904). *Contributions to the study of the behavior of lower organisms*. Washington, DC: Carnegie Institution.

Kinnaman, A. J. (1902). Mental life of two *Macacus Rhesus* monkeys in captivity. I & II. *American Journal of Psychology, 13*, 98–148, 173–218.

Livingston, B. (1967). *Zoo animals, people, places*. New York: Arbor House.

Lockard, R. B. (1968). The albino rat: A defensible choice or a bad habit? *American Psychologist, 23*, 734–742.

Markowitz, H. (1982). *Behavioral enrichment in the zoo.* New York: Van Nostrand.

Miles, W. R. (1930). On the history of research with rats and mazes. *Journal of General Psychology, 3,* 324–337.

Mills, T. W. (1899). The nature of animal intelligence and the methods of investigating it. *Psychological Review, 6,* 262–274.

Morgan, C. L. (1899). *Introduction to comparative psychology.* London: Walter Scott.

Romanes, G. J. (1895). *Animal intelligence.* New York: Appleton.

Schneirla, T. C. (1950). The relationship between observation and experimentation in the field study of behavior. *Annals of the New York Academy of Science, 51,* 1022–1044.

Shannon, J. A. (1971). Primates in U. S. biomedical research. In International Committee of Laboratory Animals (Eds.), *Defining the laboratory animal* (pp. 477–480). Washington, DC: National Academy of Sciences.

Spencer, H. (1886). *The principles of psychology.* New York: Appleton.

Thorndike, E. L. (1898). Animal intelligence: An experimental study of the associative processes in animals. *Psychological Monographs, 2* (Whole No. 8).

Warden, C. J. (1927). The historical development of comparative psychology. *Psychological Review, 34,* 57–85, 135–168.

Warden, C. J., & Warner, L. H. (1927). The development of animal psychology in the United States during the past three decades. *Psychological Review, 34,* 196–205.

Watson, J. B. (1906). The need of an experimental station for the study of certain problems in animal behavior. *Psychological Review, 3,* 149–156.

Yerkes, R. M. (1916). Provision for the study of monkeys and apes. *Science, 43,* 231–234.

6 Robert M. Yerkes and the Comparative Method[1]

James Reed
Rutgers University

In an autobiographical manuscript, Robert M. Yerkes declared: "I shall view myself as an experimental animal whose solution of daily problems ultimately spells out a way of life" (hereafter referred to as RMY); (Burnham, 1976; Hilgard, 1965; Yerkes, 1956, p. 2). Yerkes was a pioneer in uncharted fields. He was guided by some large and abstract assumptions—faith in Darwin, faith in scientific method, faith in the promise of human engineering—but the specifics of his research—the subjects, the methods, the interpretations—reflected pragmatic responses to a complex range of stimuli, including professional mentors, institutional situations, and perceived social needs or opportunities. In Yerkes' hands the comparative method was not a dictator of specific research agendas but a wide-ranging search for possible patterns in behavior and thought across species. Like many comparative psychologists, Yerkes always had his eye on man and was fairly accused of anthropomorphic tendencies, but he was also an "objectivist" who persistently sought to create a methodology that would command the respect of other scientists, and few scientists could match the variety of his hands-on knowledge of animal behavior or his eclectic inventiveness in research design.

In this chapter I hope to convey my sense of the complex interaction in Yerkes' work between scientific ideals and social pressures. His research can be seen, at least in retrospect, as the working out of logical scientific agenda, yet the apparent internal logic of his career owed a great deal to his remarkable ability to find opportunities and order in situations that were neither planned nor necessarily conducive to the development of comparative psychology. In short,

---

[1]Presented at Second International Conference, Acapulco, 1984

Yerkes' comparative psychology was a product of historical experience; its structure evolved as a dialectic between the scientist's need to find order and the demands of a changing and diverse social environment.

Yerkes' role in the World War I Army mental testing program has received more attention from historians than any other aspect of his career. Yerkes regarded his leadership of the Army testing as "vastly more than an episode in my life. In endless ways it transformed me" (RMY, p. 166) but in retrospect his work as a tester of human intelligence marks that point in a distinguished career when social pressures most distorted research design and interpretation. I argue that Yerkes was a better scientist before and after his World War I work, and that at his best he was a comparative psychologist, and at his worst he forgot lessons that he himself had drawn from the comparative method.

Before World War I and leadership of the Army testing program Yerkes had enjoyed only modest support and recognition during his 15 years as an instructor and assistant professor of comparative psychology at Harvard. His failure to gain promotion to higher rank in large part reflected administrative lack of appreciation for Yerkes' biological orientation. He called himself a "psychobiologist" at a time when psychology at Harvard was still merely an orientation within the Department of Philosophy. Yerkes was convinced, however, that evolutionary naturalism was the model that provided means for understanding human experience in both its biological and social aspects. Although I have not been able to precisely date his conversion to the Darwinian faith, he was certainly on his way when he arrived in Cambridge in the fall of 1897 (RMY, p. 79). In his origins he was typical of his generation of professional academicians—a farm boy from Bucks County, Pennsylvania in rebellion against his father and the narrow provincialism of rural and Protestant America. He got from the farm to Ursinus College by claiming that he wanted to be a doctor, but, after graduation, decided to put off medical school to get a better scientific background through study at Harvard. After 1 year in Cambridge, he was no longer hesitant to declare his intent to be a professional researcher, but vestiges of his Protestant background continued to shape his life in many forms, including his vision of science as a form of service to others. However, his was a secular altruism, superior, he believed, to that of the preacher. He would search for root causes and radical solutions.

Two biology professors, Charles Davenport and William Castle, both of whom were prominent figures in the Mendelian revival that seemed to offer the key to understanding the hereditary factor in evolution, were sponsors and models for the scientific novice. His immediate problem was to find a place for himself in the scientific division of labor that was emerging among exponents of evolutionary naturalism. His mentors in zoology had already taken for themselves the task of explaining variation or the mechanisms of heredity. A second major gap in understanding the history of life was the lack of a satisfactory account of the significance of behavior in evolution—that is, an analysis of the role of intelligence or effective response to environment in the evolutionary process. The role of consciousness or mind or behavior in the evolution of life was a live topic in an intellectual community that included William James and Josiah Royce, and remembered Chauncey Wright. In 1896 Lloyd Morgan visited Boston and soon afterward James' student Edward Lee Thorndike started experimenting with chicks in James' basement. Thorndike soon moved on to Columbia University where more support was available for animal work, leaving intellectual space for someone who could bring rigorous experimental methods to the study of the evolution of consciousness (Hale, Jr., 1980; Joncich, 1968; Kuklich, 1977; RMY, pp. 92–98).

On the advice of Josiah Royce, Yerkes defined his intellectual mission as the mapping of the uncharted regions between mind and body (RMY, p. 89). He would delineate the relationship between "material" and "mental" evolutionary process. The study of mind needed a methodology and subjects for study equivalent to the fossils of paleontologists. Yerkes believed that simpler forms of life might be viewed as living fossils and began the task of tracing human intellectual capacity back through lower forms of life to its origins with studies of the behavior and "mental life" of frogs, jelly fish, crustaceans, worms, mice, crows, pigs, racoons—and eventually insane persons, soldiers, schoolchildren, orangutans, chimpanzees, and gorillas.

Yerkes never forgot his original scientific mission, despite his prominence as a scientific bureaucrat and applied psychologist. One of Yerkes' great strengths as a builder of behavioral science was his eclecticism and aversion to extreme forms of reductionism. This trait becomes more salient in examining Yerkes' remarkable relationships with Lewis Terman and John Watson. Like Terman, Yerkes was a key exponent of intelligence testing, but testing was never his primary goal or interest. Like Watson, Yerkes was a prime mover in the development of animal behavior studies, but he was always simply an "objectivist," or one who wanted to bring a more rigorous experimental methodology to psychology, and never a "behaviorist" in the Watsonian mode.

As Robert Boakes has observed, few of Watson's students or colleagues supported his more extreme reductionist views (Boakes, 1984). Psychometricians and Watsonians shared a willingness to define their subjects operationally; they dealt with empty organisms in the sense that the test taker—whether school boy or white rat, was known solely by response to stimulus—whether the stimulus was a maze to be run or a written question that required the selection of one out of five possible answers.

Yerkes, in contrast, was never content to limit himself to observation of behavior. Just as Jean Piaget turned from the business of estimating the mental age of children on the basis of right or wrong answer to the more fruitful question of determining why the child got a wrong answer, or what went on inside its head—Yerkes repeatedly sought empathy with his subjects and speculated about their internal states, much to the disgust of his friend John Watson. There is a rich correspondence between Yerkes and Watson in *RMY* that is most detailed during the years when their separate views on the study of behavior developed. Yerkes operated in the approved Galtonian or Watsonian mode only when the expectations of others forced him to do so. Crudely put, Yerkes honored Terman's scientific godfather, Francis Galton, and he honored Watson's scientific godfather, Jacques Loeb; he was a hereditarian and a eugenicist *à la* Galton–Terman, and an objectivist, who wanted to be able to control behavior *à la* Loeb–Watson, but Yerkes looked first and last to Darwin and the tradition of evolutionary naturalism that his Galtonian and Loebian colleagues mistrusted (Cowan, 1977; MacKenzie, 1981). In pursuit of the Darwinian paradigm, he could not afford to reject any source of insight that might advance knowledge. In contrast to Jacques Loeb or John Watson, Yerkes retained respect for the arts of ''naive'' collection and description (cf. Pauly, 1980). Much of his 1911 textbook, *Introduction to Psychology,* was devoted to structuralist or Titchnerian accounts of perception, association, and consciousness, or the, by then, traditional art of introspection (Yerkes, 1911). Thus, in matters of method Yerkes was a Jamesian pluralist despite, or perhaps because of, his Darwinian fundamentalism. As a leader of his profession he maintained good relations with warring factions of structuralists, functionalists, behaviorists, and psychometricians (O'Donnell, 1979). Their various insights and social contacts might be needed in the pursuit of his largest ambition—to develop a natural history of behavior that would provide the basis for a science of man—a behavioral science that would be as useful as physics or chemistry because one could use it to predict and to control human behavior and to redesign human nature along more satisfactory lines.

By 1915, when John Watson's election as President of the American Psychological Association symbolized the coming of age of Yerkes' generation of biologically oriented psychologists, Yerkes had gone a long way toward his goal of charting natural hierarchies of intelligence or adaptive behavior. He was ready to move from dancing mice and racoons to primates, but the resources for acquiring such expensive subjects had not materialized. In fact, even his position at Harvard was shaky. His colleagues in the philosophy department resisted awarding their PhD to those who studied only animals, and dilettante philosophers got promoted while Yerkes remained a junior colleague. President Lowell saw no future in Yerkes' brand of comparative psychology. It was smelly and expensive and seemed to have no relation to practical public service. Word came to Yerkes that the way to promotion might lie through educational psychology. Yerkes' reply was unequivocal, and it illustrates why it is a mistake to view his involvement in applied psychology as simple professional opportunism. He would become involved in public service or practical work only when it seemed to further his Darwinian goals. He told his Harvard superiors that he would not concentrate on educational psychology because he was not interested in nurture but in nature (RMY, pp. 129–133). His fate at Harvard was sealed—an assistant professor for life!

The way out came through his friend and fellow eugenicist Ernest Southard, M.D., who was in charge of the new psychopathic service at the Boston State Hospital—an attempt to provide short-term diagnosis and treatment for the mentally ill—some of whom would be treated on an outpatient basis whereas others would be found in need of long-term incarceration. Southard asked Yerkes to develop methods for assessing the intellectual abilities of his patients and provided him with a means of joining "service" with real research while adding another species to his collection of subjects for comparison. For 4 years Yerkes combined teaching, unsurpassed production as an experimental animal behaviorist, and was paid as a half-time consultant by Southard. He later reflected that it was "fortunate for my health" that this divided existence was ended by World War I (RMY, pp. 140–155).

Despite competing interests, Yerkes' work in developing diagnostic mental tests attracted national attention. He attempted to improve on the techniques of Alfred Binet by developing a more nuanced scoring system; one in which subjects were rated according to how closely their answers came to being correct rather than on a simple right or wrong basis. Ironically, in view of the claims that would soon be made for the hereditability of intelligence based on the Army tests, Yerkes was extremely critical of Terman's revision of Binet's tests while he was still trying to develop his alternative Point Scale. Yerkes complained that many items in the Stanford revision were "highly dependent on education," and that chronological age was given too much emphasis in assessing performance because "sex, language, race, and social and economic status are quite as important as are norms for age" (Yerkes, 1917, p. 118). "It is, for example, not adequate for us in the school system of the American city to treat all individuals as though born to the English language" (Yerkes, March 1915, p. 150). Yerkes recommended a universal rather than age graded scale of performance, one that could be evaluated by comparison with a series of nuanced norms based on both social and biological differences (Yerkes, 1917; Yerkes & Anderson, 1915; Yerkes, Bridges, & Hardwick, 1915).

Thus, Yerkes' work in the Army testing program in many respects contradicted his own earlier work as a mental tester. During the hectic period in May–June, 1917, when the Army Alpha examination was written, Terman's Stanford Revision provided the working model of a group test because he had brought with him an improved battery of tests developed by protégé Arthur Otis, and there were used "practically in the form in which Otis had used them in his own scale " (Chapman, 1980, p. 77). The contrast between Yerkes' position before the Army Alpha was written and his foreword to *A Study of American Intelligence* of 1923 is remarkable, because in recommending Carl Brigham's book, Yerkes embraced methods and interpretations that seem incompatible with his own work conducted both before and after the Army program (Brigham, 1923). What happened? The war and the opportunities it provided for promoting psychology made it apparent that there was relatively little to be gained through *intra-*

disciplinary competition. The big prizes would go to those who could present a united front to the power brokers of the emerging American research establishment, and, in order to pursue his agenda as a comparative psychologist, Yerkes needed resources that had never before been available to psychologists. (For an excellent account of how differences between Terman and Yerkes were resolved in response to the need to present a united front to the Rockefeller funded General Education Board, see Samelson, 1979.)

By 1916 Yerkes was involved in two lines of research that were limited by their capital requirements. From February to August, 1915, he had studied *The Mental Life of Monkeys and Apes,* thanks to a former student at Harvard, G. V. Hamilton, who bought an orangutan for Yerkes' use and made his personal collection of monkeys available. The site of the research was a California estate where Hamilton served as the personal psychiatrist to a mad millionaire, and thus had the time and resources to help his former professor realize his long frustrated ambition to extend his natural history of intelligence to primates. Despite Yerkes' exciting discovery that the 5-year-old orangutan Julius engaged in "ideational" behavior that seemed to call for revision of the mechanistic interpretations of animal learning that had flourished since the publication of E. L. Thorndike's 1898 PhD dissertation, *Animal Intelligence,* Yerkes lacked the means to continue his primate research (Thorndike, 1898; Yerkes, 1916). His attempts to develop better scales for measuring human intelligence also had reached a point where large funds seemed necessary to proceed with the process of standardization. Yerkes' efforts to tap Rockefeller interests proved frustrating, however, and he found himself in competition with Lewis Terman for philanthropic dollars (Chapman, 1980). For Yerkes the solution to the lack of capital proved to be the development of close ties with a small group of scientists and philanthropists who shared Yerkes' vision that the days of the lone entrepreneur or craftsman in science were numbered. In the future, science would be capital intensive and bureaucratically organized, like the major productive sectors of the American economy. The chief exponent of this "ideology of national science" was the astronomer George Ellery Hale, the prime mover in the creation of the National Research Council, whose grant-making committees proved to be the single most important source of research funds between the world wars. (National Research Council, 1933; Tobey, 1971).

In his accounts of the origins of the Army testing program, Yerkes claimed that his efforts to involve psychologists in the war effort began in April, 1917, when Congress declared war. He was compelled by duty as President of the American Psychological Association to lead his profession into national service despite personal modesty and lack of social skills (RMY, p. 397). In fact, Yerkes began his efforts to win a place for psychology in the National Research Council, and in the preparedness campaign, much earlier than he later remembered, and these promotional efforts were part of a general search for institutional support that sprang from the capital intensive nature of his research, his ambitions as a social engineer, and his sensitivity to the need to sell his discipline to any potential sponsors, whether politicians, rich patrician nativists, government bureaucrats, or corporate philanthropists.

In February 1916, while Congress debated the issue of military preparedness, Yerkes wrote to the War Department to suggest that psychological testing ought to be part of military recruiting. Rebuffed by U.S. officials, he responded to a letter from a colleague in Canada concerning the possible employment of intelligence tests in evaluating incapacitated soldiers by offering to travel North at his own expense. He reacted to the April 4 Congressional declaration of war by turning a meeting of experimental psychologists in Cambridge into a prowar rally that ended with Yerkes in charge of a committee to investigate possible contributions of psychology to mobilization, made his trip to Canada to inspect the work of its Military Hospitals Commission, and wrote to George E. Hale, President of the National Research Council, asking that psychologists be drafted into government service. The problem was to convince Hale that they had something to offer. It helped that Yerkes could confide that he had been "summoned" to Ottawa where, "their psychology workers desire my advice concerning methods of dealing with the returned soldiers" (Camfield, 1969, p. 89).

Yerkes got an audience with Hale and, happily, Hale sought a reference from Harvard physiologist Walter B. Cannon, a close Yerkes friend since their apprenticeships in biological science under Charles B. Davenport (Camfield, 1969). In short, when Yerkes emerged as a protégé of Hale, Chairman of the National Research Council Psychology Committee, leader of the Army testing program, and an officer of the National Research Council in various capacities during the rest of his career, it was the result of aggressive and skillful lobbying campaigns that succeeded despite the indifference of many fellow psychologists and the skepticism of "hard" scientists about the ability of behavioral scientists to deliver on their promises.

It is now clear that Yerkes' greatest coup as a scientific bureaucrat and promoter was not in getting the Surgeon General to find a place for psychologists in the Army, although that was a notable accomplishment, nor in writing tests, recruiting several hundred officers and technicians, and administering examinations to over 1.7 million individuals, despite fierce competition for resources and status from Army officers and psychiatrists, although that too was a notable accomplishment. His most remarkable achievement was the myth that the Army testing program had been a great practical success and that it provided a "goldmine" of data on the heritability of intelligence.

Beginning with the work of Daniel Kevles and Thomas Camfield in 1968–69, historians have provided detailed and nuanced critical accounts of the Army testing program. It is now clear that the Army testing program contributed little to the war effort (Gould, 1981; Kevles, 1968; Samelson, 1979). Test scores were never used consistently in the assignment or rating of recruits, and the program was probably saved from separate termination by the armistice and general demobilization. The fact that the data gathered from the examinations has been cited so often and for so long in support of the Galtonian paradigm is a commentary on the will to believe among psychometricians and others that ought to know better. The tests may have predicted "practical soldier value," with a bit less precision than traditional army procedures, but there was and is no way to separate the influence of learning, acculturation, class, racial caste, or motivation from native ability in evaluation of performance on the Army examinations. Moreover, the testers repeatedly violated their own protocols, for example, by failing to retest men who scored zero on one or more parts of an examination. The scores of these men were included in the invidious group comparisons that received so much attention, and they account in part for the differences in ratings that eugenicists and nativists found so meaningful. The testers could hardly have excluded and/or retested the thousands of individuals who were not willing or able to participate in the examination (and thus got zero or suspiciously low scores) because there were so many of them. To discard them from the Army or from the data base would have been to risk the legitimacy of the whole program. Despite this, Yerkes not only saved face, he emerged as an Influential in the affairs of the National Research Council.

George Hale had grand plans to reorganize the National Research Council as an instrument for promoting and integrating postwar American scientific research and recruited Yerkes for the key position of Chairman of the Research Information Service. This division was eventually downgraded, but originally Hale and Yerkes saw it as a kind of master intelligence unit that would point the way for philanthropists and researchers. In a sense Yerkes "failed" again, because he was never able to find the vast funds needed to realize the original plan for the Research Information Service, but 5 years with the NRC made it possible for him to publicize his version of the Army testing program and to assume the chairmanship of several grant-making committees—especially the Committee for Research in Problems of Sex and the Committee on Problems of Human Migration—that were working models of the ideology of national science (RMY, pp. 215–235).

Yerkes' salience as a good organization man who had an unsurpassed knowledge of the network of foundations that subsidized research, an insider's knowledge of the latest developments in biosocial science, and imaginative plans that might attract large funds, finally paid off after James R. Angell assumed the Presidency of Yale in 1921. This essay cannot include a description of the complex network of associations and negotiations that led to Yerkes' appointment as a research professor at Yale in 1924 and the generous funding from Rockefeller interests that were part of the transaction. By 1925, however, Yerkes had at last found the institutional base that he needed to become the founder of American primatology. In resuming full-time pursuit of his agenda as a Darwinian comparative psychologist, Yerkes once again displayed the methodological eclecticism and common sense that marked his best work before the war. Although evaluation of Yerkes' work on the mental ability of primates cannot be attempted here, Yerkes the primatologist stands in stark contrast to the popular image of the intelligence tester that has emerged from contemporary criticism of the Galtonian paradigm. For example, Stephen Jay Gould, in *The Mismeasure of Man* has pointed to *reification* and *ranking* as the two fundamental errors or abuses of scientific method characteristic of Galtonians (Gould, 1981). I have already mentioned Yerkes' prewar criticism of Terman's Stanford Revision. As late as March 19, 1917, Yerkes attacked Terman's work in G. Stanley Hall's Clark University seminar. In the Binet-Terman scales, Yerkes (1917) complained:

> the process of selecting tests according to percentage of passes and of grouping them according to age constitutes standardization. The result of this method of selecting and standardizing tests is an inflexible scale, which however accurate it may be for the race, social stratum, or sex for which it is constructed, cannot possibly yield reliable results when applied to widely differing groups of individuals. (p. 114)

Thus, Yerkes was apparently sensitive to dangers of making group comparisons or ranking individuals by standards inappropriate to their experience.

Yerkes the primatologist also exhibited considerable caution when comparing the test scores of individuals of different species. In his work with primates Yerkes administered individual tests, instead of the group examinations that the Army program demanded. He was interested in developing methods that would generate good statistics, usually in the form of learning curves that represented the number of trials that a subject required to master a particular problem. He understood, however, that the numbers generated by his tests were simply indicators that required careful assessment—only one of a series of signs generated by a good experiment.

Yerkes' famous multiple choice apparatus was the first successful attempt at a method for studying learning in different kinds of animals, where performance would not depend on the subject's perceptual or motor abilities or on its level of activity. Having tried the method on crows, pigs, and humans at the Boston State Hospital, Yerkes was ready in 1915 for his long anticipated attempt to demonstrate that Edward Thorndike had been wrong in asserting that no animal could think (Yerkes, 1915b, 1915c, 1916).

Julius, a 5-year old orangutan provided Yerkes with the first "hard" evidence that there were qualitative differences in learning patterns between species. Julius did not achieve a higher score, however, than other creatures, in this case pigs and monkeys, who were presented with the same problem. Rather, he took many more trials to learn the "right answer" was always the door or compartment on the extreme left. But Julius did provide Yerkes with a different kind of learning curve. He abruptly stopped making errors, in contrast to the pigs and monkeys who gradually learned the correct response. Julius's learning curve provided Yerkes with the first of many indicators of "ideation" in the ape (Yerkes, 1916).

As a primatologist Yerkes did not reify statistical indexes, and he was careful about drawing invidious distinctions between individuals or groups, despite the mighty demands on the patience of experimenter and reader alike imposed by such subjects as Congo the gorilla or a pair of chimpanzees that never learned to talk. I conclude that Yerkes' career as a mental tester and comparative psychologist provides some contradictions that require explanation. The man who tolerated and rationalized questionable methods and interpretations in the Army testing program—and who made harsh judgments about the native capacity of human beings—was in other situations a more self-conscious methodologist and an eager defender of the "intelligence" of other creatures.

Part of the explanation for the contradictions in Yerkes' career may lie in the deeply felt need to prove that psychologists had technologies analogous to those of physical scientists and thus deserved higher levels of status and support. In Yerkes' case, bad science led to generous support for better work that marks the founding of primate studies on a significant scale. Social pressure may have shaped Yerkes' work at a more profound level than the scramble for dollars and relevance. I look for additional insights in the historical literature on paternalistic relationships, including race relations in the American South. Perhaps I am dealing with a phenomenon that has some parallels with the rise of virulent racism in turn of the century America and the transition from a paternalistic to a competitive racial caste system in the American south—an event that occurred during the period when psychology became an academic profession (Woodward, 1971).

REFERENCES

Boakes, R. (1984). *From darwin to behaviorism: Psychology and the minds of animals* (pp. 145, 172–173, 235). Cambridge, England: Cambridge University Press.

Brigham, C. C. (1923). *A study of american intelligence* (pp. v–viii). Princeton: Princeton University Press.

Burnham, J. C. (1976). Robert M. Yerkes. *Dictionary of American Biography, 14,* 549–551.

Camfield, T. M. (1969). *Psychologists at war: The history of american psychologists and the first world war.* Doctoral dissertation (pp. 79–80, 83–89). University of Texas at Austin.

Chapman, P. D. (1980). *Schools as sorters: Lewis M. Terman and the intelligence testing movement, 1890–1930.* Doctoral dissertation (pp. 77, 91–93). Stanford University.

Cowan, R. S. (1977). Nature and nurture: The interplay of biology and politics in the work of Francis Galton. *Studies in the history of biology* (pp. 79–80, 83–89). Baltimore: Johns Hopkins University Press.

Gould, S. J. (1981). *The mismeasure of man* (pp. 24, 30–31, 151, 158–159, 192–233, 238–239, 250–252, 268–269, 273–274, 288–292). New York: W. W. Norton & Company.

Hale, M. (Jr.). (1980). *Human science and social order: Hugo Munsterberg and the Origins of Applied Psychology.* Philadelphia: Temple University Press.

Hilgard, E. R. (1965). Robert Mearns Yerkes, National Academy of Sciences, *Biographical memoirs* (vol. 38, pp. 385–411). New York: Columbia University Press.

Joncich, G. (1968). *The sane positivist: A biography of Edward L. Thorndike* (pp. 79–103). Middletown, CT: Wesleyan University Press.

Kevles, D. J. (1968). Testing the Army's Intelligence: Psychologists and the Military in World War I. *Journal of American History, 55,* 565–581.

Kuklich, B. (1977). *The rise of american philosophy: Cambridge, Massachusetts, 1860–1930.* New Haven, CT: Yale University Press.

Lewis M. Terman Papers. (1920, May 18). Lewis M. Terman to O. S. Reimbold. Stanford, CA: Stanford University Library.

Mackenzie, D. A. (1981). *Statistics in Great Britain.* Edinburgh: Edinburgh University Press.

National Research Council (1933). *A History of the National Research Council, 1919–1923.* Washington, D.C.: National Research Council.

O'Donnell, J. (1985). *The origins of behaviorism: American psychology, 1870–1920.* New York: New York University Press.

Pauly, P. J. (1980). *Jacques Loeb and the control of life: Experimental biology in Germany and America, 1890–1920.* Doctoral dissertation, Johns Hopkins University.

Samelson, F. (1979). Putting psychology on the map: Ideology and intelligence testing. In A. Buss. (Ed.), *Psychology in social context,* (pp. 112–114, 142–158). New York: Irvington Publishers.

Thorndike, E. (1898). *Animal intelligence: An experimental study of the associative processes in animals* (Monograph Supplement No. 8). Psychological Review.

Tobey, R. C. (1971). *The American ideology of national science, 1919–1930* (chapter 2). Pittsburgh: University of Pittsburgh Press.

Woodward, C. V. (1971). The strange career of a historical controversy. *American Counterpoint: Slavery and Racism in the North-South Dialogue* (pp. 234–260). Boston: Little, Brown.

Yerkes, R. M. (1911). *Introduction to psychology.* New York: Henry Holt.

Yerkes, R. M., & Anderson, H. l. (March 1915). The importance of social status as indicated by the results of the Point Scale Method of measuring mental capacity. *Journal of Education Psychology, 6,* 150.

Yerkes, R. M., & Bridges, J. W. & Hardwick, R. S. (1915a). *A Point Scale for measuring mental ability* (p. 82 and passim). Baltimore: Warwick & York.

Yerkes, R. M., & Coburn, C. A. (1915b). A study of the behavior of the crow, *Corvus americanus* Aud. by the Multiple Choice Method. *Journal of Animal Behavior, 5,* 75–114.

Yerkes, R. M. (1915c). A study of the behavior of the pig, *Sus scrofa* by the Multiple Choice Method. *Journal of Animal Behavior, 5,* 185–225.

Yerkes, R. M. (1916). *The mental life of monkeys and apes: A study of ideational behavior.* Cambridge, MA: Henry Holt.

Yerkes, R. M. (1916a). A new method for studying ideational and allied forms of behavior in man and other animals. *Proceedings of the National Academy of Sciences, 2,* 231–233.

Yerkes, R. M. (1917). The Binet versus the Point Scale Method of measuring intelligence. *Journal of Applied Psychology, 1,* 118.

Yerkes, R. M. (1923). A Foreword to Carl C. Brigham, *A study of American intelligence* (p. v–viii). Princeton: Princeton University Press.

Yerkes, R. M. (1932). In C. Murchison (Ed.), *Psychology in autobiography* (vol. 2). Worcester, MA: Clark University Press.

Yerkes, R. M. (1956). *The Scientific Way* (pp. 89, 92–98, 167–168, 215–235). New Haven, CT: Sterling Library, Yale University.

7

Placing Women in the History of Comparative Psychology: Margaret Floy Washburn and Margaret Morse Nice[1]

Laurel Furumoto
Wellesley College

Elizabeth Scarborough[2]
State University of New York College at Fredonia

Women tend to be invisible in the history of psychology, and women in comparative psychology are no exception. A recent example of this practice is provided by Gottlieb in his chapter "Comparative Psychology and Ethology" included in a collection of historical papers marking the first century of experimental psychology (Hearst, 1979). He does not identify any contributors to the fields of comparative psychology or ethology as women. Although names of some women are listed in the references (e.g., S. J. Shettleworth, J. Stevenson-Hinde, M. F. Washburn), there is no way of knowing that they are women from the contents of the chapter or the initials-only style used in the reference list. Furthermore, the dozen photographs of contributors to the field appearing at the end of the chapter are all of men.

Why do histories of psychology tend to be written as womanless history even though it can be documented that women have participated in and contributed to the discipline for almost a century? (See Furumoto & Scarborough, 1986.) Gerda Lerner, American historian and a pioneer in the field of women's history, sees the omission of women as a general phenomenon in historical writing. In a collection of her essays titled *The Majority Finds its Past: Placing Women in History* Lerner (1979) discusses the problem:

---

[1]This chapter is based in part on a paper by Elizabeth S. Goodman titled: "Margaret Washburn, *The Animal Mind*, and Comparative Psychology" presented at the meeting of the Cheiron Society, River Falls, WI, June 1981 and on a paper by Laurel Furumoto titled: "Margaret Morse Nice: Watcher at the Nest" presented at the joint meeting of the Cheiron Society and the International Society for Comparative Psychology, Toronto, June 1983.

[2]Prior to 1984, Elizabeth Scarborough used the name Elizabeth S. Goodman.

Traditional history has been written and interpreted by men in an androcentric frame of reference; it might quite properly be described as the history of men. The very term "Women's History" calls attention to the fact that something is missing from historical scholarship and it aims to document and reinterpret that which is missing. Seen in that light, Women's History is simply "the history of women." (p. xiv)

In Lerner's (1979) view, the task of women's history is not only to identify women and their contributions but also to reconstruct the experience of women in the past. This reconstruction is necessitated by the fact that women's "culturally determined and psychologically internalized marginality . . . makes their historical experience different from men" (p. xxxi).

In this chapter we adopt a women's history perspective and begin to create a place for women in the history of comparative psychology by discussing the lives and contributions of Margaret Floy Washburn (1871–1939) and Margaret Morse Nice (1883–1974). These particular women have been chosen because they were recognized by their contemporaries as having produced significant work in the field and because they have been identified as important contributors by historians studying American women and women scientists.[3] Another reason we chose them is because their life histories vividly illustrate ways in which their gender dictated experiences for them different from those of men in the field.

MARGARET FLOY WASHBURN

As noted in an earlier paper (Goodman, 1980), Margaret Washburn "held a life long fascination with the minds of humans and animals and was convinced that experimental psychology provided the appropriate methodology for exploring the topic" (p. 69). With the strong support of both her father, who was an Episcopal minister, and her mother, whose sister was an early graduate of Vassar College, she steadfastly pursued an uninterrupted academic career. As Washburn (1932) recalled in her autobiography: "Both my parents always took pleasure in my work" (p. 349).

Born in New York City in 1871, she was an only child who in her early years was encouraged by her parents in her favorite pursuit—reading. At 15 she entered Vassar College where she concentrated in chemistry and French. Commenting on her Vassar experience Washburn (1932) observed: "At the end of my senior year I had two dominant intellectual interests, science and philosophy.

---

[3]See *Notable American women* entry for Washburn in Vol. 3, pp. 546–548 (James, James, & Boyer, Eds., 1971) and for Nice in Vol. 4, pp. 506–507 (Sicherman & Green, Eds., 1980); see also Rossiter, *Women scientists in America* (1982).

They seemed to be combined in what I heard of the wonderful new science of experimental psychology'' (p. 338).

After graduating from Vassar at the age of 20, Washburn (1932) decided to study this ''wonderful new science'' at Columbia University with James McKeen Cattell, newly appointed head of the psychological laboratory there: ''I determined to be his pupil. . . . but Columbia had never admitted a woman graduate student: the most I would hope for was to be tolerated as a 'hearer', and even that would not be possible until after Christmas when the trustees had met'' (p. 338). After a year of study at Columbia, Washburn took Cattell's advice and transferred to Cornell University where women were being admitted as degree candidates and were eligible for fellowships as well. Washburn's arrival at Cornell for the 1892–93 academic year coincided with E. B. Titchener's who had come from Oxford and Leipzig, to direct the psychological laboratory. Under his direction she completed her PhD with a thesis on the influence of visual imagery on judgments of tactual distance and direction. Receiving the degree in June 1894, she became the first woman to be awarded a doctorate in psychology.

In 1903, after nearly a decade of teaching that included a 6-year post at Wells College and brief appointments at Cornell as Warden of Sage College (the women's residence hall) and the University of Cincinnati as Assistant Professor, Washburn returned to Vassar College as Associate Professor of Psychology. By that time, at the age of 32, she had already contributed enough to the field of psychology as an experimentalist and critic to be included in a list compiled in 1903 of the 50 most distinguished psychologists in the United States (Cattell & Cattell, 1933).

Washburn would spend the rest of her career at Vassar College and would become a leading figure in American psychology. As a professor and head of the psychological laboratory at Vassar, she taught and influenced several generations of women students, many of whom were junior collaborators in her experimental work and shared authorship with Washburn on articles published in the *American Journal of Psychology*. In all, 69 such studies appeared with 119 students as joint authors. A significant portion of these papers explored topics in animal psychology.

Washburn also held editorial positions on several journals including the *American Journal of Psychology* and the *Journal of Animal Behavior*. She was elected President of the American Psychological Association in 1921, and in 1931 was the second woman elected to the National Academy of Sciences.

Although Washburn's published work covers a wide spectrum of topics in experimental psychology (see bibliographies by Kambouropoulo, 1940; Mull, 1927; & Woodworth, 1949), much of her work was focused on comparative psychology. Her major publication was *The Animal Mind*, initially published in 1908 with subsequent editions in 1917, 1926, and 1936. Her interest in comparative psychology began when she taught a course in the subject at Cornell in 1901–02. It intensified a few years later when, as Washburn (1932) recalled:

> During a six-weeks' stay at Ithaca in the summer of 1905, I collaborated with Dr. Bentley in some experiments on color vision in a brook fish which he captured from a neighboring stream. . . . Shortly after this, I began to collect and organize literature on animal behavior. The Animal Behavior Series, which the Macmillans published under Dr. Yerkes' editorship, brought out the first edition of *The Animal Mind* in 1908. . . . the patterns of animal consciousness seemed to me then, as they do now, well worth investigating and perfectly open to investigation. (p. 347)

This book, as noted earlier (Goodman, 1980) "reflected two vital elements in (Washburn's) life—an intense love for animals (especially cats) and a fascination with consciousness and introspection" (p. 75).

In a series of lectures on the evolution of comparative psychology, Julian Jaynes (1968) referred to *The Animal Mind* as the first real textbook of comparative psychology—"a careful, thorough, extensive, and fascinating review of the facts of the field, embedded in an intelligent discussion of the major principles and issues of the time." He also pointed out that the work, as it went through successive editions, was more than a handbook. It made a considerable original contribution to the field. This is especially evident in Washburn's discussions of learning, as her interpretations and terminology became the "common ware of the future."

E. G. Boring much earlier also identified Washburn and *The Animal Mind* as important in the history of comparative, or animal psychology, as he called it. He pointed out that she had not only contributed research to the movement but had become its secretary and encyclopedist as well. The book was a thorough treatment of research results and also a systematic orientation to the "dominating problems." Boring (1929) notes that a "movement in a field of research can hardly be said to have passed adolescence until there is a compendium that represents it, and Washburn's book constitutes just such a symbol of self-conscious unity and also a history of the movement" (p. 561). The comprehensiveness of Washburn's literature review is indicated in Boring's "notes" section of *A History of Experimental Psychology*, where he repeatedly refers the reader to *The Animal Mind* for bibliographies (of comparative psychology in general, and of the research of specific persons: Loeb, Jennings, Yerkes, and others).

How is it that *The Animal Mind* may be seen as "the first textbook in comparative psychology"? There had, of course, been earlier works of importance, even books dealing directly with intelligence in animals. Attention must be paid to G. J. Romanes, C. L. Morgan, and E. L. Thorndike, in particular, before answering the question. Romanes's book entitled *Animal Intelligence* (1882) is cited by Boring (1929) as the first comparative psychology. Romanes reviewed a prodigious amount of data gleaned from both scientific and popular literature. Following Darwin, his ultimate aim was to establish continuity of mind in defense of mental evolution. Though Romanes's work provided an impetus for later studies, it was flawed by dependence on the anecdotal method that encourages anthropomorphizing the animal and the inadequacy of the psychological system with which he worked.

Recognition of the limitations of the anecdotal method brought a quick reaction from Morgan. His *Animal Life and Intelligence* (1890–91) was followed by the *Introduction to Comparative Psychology* (1894) in which he presented his now famous canon. This appeal to the law of parsimony when interpreting observations of animal behavior then became an important methodological consideration for further work in comparative psychology. Morgan also presented the results of his own careful observational studies of behavior under conditions of specially modified environments, perhaps the first systematic efforts to apply the experimental method to animal psychology. In this way Morgan may be credited with founding the scientific school of comparative studies.

It was Thorndike, however, who performed the classical experiments that brought the experimental method to comparative psychology, for he studied animals in the laboratory with special apparatus. His first publication was printed as a monograph in 1898 and was titled *Animal Intelligence*, the same title used by Romanes. His further studies appeared in close succession and encouraged others to work in the same vein. The explosion of research that took place around 1900 is documented by a citation analysis of the 476 references listed by Washburn in the first edition of *The Animal Mind*. Fifty-six percent of those (266) were published between 1900 and 1907. In those 8 years there were twice as many studies as in the decade of the 1890s, which produced almost three times as many as the 1880s. In all, 95% of Washburn's references were published after 1880, thereby dating from about the time of Romanes's publication.

Now it may be noted why it is appropriate to designate *The Animal Mind, a Textbook of Comparative Psychology* as the first textbook in the field. In her preface, Washburn points out that the title might more appropriately have been "The Animal Mind as Deduced from Experimental Evidence." Hers was a comprehensive collection of the facts that had resulted largely from use of the experimental method in comparative psychology. This set it apart from the earlier works. It served a critical need of the burgeoning movement, for it provided in one source the wealth of material that was accumulating. Much of the material coming then from physiologists and psychologists was inaccessible, being widely scattered in a diverse set of journals.

The increased interest and activity in the field called for just such a volume. By 1908, the publication date of *The Animal Mind*, there were already courses in comparative psychology being taught in at least eight institutions (Warden & Warner, 1927). Clark and Chicago had offered the first courses, both begun in 1899, taught by E. C. Sanford and G. H. Mead, respectively. Harvard and Iowa came next, both offering the course in 1902, with R. M. Yerkes at Harvard and Mabel C. Williams at Iowa. Apparently only one institution had by then established a specialized research laboratory for animal study. This was at Chicago, begun by John B. Watson in 1903. Courses under the title of "Genetic Psychology" may also have been mainly or entirely focused on comparative, as was the course that Washburn initiated at Cornell in 1901.

The Animal Mind (1908) was received as an immensely important contribution and became a classic text. The review in the *American Journal of Psychology* concluded "altogether it is a Godsend to the student and teacher of psychology at the present day" (p. 279). Yerkes adopted it as a text for his class at Harvard and emphasized that comparative psychology should study conscious behavior "after the manner of Jennings and Washburn."

As the literature grew and the focus of the field shifted, Washburn kept at the task. The three revisions incorporated new facts and showed considerable rearrangement of material, with new subjects being introduced appropriately. Carr's (1918) review of the second edition reaffirmed its importance: "The book represents the most exhaustive and complete summary of the experimental literature now extant. For the serious student of comparative psychology the book has proved to be invaluable" (p. 290).

In the course on the "History of Psychology" taught at Ohio State in 1927 *The Animal Mind* held ninth place in a list of "great psychological treatises in America." It was not then, however, of only historical interest, for the year before Harvey Carr, in his presidential address to the American Psychological Association entitled "The Interpretation of the Animal Mind," had dealt entirely and directly with Washburn's position, urging the younger generation to come to grips with the issues involved.

MARGARET MORSE NICE

Growing up in Massachusetts during the last 2 decades of the 19th century, Margaret Morse, who did not acquire the name Nice until she married in 1909, was one of seven children in the family of Margaret Duncan and Anson Daniel Morse, a professor of history at Amherst College. As a child, in contrast to Margaret Washburn, she was discouraged by her parents in her scholarly interests and her outdoor pursuits. In her autobiography, written when she was in her eighties, Nice (1979) remembered her childhood in expansive terms as a "very happy one with wonderful parents, a flock of congenial brothers and sisters, and the glories of nature" in rural New England (p. 15). She also recalled that the three girls in the family, despite their long skirts, "led active, out-of-doors lives, taking long walks, riding our bicycles, as well as our intelligent but rather temperamental horse Rex" (p. 14). In her teens, however, Margaret often felt depressed, which she attributed to the old fashioned and over protective attitudes of her parents. They did not believe that their daughters should prepare themselves for professions. Rather, they sought to prepare them to be perfect housekeepers and homemakers. For Margaret and her two sisters, this was a dreary prospect and she remembered that all three of them wished they "had been boys, since boys had far more freedom than girls did to explore the world and to choose exciting careers" (p. 15).

When she entered nearby Mount Holyoke College in the fall of 1901, Margaret Morse (Nice, 1979) experienced a kind of liberation: "I had for the first time, freedom to arrange my life pretty much as I wanted it unhampered by parental solicitude" (p. 16). She looked back on her 4 years at this liberal arts college for women as very happy ones "with excellent courses under stimulating teachers, the companionship of true friends, and carefree exploration of the lovely country" (p. 21). Despite the new sense of freedom she experienced in college, Margaret found herself, upon graduation, returning to Amherst to be a daughter-at-home as her parents wished. She had made no plans either immediate or future for supporting herself. After a year back at home she remembers becoming desperately dissatisfied with what seemed to her to be an aimless existence—attending her father's daily class in American history, caring for his greenhouse, riding horseback, and telling the family cook what to prepare for meals.

Then, in a summer school course she attended in 1907 at the nearby Massachusetts Agricultural College, she heard two lectures by Clifton F. Hodge of Clark University that she remembers as having a profound effect on her and giving direction to her whole life. Hodge lectured to the class on the study of live animals, using the toad as the chief example—how much and what they ate and how they affected humankind. Nice (1979) remembered thinking "If I could study such things in a university, life would have a real purpose for me" (p. 23). She approached Hodge to ask about the possibility of studying at Clark and found him most encouraging. He even had animals available and a problem for her to study, suggesting that she investigate the food of the bobwhite. Margaret was very excited by this opportunity; her parents, however, were full of doubts about the undertaking. It was not until late summer, when she and her younger brother, Ted, were setting out for a long awaited camping trip, that her parents gave reluctant approval to her plan to enter graduate school at Clark. Arising for a very early breakfast, she found a note from her father that read "I am verging to the conclusion that in view of all your talents, proclivities, likings and dislikings and accomplishments, it may be advisable for you to specialize in the field of biology with the purpose of teaching and writing" (p. 23).

Entering Clark University that fall, Margaret Morse found the sense of life purpose she had previously lacked. Recalling this period, Nice (1979) writes: "Dr. Hodge, Dr. Hall, and my fellow students showed me that the world was full of problems crying to be solved; at every turn there was a challenge—nature waiting to be studied and understood. . . . Clark University gave me my first awakening. I had found my goal" (p. 26). She saw Clark in that fall of 1907 as a strange and wonderful place "devoted entirely to graduate work, with 16 men on the faculty and 64 graduate students hampered by few rules and imbued with the most democratic spirit, it was a haven from the hurried, worried, materialistic world, a place where truth could be pursued in freedom" (p. 28).

Margaret Morse spent her first year at Clark studying the food of the bobwhite, trying to add species of weed seeds and insects to those already reported in earlier work by Sylvester D. Judd, and finding out what quantity of seeds and insects a bobwhite would eat in a meal or during a day. "Hunting weed seeds, catching grasshoppers, and feeding them to appreciative bobwhites: attending lectures, seminars, and journal club; taking informal courses in bacteriology, neurology, and histology; reading in the splendid library; walking in the country and attending parties with fellow students—all these activities" Nice (1979) recalled "made it a happy year" (p. 28). In fact, she found it such a happy year that she decided to use the topic of "the food of the bobwhite" as the subject for a PhD thesis instead of the M.A. she had originally intended. This plan, however, like previous plans, encountered strong family opposition; her parents "urged her unceasingly to return to Amherst and again be daughter-at-home" (p. 33).

In her second year at Clark, she continued her feeding tests and made plans to carry out a large series of these tests in the summer of 1909 with young bobwhites at a nearby state hatchery. Only hinting at the reasons behind her decision, Nice (1979) records how she changed her mind:

> Instead of raising bobwhites, I was married; instead of working for a Ph.D. I kept house . . . sometimes I rather regretted that I had not gone ahead and obtained this degree. . . . But no one had ever encouraged me to study for a doctor's degree: all the propaganda had been against it. My parents were more than happy to have me give up thoughts of a career and take up homemaking, and in every way they helped us in this new venture. (p. 33)

Margaret Morse married Leonard Blaine Nice, a fellow graduate student at Clark whom she had known for a year. They stayed on at Clark for 2 more years while Leonard completed his work for the PhD in physiology and then moved to Cambridge for another 2 years so that he could teach physiology at the Harvard Medical School. In September 1913, the couple headed for Norman, Oklahoma, where Leonard had been appointed Professor of Physiology and Pharmacology at the University of Oklahoma. In 1927 there was another move, this time to Columbus, Ohio where Nice's husband had been offered an appointment in the Ohio State University Medical School. A final move occurred in 1936 when he was appointed head of the Physiological and Pharmaceutical Departments in the University of Chicago Medical School.

As her husband advanced in his education and career, Margaret Nice struggled to reconcile her strong desire for research and intellectual activity with the demands of domesticity. Between 1910 and 1923, she gave birth to five daughters and the burden of caring for them as well as the housework weighed heavily on her, especially when the children were very young and her husband's income was small. She described her plight in the fall of 1918 (Nice, 1979):

> With four children aged six months to eight years, in what seemed to be cramped quarters, no one enjoying housework, and much of the time without even a college girl to come in an hour a day to wash the dishes, with no means of transportation but our own legs and the baby carriage, and no free Sunday afternoon for tramps to the river, I was truly frustrated. I resented the implication that my husband and children had brains, and I had none. He taught, they studied, I did housework. (p. 41)

In spite of these difficulties, Nice was able to persist in her research and writing by combining two strategies—spending as little time and energy on housework as possible and finding the subjects of her research in her immediate environment. She described her approach to her domestic responsibilities as follows (Nice, 1979): "My technique of housework . . . was based on efficient preparation of good and simple meals, scalding water instead of dishtowels, sending out the washing and ironing and dispatch in the matter of cleaning. Most of my time was free for activities of more lasting value" (p. 34–35).

Margaret Nice made laboratories of her nursery and her backyard where she carried out research in two different areas. One of these was language acquisition, on which she published more than a dozen papers between 1915 and 1933 based on observation of her five daughters. The other and more prominent line of research was on bird behavior. Indeed, her most notable work was the study she made of the life history of the song sparrow—carried out almost literally at her doorstep in Columbus, Ohio.

Nice's publications on birds span a half century, beginning in 1910 with a paper on the food of the bobwhite and ending in 1962 with a paper on the development of the precocial birds.[4] Over the years her ornithological investigations became more and more concentrated on behavior. Milton B. Trautman, a zoologist with interests in the life histories of North American birds and fishes who became acquainted with Nice when she was living in Ohio, has commented on this trend in her research. Trautman (1977) writes: "during the early 1920s she began to display an ever-increasing interest, eventually amounting to almost a passion for behavioral studies" (p. 433). More than 50 papers and three books comprise her contribution to the literature on bird behavior. (See Trautman, 1976, for a bibliography of Margaret Nice.)

---

[4]Nice was remarkably prolific and produced not only empirical and theoretical papers in bird behavior and language acquisition but also articles, notes, and reviews, primarily in the area of ornithology. Her expert knowledge of German, Dutch, and other languages was employed in writing countless reviews of the European literature for an American audience.

In addition to her studies of imprinting, incubation periods, and of nesting in a variety of species, Nice is remembered for her important work on territorialism reported in a 1941 paper "The Role of Territory in Bird Life." Her investigations of the life history of the song sparrow, which resulted in a two volume work published in 1937 and 1943, are regarded as classics in the field. Using the technique of banding in her song sparrow studies, she was able to identify and to follow the life histories of individual birds. Nice is recognized as having made a significant methodological contribution to animal behavior research in this pioneering work (see Streseman, 1975).

Two major ornithological societies acknowledged the accomplishments of Margaret Nice in the study of birds: the Wilson Ornithological Club elected her as its first woman president for two terms in 1938 and 1939 and the American Ornithological Union bestowed on her its highest honor, the Brewster medal, for her work on the life history of the song sparrow. In a foreward to Nice's autobiography, Konrad Lorenz (Nice, 1979) also paid tribute to this work, recalling their first meeting in 1934 at the International Ornithological Congress held in Oxford.

At that time she had already begun her field studies on the song sparrow *Melospiza melodia* which occupied her for many years and which turned out to be a major break-through in the methods of studying animal behaviour. Her paper on the song sparrow was, to the best of my knowledge, the first long term field investigation of the individual life of any free-living wild animal. (p. IX)

CONCLUSION

Both Nice and Washburn were talented and dedicated scientists and both were subject to restrictions affecting their professional development and personal lives because they were women. We see, however, significant differences between the two women in the kinds of restrictions they faced, differences which stem, in part, from parental attitudes and, in part, from marital status.

Nice's overbearing parents did not support any independent initiative taken by their daughter. In contrast, Washburn's parents fostered her intellectual development and career aspirations. Nice, unlike Washburn, chose to marry and disrupted her education to do so. Nice, with neither a PhD nor institutional affiliation, shouldering the duties of the wife of an upwardly mobile academician and the mother of five daughters, dealt with obstacles vastly more trying, it would seem, than Washburn. Yet Washburn's career, although unencumbered by husband and children and helped by her doctorate and an academic appointment, was hardly free from gender restrictions.

Washburn's professional attainment was clearly limited by her employment at a women's college. Conditions there were far from optimal for research and scholarly development—teaching loads were heavy, salaries low, support for research was meager, students were minimally prepared to serve as assistants, collegial contacts were few. Washburn nevertheless persevered. Employment at a major university research center was not a possibility for her, as such institutions were unwilling to hire women for their faculties (see Rossiter, 1982). Her career commitment, however, was unflagging and she "made do" with what she had (see Scarborough & Furumoto, 1987).

Another gender-linked factor affecting Washburn was the socially prescribed role of daughter that prevailed in late 19th century American middle-class families. This role embodied something Jane Addams (1964) identified as "the family claim," a constellation of duties expected of a daughter—but not necessarily of a son—to her family (pp. 71–101). Washburn (1913) was not exempt from this claim and voiced it poignantly in a letter to Robert Yerkes which contained her resignation as review editor for the *Journal of Animal Behavior:* "I doubt if anyone else on the board is teaching eighteen hours a week, as I am. I simply must cut down my work somewhere. If I am ever to accomplish anything in psychology, it must be done in the next five years, for as my parents get older, I shall have less and less command of my time."

Finally in the field of psychology itself, gender-specific barriers worked to exclude women. For example, Washburn's PhD advisor, E. B. Titchener, in 1904 established an elite group of experimentalists who met yearly in the psychological laboratories of the prestigious Eastern universities to discuss research in progress and matters of current interest and importance to the field. All the prominent experimental psychologists, including comparative psychologists such as J. B. Watson and R. M. Yerkes, participated in the group. From the beginning, however, Titchener insisted that women, regardless of their qualifications as experimentalists, be excluded. This policy of exclusion was maintained, apparently with little or no protest from the other members, until 1929—two years after Titchener's death—when the society was reorganized and elected two women members, one of whom was Margaret Floy Washburn (see Scarborough & Furumoto, 1987).

Margaret Nice's scientific ambitions were frustrated by gender-linked problems in addition to the demands of domestic life. One of these was the difficulty she had in making contact with and being accepted by a scientific peer group. Another was related to her social identity because many of those whom she considered her scientific peers insisted on seeing her as a housewife.

During her Oklahoma years (1913–1927), excluded from the academic community which her husband enjoyed, Nice depended heavily on collaboration with her husband and correspondence with an amateur ornithologist in Eastern Iowa, Althea Sherman, to support her scientific work. Nice (1952) described Althea Sherman as "an extraordinary woman . . . tireless in her seach for truth" (p. 51) who, for 35 years, watched birds in her country home:

My correspondence with Miss Sherman started in 1921 when I wrote to her inquir-
ing about the exceptional length of fledging of two Mourning Doves—18 and 19
days—reported by her in the *Condor*. I received a long and detailed letter in which
she made me happy by saying: ''I am glad there is another woman to join our ranks
who is doing serious study.'' This was the beginning of a close and inspiring
friendship. We met but twice—at A(merican) O(rnithological) U(nion) meetings in
Chicago in 1922 and in Detroit in 1931. (p. 51)

Sherman, never married and 68 at the time she began corresponding with
Nice, shared with the younger woman not only a passion for studying birds, but
also a hearty distaste for the drudgery of housework. As Sherman (1926) con-
fided to Nice, ''Like you I rebel against spending time on menial tasks that I
ought to hire another to do.'' Letters from Sherman to Nice in the period from
1921 to 1932 are filled with detailed discussions of observations made on birds,
and current ornithological literature and meetings, and are liberal in their praise
for Nice's accomplishments as a scientist and mother. In one, for example,
Sherman (1921) remarked: ''When congratulating you upon your work done, I
do not for a minute forget the greatest task, the rearing a family of children. That
alone seems too great a task for many women. To this work I add the numerous
articles that have appeared in the bird magazines.''

The Sherman–Nice correspondence continued without interruption after the
Nices moved from Oklahoma to Ohio in 1927, but Sherman's letters end
abruptly without explanation in 1932, one presumes because of her failing
health. Althea Sherman is credited as being a strong influence on Margaret
Nice's scientific career (Trautman, 1977). Not only did she provide praise,
encouragement, and intellectual comradeship to Nice as the younger woman was
entering a critical stage in her study of bird behavior, but also certain aspects of
Sherman's life may have served as a warning to Nice. Most important, Sherman
never fulfilled her ambition to write a book on the life histories of several species
of birds based on the results of her intensive, long-term studies. Nice (1952) saw
two chief reasons for this failure: ''Her time was frittered away in activities of
lesser importance, and the task was intrinsically too great'' (p. 55). And she
lamented Sherman's fate as well as that of other talented women:

> It is a tragic thing that a woman of her intellect, gifts, and character should have
> had to spend so much time in manual labor that she could not give her message to
> the world. This problem is an increasingly serious one in our civilization. Our
> highly-educated, gifted women, have to be cooks, cleaning women, nurse maids.
> (p. 55)

Nice herself managed to avoid the pitfalls that to her mind accounted for
Sherman's unwritten book. Soon after moving to Ohio, she began her long-term
study of the life history of a single species, the song sparrow, and according to
Trautman (1977) for the following decade (1927–1936) until the family moved

to Chicago, she "had four principal objectives: (1) spending innumerable hours in the field gathering data, sometimes all day or before daylight or after dark; (2) researching in the libraries housed at the Ohio State University, Ohio Historical Society, Columbus Public or smaller libraries; (3) discussing avian problems with qualified persons; (4) working up data into manuscript form for publishing" (p. 435).

It was in the third of these four objectives—discussing avian problems with qualified persons—that Nice was frustrated during most of her time in Columbus. Her correspondence with Sherman ended, and she was unable to fill the void. Recalling the benefits of being able to visit Berlin in 1932 for discussions with the ornithologist Erwin Streseman, Nice (1979) remarked: "At Columbus I had missed the stimulus of talking over my Song Sparrow problems with other naturalists for these were organized into the strictly masculine Wheaton Club, of which Blaine was a member but from which I was excluded" (p. 116). Although Margaret Nice was finally admitted to the monthly meetings of the Wheaton Club, as an "unofficial honorary member" she recalled her years of exclusion with sharp regret: "How I would have benefited from this opportunity for discussion of my problems earlier in the study of Song Sparrows!" (p. 151).

Nice was eventually successful in establishing a place for herself among scientists whom she considered her peers, despite the handicaps of being female, lacking a PhD and an institutional affiliation. Yet she was apparently unable to escape being stereotyped by them as a housewife. She is remembered by her long-time ornithological friend, Milton B. Trautman (1977), as especially resenting being referred to as a housewife: "Several of us have heard her exclaim, 'I am not a housewife, I am a trained zoologist' " (p. 440). Yet in an obituary by Parkes (quoted in Trautman, 1977) and in Trautman's (1977) as well, she is identified as being (among other things) "a housewife."

When seen together, the lives of Margaret Floy Washburn and Margaret Morse Nice reveal in an impressive way the complex and pervasive influence that being a woman has in shaping an individual's experience. The woman who pursued a career and the woman who chose marriage and motherhood followed separate paths, necessitating different adaptations by each as she comfronted her own peculiar set of gender-linked obstacles to professional development and scientific achievement. Viewed in this context of restriction and accommodation, the contributions of Washburn and Nice to comparative psychology loom large indeed.

ACKNOWLEDGMENTS

We would like to acknowledge the skillful editorial assistance of Barbara Kneubuhl in preparing this chapter and to express our appreciation to Grace Kinchla for typing the manuscript.

REFERENCES

Addams, J. (1964). *Democracy and social ethics*. Cambridge, MA: Harvard University Press.

The animal mind. (1908). *American Journal of Psychology, 19,* 279.

Boring, E. G. (1929). *A history of experimental psychology*. New York: Century.

Carr, H. (1918). Washburn's Animal Mind. *Psychological Bulletin, 16,* 288–290.

Cattell, J. McK., & Cattell, J. (Eds.). (1933). *American men of science: A biographical directory* (5th ed.). New York: Science Press.

Furumoto, L., & Scarborough, E. (1986). Placing women in the history of psychology: The first American women psychologists. *American Psychologist, 41,* 35–42.

Goodman, E. S. (1980). Margaret F. Washburn (1871–1939): First woman PhD in psychology. *Psychology of Women Quarterly, 5,* 69–80.

Hearst, E. (Ed.). (1979). *The first century of experimental psychology*. Hillsdale, NJ: Lawrence Erlbaum Associates.

James, E. T., James, J. W., & Boyer, P. S. (Eds.). (1971). *Notable American women 1607–1950: A biographical dictionary* (Vol. 3). Cambridge, MA: Harvard University Press.

Jaynes, J. (1968, Summer) *Lectures on the evolution of comparative psychology*. Presented at the NSF Institute for the Teaching of the History of Psychology, Durham, NH.

Kambouropoulou, P. (1940). A bibliography of the writings of Margaret Floy Washburn: 1928–1939. *American Journal of Psychology, 53,* 19–20.

Lerner, G. (1979). *The majority finds its past: Placing women in history*. New York: Oxford University Press.

Morgan, C. L. (1890–91). *Animal life and intelligence*. London: E. Arnold.

Morgan, C. L. (1894). *An introduction to comparative psychology*. London: W. Scott.

Mull, H. K. (1927). A bibliography of the writings of Margaret Floy Washburn, 1894–1927. *American Journal of Psychology, 39,* 428–436.

Nice, M. M. (1937). Studies in the life history of the song sparrow I, a population study of the song sparrow. *Transactions of the Linnaean Society of New York, 4,* 1–247 (Reprinted by Dover, 1964).

Nice, M. M. (1941). The role of territory in bird life. *American Midland Naturalist, 26,* 441–487.

Nice, M. M. (1943). Studies in the life history of the song sparrow II, the behavior of the song sparrow and other passerines. *Transactions of the Linnaean Society of New York, 6,* 1–328 (Reprinted by Dover, 1964).

Nice, M. M. (1952). Some letters of Althea Sherman. *Iowa Bird Life. 22,* 50–55.

Nice, M. M. (1979). *Research is a passion with me: The autobiography of Margaret Morse Nice*. Toronto: Consolidated Amethyst Communications.

Romanes, G. J. (1882). *Animal intelligence*. London: Kegan Paul, Trench.

Rossiter, M. W. (1982). *Women scientists in America: Struggles and strategies to 1940*. Baltimore: Johns Hopkins University Press.

Scarborough, E., & Furumoto, L. (1987). *Untold lives: The first generation of American women psychologists*. New York: Columbia University Press.

Sherman, A. *Letter to M. M. Nice, December 30, 1921*. (From the M. M. Nice papers, Cornell University, Ithaca, NY).

Sherman, A. *Letter to M. M. Nice, March 10, 1926*. (From the M. M. Nice papers, Cornell University, Ithaca, NY).

Sicherman, B., & Green, C. H. (Eds.). (1980). *Notable American women: The modern period* (Vol. 4). Cambridge, MA: Harvard University Press.

Streseman, E. (1975). *Ornithology: From Aristotle to the present*. Cambridge, MA: Harvard University Press.

Thorndike, E. L. (1898). *Animal intelligence, an experimental study of the associative processes in animals*. New York: Macmillan.

Trautman, M. B. (1976). *A partial bibliography of Margaret Morse Nice.* The Ohio State University Museum of Zoology Report for 1976, Number 7.

Trautman, M. B. (1977). In memoriam: Margaret Morse Nice. *The Auk, 94,* 430–441.

Warden, C. J., & Warner, L. H. (1927). The development of animal psychology in the United States during the past three decades. *Psychological Review, 34,* 196–205.

Washburn, M. F. (1908). *The animal mind.* New York: Macmillan.

Washburn, M. F. *Letter to R. M. Yerkes, October 24, 1913.* (From the R. M. Yerkes papers, Yale University, New Haven, CT).

Washburn, M. F. (1932). Margaret Floy Washburn: Some recollections. In C. Murchison (Ed.), *A history of psychology in autobiography* (Vol. 2, pp. 333–358). Worcester, MA: Clark University Press.

Woodworth, R. S. (1949). Margaret Floy Washburn. In *National Academy of Sciences biographical memoirs* (Vol. 25). Washington, DC: National Academy of Sciences.

8 Edward C. Tolman: Comparative Psychologist?

Nancy K. Innis
University of Western Ontario, Canada

INTRODUCTION

In 1911, having just graduated from M.I.T. with a B.S. in electrochemistry, Edward Tolman enrolled in two summer courses in the Philosophy Department at Harvard College. One was a course in introductory philosophy taught by Ralph Barton Perry and the other a course in introductory psychology given by Robert Yerkes. In fact, both men were to have a lasting influence on Edward Tolman.

At the end of that summer, Tolman decided to enter the graduate program at Harvard specializing in psychology. He (Tolman, 1952) felt that psychology "offered a nice compromise between philosophy and science" and that it was nearer his "capacities and interests" than philosophy. In his characteristic self-deprecating style he claimed in his autobiography "I did not have brains enough to become a philosopher" (p. 323). More to the point was the fact that experimental psychology would permit him to engage in scientific pursuits, while at the same time maintaining a strong interest in social issues. Tolman's relationship with his older brother, Richard, later to become a noted physicist, also influenced his choice of psychology and his desire to become a researcher. Tolman both admired and competed with his brother. A career in psychology, rather than one in the physical sciences, meant he need not compete directly (Tolman, 1954).

During his years as a graduate student at Harvard, Tolman's research, under the supervision of the eminent Hugo Münsterberg and his associate Herbert Langfeld, involved studies of the effect of olfactory cues on human memory. He continued to do research on human memory during the 3 years he was on the faculty at Northwestern University (1915 to 1918) and when he first arrived at the University of California.

However, he was asked to introduce a new course when he joined the Berkeley Department, and he decided on a course in comparative psychology. Whether this initiated a change in his research interests or was the result of such a change is difficult to document. In any case, from this time on Tolman's work, and that of his students, was to center on the study of animal learning. We are concerned with examining the importance of this work for the field of comparative psychology. Was Tolman, in fact, a comparative psychologist?

To determine an individual's impact on a particular field, several aspects of his career must be examined. Most important is the nature of the research being carried out in his laboratory. Following this, one can examine the emphasis of the journals in which reports of this research are published and the professional associations to which the individual belongs. Another major area is the training of students, both at the undergraduate and graduate level. The nature of the courses taught, the textbooks used, and the textbooks written provide a good indication of the emphasis placed on certain aspects of the field by the individual in question. In this chapter I consider Edward Tolman's contribution to comparative psychology by examining his research, writing, and teaching.

One problem, and it is a problem that persists today, is the lack of a clear definition of comparative psychology. More specifically, what did psychologists, during the 2 decades between 1920 and 1940, consider as constituting comparative psychology? We mainly limit our discussion to this period, because it was during these years that Tolman's work most directly impinged on comparative psychology. An examination of the comparative psychology textbooks used in the courses being taught at this time, as well as those popular in the previous decade or so, when the teachers of these courses were being trained, indicates that the study of comparative psychology had become equated with the study of animal psychology. Earlier in the century, the definition was much broader, emphasizing race, child, and individual differences, as much as animal psychology. For example, Yerkes' courses in comparative psychology emphasized race and child psychology (Course Catalogues, 1911–1914).

The first comparative psychology textbook to be used extensively in this century was Margaret Floy Washburn's *The Animal Mind: A Textbook of Comparative Psychology,* which first appeared in 1908 and was reprinted in 1909 and 1913. We know that this text was used in the course in animal psychology taught by Tolman in the mid 1920s. The second text of importance during the early part of the century was John B. Watson's *Behavior: An Introduction to Comparative Psychology,* published in 1914 and based on a series of lectures presented at Columbia University in 1912. Tolman states in his autobiography that this text was used in a course in comparative psychology that he took with Yerkes in 1914 (Tolman, 1952). This was possibly Yerkes' Animal Psychology course. Yerkes also taught a course in Advanced Comparative Psychology (Psychology 22), which examined child, animal, and race psychology; however, it was not scheduled to be given in 1914–15 when Watson's text was first available (Course Catalogues 1911–1915). Whatever the actual relationship between the course taken by Tolman from Yerkes and Watson's text, both of these had an important influence on Tolman as we see later.

A text by A. J. Warden (1927), Munn's (1933) *Introduction to Animal Psychology,* and a collaborative volume edited by Fred A. Moss (1934) entitled *Comparative Psychology* appeared in the late 1920s and early 1930s. Tolman was a contributor to the latter text. All these books were almost entirely devoted to an examination of animal psychology; usually examining a number of species, and considering sensory systems, learning, and what was sometimes referred to as mental development. Thus, throughout this time comparative psychology and animal psychology seemed to be synonymous terms. The statement in the Preface of the 1934 Moss text is indicative of this approach:

> The increasing number of courses offered in Comparative Psychology gives some indication of the importance of the subject. Realizing the need for a satisfactory textbook in this field, a number of men who had been working in Animal Psychology convened at the Cornell meeting of the American Psychological Association and planned an introductory textbook.

It should be noted that the study of animal psychology at this time was tacitly assumed to be directed at the understanding of human behavior, rather than emphasizing a comparison among animal species, as was later the case. Within this perspective then, we examine Edward Tolman's contribution to comparative or animal psychology. We begin by considering the courses he taught in this area.

TEACHING

Undergraduate

When Edward Tolman was hired as an instructor at the University of California in 1918 he was asked to suggest a new course. "Remembering Yerkes' course and Watson's textbook," Tolman (1952) recalls in his autobiography, "I proposed 'comparative psychology'." This course, to become Psychology 150, was listed in the 1918 course catalogue as "Animal Psychology" and described as studying "Sensation, perception and attention in animals; their methods of learning" (Course Catalogues, 1918–1950). However, because of the war, teaching assignments were disrupted in the fall of 1918 and it is unlikely the course was given that year. Animal Psychology was offered in the fall of 1919, however, and, although there is no record of the textbook used, it may very well have been

Watson's *Behavior* because the course description coincides very well with the topics covered in this book.

Initially Watson's book had a profound influence on Tolman. Behaviorism was for Tolman a congenial solution to the many problems of Introspection, the then predominant method of Psychology; problems that had nagged him since he was a graduate student at Harvard. By the time Tolman joined the faculty of Berkeley he "had become a confirmed behaviorist" (Tolman, 1952). Soon, however, he became uncomfortable with Watson's "muscle twitch psychology" and began to develop his own form of behaviorism. Tolman presented these ideas in a paper entitled "A New Formula for Behaviorism" that appeared in the Psychological Review in 1922. He took the position that consciousness, or cognitive factors, need not be rejected by those studying either human or animal behavior. Throughout his career, Tolman continued to espouse a behaviorism that incorporated cognition and purpose.

This development in Tolman's thinking is indicated in the course description for Animal Psychology that appeared in the 1920–1921 course catalogue. Now the course was to consider "Problems in the behavior and consciousness of animals; sensation, ideation, learning. Methods and results" (Course Catalogues, 1918–1950). It may be that Washburn's text *Animal Mind* was introduced at this time; there is evidence that it was the book used in the course in 1926 and 1927.

In 1923 a more neutral course description appeared. Animal Psychology (Course Catalogues, 1918–1950) involved "A survey of the psychology of the higher forms; experimental methods and results bearing on human psychology." That fall, Tolman was on sabbatical leave and the course description may have been suggested by his replacement. Nevertheless, this description for Psychology 150 was not changed for the next 15 years. Tolman, as most other comparative psychologists of the day, viewed the study of animal behavior primarily as a means for gaining an understanding of human behavior, as was previously mentioned. This was one of the justifications for studying only a few animal species such as primates and the rat.

In 1920 Tolman introduced a full year laboratory course, Psychology 151, to accompany Psychology 150. In this course, entitled "Experiments in Animal Behavior," each student was to "conduct a special investigation on the sensations, instincts, or learning of the higher vertebrates." The course included "Experiments, reading and discussion" (Course Catalogues, 1918–1950).

A second term more advanced section of Psychology 150 was added in 1938. The description of the old first term course now read (Course Catalogues, 1918–1950) "General survey of the behavior of the lower and higher animal forms. Tropisms, instincts, sensory capacities, learning and problem solving," while the new course involved a "more intensive survey of the experimental literature on learning and problem solving in the higher forms." This increase in course offerings in animal psychology indicates the growth in research in animal psychology over the preceding 20 years.

Tolman taught Psychology 150, with few exceptions, every year from 1919 to 1949. He also occasionally gave a course in Animal Psychology at other universities, when visiting during summer school or during his leaves. He continued to offer Psychology 151 until 1942–43 when, because of the war, enrollment was falling. It was not given again until 1948–49, when seven students were enrolled, and this was likely the last time Tolman taught it. In summary then, throughout most of Tolman's career about one third to one half of his undergraduate teaching load comprised courses in animal or comparative psychology.

Graduate Teaching

Graduate training at Berkeley during the years before the second world war was research, not course, oriented. Tolman's graduate seminar seemed to begin informally in the fall of 1921. His students came to his home every Thursday evening "to talk psychology" (Letter to M. C. Tolman, Sept. 15, 1921). As the seminar developed over the years, it became the high point of the week for Tolman's graduate students. The lively discussions usually centered on the research going on in the laboratory and related research, reported in the literature. It was not listed as a formal seminar until 1937–38, when it appeared as Seminar in Animal Psychology, meeting on Tuesday nights. The 1920s and 1930s were a most productive time in terms of both research and graduate training for Tolman.

RESEARCH

Early in July of 1919 Tolman acquired 6 rats from the Anatomy Department at Berkeley and by November of that year had a colony of 50 white rats, and two students doing research under his supervision (Letters to M.C.T., 1919). One of the issues of the day in which he was particularly interested was the role of instincts in determining behavior. Following this theoretical interest in whether the propensity to behave in certain ways could be inherited, Tolman (1924) began what was later to become a major research project, examining the role of genetic factors in maze-learning ability. This project may have been fostered by discussions with Zing Yang Kuo, his first doctoral student. Kuo, later to become a well-known comparative psychologist, maintained a behavioristic position even more extreme than Watson's, asserting that all behavior was the result of learning. Kuo (1921) and Tolman (1922) exchanged views in published papers and most likely had many informal discussions on the topic as well. Tolman considered Kuo an excellent student and when Kuo's dissertation, "A Behavioristic Experiment on Inductive Inference" was rejected by the philosophers on his dissertation committee, Tolman made an appeal to the Graduate Council of the university (Letter to M.C.T., March 1, 1923). The thesis was accepted by them by a vote of 9 to 1 in the spring of 1923, however, because Kuo had returned to China before the decision was reached, the degree was not conferred until 1936 when he returned to the United States.

Between 1925, when Hugh Blodgett received a PhD, and 1940, more than a dozen students obtained doctoral degrees carrying out animal research under Tolman's direction. With one exception these studies used rats as subjects and generally involved maze-learning problems. The exception was the work of Otto Tinklepaugh (1928a) with monkeys, including Cupid and Psyche (Tinklepaugh, 1928b). Although Tinklepaugh's work is the only primate research from Tolman's laboratory that I have found in print, Tolman was still interested in maintaining a primate colony in 1928 after Tinklepaugh had left for Yale taking his monkeys with him. In a letter discussing plans for the new Life Sciences building, which would house the Psychology Department, Tolman indicated that there would be facilities for housing and doing research with monkeys and chimps.

Tinklepaugh received his PhD in 1927. Among others completing doctorates at this time, who would later contribute to comparative psychology, were Joseph Yoshioka in 1928, M. H. Elliott and Robert Tryon in 1929, and I. Krechevsky (later, David Krech) and Charles Honzik in 1933. Tryon's work, which involved a study of individual differences, Tolman felt to be of particular importance. This research involved the continuation of the project on the role of heredity in maze-learning ability begun by Tolman in the early 1920s, and reported in the Journal of Comparative Psychology in 1924. During the late 1920s and early 1930s, having examined the performance of many generations of rats, Tryon published several papers on individual differences in the learning ability of "maze dull" and "maze bright" rats, most of which also appeared in this journal.

Tolman's strong involvement in the genetic project is indicated by the fact that, on two occasions, the continuation of this research was one of the main reasons Tolman gave for refusing the offer of an appointment at Harvard. He was also to use these job offers as leverage for getting more support for Tryon at Berkeley. In March of 1928, in a letter to E. G. Boring, Chairman of the Harvard Psychology Department, Tolman outlined the extent of his research program, involving "seven major researches in progress" and "a colony of some thousand rats" (March 16, 1928). Even if it were possible to transport the large automatic maze and the animal colony, and to find financial support for Tryon, Tolman was dubious that Harvard could afford the cost of maintaining such an operation. For example, he was spending some $2,700 that year for the care and maintenance of animals.

Later, in 1931, when refusing the second offer of a position at Harvard, Tolman wrote to Boring (March 28, 1931): "It would be absolutely criminal for Tryon's research to stop now. I feel this so strongly that this year my brother,

Richard, and I have contributed the money for Tryon's research associateship out of our own pockets, having been unable up until now to wangle anything here.'' The following year Tryon was appointed Assistant Professor in the Berkeley department where he remained for the rest of his career, continuing this research. Tryon played a role in training others, such as Calvin Hall, who also have made contributions to comparative psychology. Hall has acknowledged Tolman's influence, as has Jerry Hirsch (a recent editor of the Journal of Comparative Psychology), who at a much later date was also a student in the Berkeley laboratories.

JOURNAL PUBLICATIONS

The Journal of Comparative Psychology was one of the journals published by the American Psychological Association in which papers by Tolman and his students frequently appeared. Between 1923 and 1940 nine papers on which Tolman was author were published in this journal. As well, in 1936, Tolman became an Associate Editor of the Journal of Comparative Psychology, although it is not known how frequently he reviewed papers for this journal.

TEXTBOOKS

Tolman was one of the men working in animal psychology who got together at the APA Meeting at Cornell to plan the comparative psychology text edited by Moss in 1934. Tolman's contribution was a chapter on Theories of Learning. Tinklepaugh and Tryon also had chapters in the book; in fact, the chapters written by Tolman and his former students comprise over one quarter of the pages in the text. Moss's Comparative Psychology appears to have been quite popular, and it is fair to assume that Tolman and those he trained had a considerable influence on the comparative psychology being taught in many colleges and universities during the 1930s and later. Tryon and Tinklepaugh had chapters in the 1942 revision of the book, while Calvin Hall continued the tradition with a chapter in Stone's 1951 revision.

Tolman's theoretical ideas, which are mainly presented in papers published in the Psychological Review and in his first book, *Purposive Behavior in Animals and Men,* indicate, I believe, that his main interest in studying rat behavior was to be able to make generalizations applicable to all, and especially to human behavior. Tolman was primarily a learning theorist. Whether he would have called himself a comparative psychologist is difficult to say; I somehow think not. However, the preceding facts indicate that as a teacher, graduate supervisor, and researcher, he contributed immensely to comparative psychology and thus deserves a well-earned placed in the history of this discipline.

REFERENCES

Course Catalogues (1911–1915). Harvard University.

Course Catalogues. (1918–1950). University of California, Berkeley.

Kuo, Z. Y. (1921). Giving up instincts in psychology. *Journal of Philosophy, 18,* 645–664.

Moss, F. A. (Ed.). (1934). *Comparative psychology.* New York: Prentice–Hall.

Moss, F. A. (Ed.). (1942). *Comparative psychology* (2nd ed.) New York: Prentice–Hall.

Munn, N. L. (1933). *An introduction to animal psychology.* New York: Houghton Mifflin.

Stone, C. P. (Ed.). (1951). *Comparative psychology* (3rd ed.) Westport, CT: Greenwood Publisher.

Tinklepaugh, O. L. (1928a). An experimental study of representative factors in monkeys. *Journal of Comparative Psychology, 8,* 197–236.

Tinklepaugh, O. L. (1928b). The self-mutilation of a male macacus rhesus monkey. *Journal of Mammalogy, 9,* 293–300.

Tolman, E. C. (1922). Can instincts be given up in psychology? *Journal of Abnormal Psychology, 17,* 139–152.

Tolman, E. C. (1924). The inheritance of maze-learning ability in rats. *Journal of Comparative Psychology, 4,* 1–18.

Tolman, E. C. (1932). *Purposive behavior in animals and men.* New York: Century.

Tolman, E. C. (1952). Edward Chace Tolman in *History of psychology in autobiography* (Vol. IV.). Worcester: Clark University Press.

Tolman, E. C. (1954). *Compilation of biobibliographical data.* Unpublished.

Warden, C. J. (1927). *A short outline of comparative psychology.* New York: Norton.

Washburn, M. F. (1908). *The animal mind: A textbook of comparative psychology.* New York: Macmillan.

Watson, J. B. (1914). *Behavior: An introduction to comparative psychology.* New York: Henry Holt.

9 Two Comparative Psychologies

Jack Demarest
Monmouth College, NJ

If the doctrine of evolution is true, the inevitable implication is that mind can be understood only by observing how mind is evolved.
—Spencer, 1886, p. 291

Even if we were in possession of a scientific phylogeny instead of the fairy tales that go by that name at present, it would not relieve us of the task of explaining the instincts on the basis of the physical and chemical qualities of protoplasm.
—Loeb, 1900, p. 198

From a discussion of the behavior of the lower organisms in objective terms, compared with a discussion of the behavior of man in subjective terms, we get the impression of complete discontinuity between the two . . . Only by comparing the objective factors can we determine whether there is continuity or a gulf between the behavior of lower and higher organisms (including man)
—Jennings, 1906, p. 329

INTRODUCTION

The history of psychology is written primarily by avocational, rather than professional, historians. For the most part, we still continue to write stories rather than explore issues, and our interest in the past is primarily dictated by our concern with the present (Hyman, 1982). I do not pretend to be any different in the approach taken in this chapter, but I hope to demonstrate that the story behind the current identity crisis in comparative psychology can be best understood as the result of our tendency as scientists to view history from only one perspective. "The study of the history of psychology," it has been said, "has suffered mightily from those who have taken it literally" (Young, 1966, p. 14), and our positivist attitude has led us to identify the field with one historian's comparative psychology when, in actuality, there were and still are at least two.

It has often been stated that comparative psychology was fathered by Darwin, by way of Romanes, and that its research program from the start has been to establish continuity of mind in defense of mental evolution (Boring, 1950). Lloyd Morgan is typically cast in the role of midwife in this scenario, delivering the philosopher's concern with the developmental history of consciousness from the realm of natural history into the hands of experimentalists like Thorndike, Watson, and Yerkes. Biologists like Jennings, Loeb, and Wesley Mills are recognized for their research contributions and their participation in the development of the psychological study of animal life, but they are usually portrayed as bit players having but a transitory influence on the conceptual growth of the field. This is the version of history as given by E. G. Boring, and it will be found in almost any compendium on comparative psychology that one can find published after 1930 (e.g., Carmichael, 1968; Stone, 1951; Warden, 1928; Waters, 1934; but see Gottlieb, 1979).

A recent paper by Pauly (1981) casts a different light on this scene. In this light, comparative psychology was initially viewed as a division of biology concerned with the integration of structure and function, primarily in primitive life forms (Loeb, 1890; Verworn, 1894; Yerkes, 1904). Although Lloyd Morgan retains his position as midwife in the birth of experimental comparative psychology, there was not one but two opposing conceptualizations that resulted, represented by Loeb on the one hand and Jennings on the other.

Consciousness and the Continuity Doctrine

Allow me to place the Loeb–Jennings dichotomy in a conceptual context. By the late 1800s the belief in the continuity of mind could be found everywhere. Herbert Spencer (1886), popularizer of evolutionary ideas, wrote that consciousness evolved through a succession of changes in the nervous system permitting greater correspondence between the organism and its environment: "by so doing evolves a distinct consciousness—a consciousness that becomes higher as the succession becomes more rapid and the correspondence more complete" (p. 179). Naturalists literally flooded bookstores, popular magazines, and natural history journals with a descriptive studies of organisms, primarily insects, using conscious choice and other humanizing characteristics to explain the activities and movements of these creatures (e.g., Binet, 1894; Forel, 1904; Lubbock, 1882). Romanes book entitled *Animal Intelligence* (1882) specifically focused on proving the mental continuity hypothesis.

Despite the wide acceptance of the Continuity Doctrine, the fundamental question of the development and distribution of consciousness became a sore point for philosophers to attack. William James (1890) was among the most outspoken:

> It is very generally admitted, though the point would be hard to prove, that consciousness grows the more complex and intense the higher we rise in the animal kingdom . . . In a general theory of evolution the inorganic comes first, then the lowest forms of animal and vegetable life, then forms of life that possess mentality, and finally those like ourselves that possess it in a high degree . . . In this story no new *natures*, no factors not present at the beginning, are introduced at any later stage.
> But with the dawn of consciousness an entirely new nature seems to slip in, something whereof the potency was *not* given in the more outward atoms of the original chaos. (p. 138, 146)

To Spencer's statement that consciousness becomes "nascent" as organisms undergo successive changes in the nervous system, James (1890) replies:

> Merely to call the consciousness 'nascent' will not serve our turn. It is true that the word signifies not yet *quite* born, and so seems to form a sort of bridge between existence and nonentity. But that is verbal quibble. The fact is that discontinuity comes in if a new nature comes in at all. The *quantity* of the latter is quite immaterial. The girl in 'Midshipman Easy' could not excuse the illegitimacy of her child by saying, 'it was a very small one'. And consciousness, however small, is an illegitimate birth in any philosophy that starts without it, and yet professes to explain all facts by continuous evolution. (148–149)

This became the first great problem for comparative psychology. How does an evolutionary psychology explain the origins and evolution of mental life from life that is otherwise insensitive. By the early 1900s there were three alternative explanations; (a) grant consciousness to all animals, (b) grant consciousness only to those animals whose behavior reveals attributes regarded as evidence of mind, or (c) deny that any animal exhibits consciousness.

Consciousness and the Biologizing of Mind

The argument that *all* animals are conscious, from simple protista to complex human beings, was based on the grounds that life implies consciousness. This was the view of the vitalists, many non-Darwinian naturalists, and even many naturalists who adopted Darwin's viewpoint and interpreted animal movements by their analogy with human conduct (e.g., Binet, 1894; Forel, 1904; Lubbock, 1882). It was an inevitable outcome of the attempt to prove mental continuity by establishing that the essence of all the higher faculties of man can be found in animals, and it led to a widespread use of psychological terms applied by different authors with wide differences in meaning. Aside from the obvious confusion that this engendered, the problem with this approach is that it was just as arbitrary to posit consciousness to animal life although denying it to practically indistinguishable vegetable life as it was to call some animals conscious but not others on the basis of their similarity to humans. Consequently, for this argument to be consistent its adherents had to believe that all life, for that matter, all atoms possess consciousness in some primitive sense. James (1890) put it this way: "If evolution is to work smoothly, consciousness in some shape must have been present at the very origin of things" (p. 149). This argument, although metaphysically sound, is not a particularly satisfying one on which to build a science of mental life, and by the turn of the century few people believed that all animals were conscious.

Similarly, few people believed that no animals were conscious. Arguing from analogy, it seemed that many organisms, especially the "higher" forms, behaved in ways that appeared to require conscious thought; that is, if a human behaved in the same way we would unhesitatingly infer conscious choice. There were other problems with this viewpoint as well, not the least of which was the unwillingness of people to deny their own consciousness. For, to be consistent, this argument also had to extend to the human species.

The remaining solution to James' (1890) dilemma was to argue that consciousness and perhaps many other mental traits are emergent properties of increasingly complex organisms. This position known as "organic selection" (Baldwin, 1902), argued that qualitative discontinuity in mental evolution goes hand in hand with quantitative continuity in physical evolution. Consciousness, as an emergent property, could therefore appear in one animal species and not in another, and the question then became simply where to draw the line, and by what criteria would the distinction be made.

The criteria used by both naturalists and the early comparative psychologists to define consciousness varied widely. Some argued that variability of response was, in itself, sufficient (Binet, 1894), others believed that adaptive modification was the important factor (Morgan, 1894), and still others believed that some evidence of purposive choice was necessary (Schneider, in Calkins, 1905). Of course, none of these criteria really addressed James (1890) crucial point that mind, if it is to have evolved at all, must manifest itself in a continuous link with the past, and it is here that we must turn to biology for a resolution. For unlike the philosophically oriented psychologists, the physiologist's solution to the problem was to abandon altogether the use of terminology garnered from human experience in favor of strictly mechanical or physiological concepts. They were not necessarily denying consciousness but rather admitting that there was no scientific way of recognizing it. Because the comparative physiologists had performed the greater part of the experiments on animals throughout the late 1800s and into the early 1900s without relying on psychological terminology, the attitude that began to prevail was that a metaphysical explanation was both unnecessary and unproductive.

The Comparative Psychologies of Jennings and Loeb

Some sort of psycho-physiological relationship had been assumed to account for mind for hundreds of years, but with Herbert Spencer we begin to see that this view can be coupled with an evolutionary theory of origins. A similar attitude was held by Romanes, Morgan, and many of the physiologists of the time. C. Lloyd Morgan (1894) is the central figure here, because his views on several important issues were the focus of much of what comparative physiology and comparative psychology would become. On the anecdotal foundations of comparative psychology, we already know his position. He believed in direct observation, and experimentation was central to this objective orientation. On the use of terminology from human psychology to explain animal behavior, we have his law of parsimony. And with respect to the psycho-physiological relationship, he argued that occurrences in the mind are so correlated with events in the body that this relationship lies at the heart of the problems of evolution. Evolution, from a scientific orientation, is progressive organization, and special features emerge in this organized advance. The following quote is found in Morgan (1961) ''Briefly stated, the hypothesis is that when certain items of ''stuff'', say o, p, q, enter into some relational organization R . . . the whole R (o, p, q) has some ''properties'' which could not be deduced from prior knowledge of the properties of o, p, and q taken severally'' (p. 253). Or, as Baldwin (1961) more colorfully put it: ''The qualities of flower and fruit . . . cannot be accounted for, much less predicted, from the chemical formulas of processes going on in the tissue of the fruit tree'' (p. 8). For Morgan, the province of comparative psychology was to investigate the nature and the mode of development of mental processes, dealing with them in their synthetic rather than their analytic aspect. The methods of comparison and analysis, particularly as relates to the psycho-physiological relationship, were to be employed with a predominantly synthetic aim. The first business of the comparative psychologist, he felt, was to establish generalizations about mental evolution with reference to progressive organization and complexity (cf. Demarest, 1983; Yarczower & Hazlett, 1977). It should be added that the corner of the field that seemed to him most likely to yield this sort of information was the study of the behavior of lower organisms. Not only were these animals simpler to study systematically, but as stated by Morgan (1961), they represented: ''the contour line below which lies all that was conventionally spoken of as instinct, while above it is the region of intelligence'' (p. 248).

Out of this synthesis of ideas that Morgan began to piece together grew two very different approaches to comparative psychology, both fostered by physiologists. The more radical view was that of the mechanistic school represented by Loeb, Beer, Bethe, Von Uexkull, Nuel, and others. The tropism theory of Loeb, as presented in his 1890 paper, was the rallying point in this movement. In that theory Loeb concentrated on how external forces controlled the actions of simple organisms, while at the same time emphasizing that internal conditions (i.e., sensory physiology) and mental activity were unimportant to this explanation. Like the plants that his colleague Julius Sachs studied, the direction and movement of an animal could be reducible to "physico-chemical" conditions in the organism's nervous system correlated with specific reflex actions. Identification of the features in the environment that produced the automatic responses was the goal of Loeb's comparative psychology, and therefore precise experimental control and objective explanation was of primary importance. Interestingly, although trained in brain physiology and the cerebral ablation techniques of Goltz, Loeb considered the nervous system little more than a transmission line in this analysis. The response to the external forces of temperature, or light, or gravity was automatic and unvarying, and the nervous system merely conveyed the impulses.

From this account of behavior arose a new type of comparative psychology. Bethe (1898), for example, attempted to explain all the complicated behavior of ants and bees, previously attributed to human-like faculties by the romantic naturalists, as a result of reflex responses to chemical stimulation. Nuel (1904) went even further in attempting to account for complex human actions according to principles of simple reflex phenomena. Although they believed that man's mind is a natural product of the evolution of animal mind, they argued that an evolutionary hypothesis and, in particular, mentalistic explanations were superfluous to this line of inquiry. In fact, a joint paper by Beer, Bethe, and Von Uexkull (1899) proposed to eliminate entirely the subjective terminology of traditional human psychology in describing nonhuman animal behavior. In its place they wanted objective, deterministic, noninferential facts: Von Uexkull (1902) stated:

> such in a few words are the problems and aspects of experimental biology. A blossoming of this hopeful science is, however, only to be expected when investigators become impressed with the conviction that psychological doctrines in so far as they relate to the animal mind are worthless and untenable speculations, and when refusing to be led astray by the siren tones of theories of mind, they limit their researchers to the facts of experience. (p. 233)

The mechanistic school was a dramatic departure from the comparative psychology of the time. It was diametrically opposed to the accounts given by Lubbock, Bert, Graber, Romanes, and others who described the behavior of insects and other invertebrates in terms of conscious choice and preference. Warden (1927) found the following: "It was a far cry from the notion of Romanes that the insect flies into the candle flame out of curiosity to the opinion of Loeb that it does so because it cannot do otherwise" (p. 153). Anticipating Lloyd Morgan's canon, the movement epitomized parsimony in interpreting animal behavior in objective terms, and it insisted that behavior should be investigated for its own sake and not simply as evidence for or against the mental continuity hypothesis. The effect was compelling, and the humanizing tendency was struck a final blow. More importantly, however, Loeb's emphasis on experimental control and on the environmental conditions triggering reflexive behavior strongly influenced the development of a nonevolutionary, behavioristic comparative psychology in which little importance was placed on sensory physiology or hypothetical cognitive processes.

The mechanistic movement soon met with energetic opposition from several sides. The apologists for the universality of consciousness (e.g., Claparede, 1901; Forel, 1904) continued their anthropomorphic babblings, though with a much diminished influence. Sensory physiologists and psychobiologists (Yerkes' terminology) objected to Loeb's dismissal of the nervous system as merely the conductor of impulses, and they began to bring together anatomical, physiological, and psychological facts to explore this relationship. Most noteworthy of these interdisciplinary marriages, by the way, was the expansion of the *Journal of Comparative Neurology* in 1904 to include comparative psychology (Yerkes, 1904). Psychologists, sometimes from unexpected sources, continued to express their chagrin over the mechanist's failure to understand that different levels of analysis yield unique and complementary explanations. Watson (1907) stated:

> When a psychologist attempts to read the writings of Loeb, he is apt to become thygmotactic and stereotropic, and lose that calm intellectual poise which he ordinarily possesses . . . (Loeb) still fails to grasp the fundamental principle of psychology, viz., that a physico-chemical statement of behavior can never *interfere with* nor be *substituted for* a psychological statement. (p. 291, 293)

But, most important of all, was the opposition engendered by the evolutionary biologists, in particular Herbert Spencer Jennings.

Jennings was literally raised on evolutionism. His father, was an itinerant Midwestern farmer–doctor, so devoted to the new ideology that he named both his sons after evolutionists (Jennings' brother was named Darwin). The evolutionist Herbert Spencer (1853) had written: "since man's mind is a product of evolution, and its achievements are the result of the accumulation of all the experiences and events of the past, psychology should study primitive men and animals and even the lowest forms of animal life—to protozoa" (p. 65). How fitting it is then that the very point on which Herbert Spencer Jennings would take Loeb to task was in explaining the reactions of protozoa to external stimuli. Jennings sought to show that protozoan behavior could be understood in terms of sensorimotor physiology, that is, in terms of internal processes rather than external physical forces. As a zoologist, Jennings was far better prepared to discuss the details of the physiology and behavior of invertebrates than was Loeb, and consequently he was able to demonstrate the errors and oversimplifications in Loeb's work. From a tremendous amount of experimental evidence he was able to show that the behavior of lower organisms is not as simple as Loeb's theory would seem to require, that their responses to the same stimulus fluctuate due to differences in inner physiological states at different times, and that instead of being directed and forced, their responses are more often of the 'trial and error' type (Jennings, 1907). Although Watson (1905) criticized Jennings' liberal use of this term, the appeal to trial and error learning was particularly significant because of the evolutionary implications that it carried. First of all, the discovery of adaptive modifications in the behavior of protozoa provided further evidence of continuity between the behavior of "lower" and "higher" organisms. Jennings (1907) stated: "It is difficult if not impossible to draw a line separating the regulatory behavior of lower organisms from the so-called intelligent behavior of higher ones; the one grades insensibly into the other" (p. 335). Secondly, Jennings made no secret of his belief in Baldwin's principle of organic selection, that the ability to learn results in adaptation to local conditions and that learning can be a major force in evolutionary adaptation. Finally, the demonstrations in these simple organisms of behavior that could not be differentiated in objective terms from perception, attention, discrimination, memory, choice, and desire implied the existence of an evolutionary hierarchy of psychological states and associated internal physiological processes. The issue of whether mental evolution was continuous or episodic rested upon the findings of comparative studies of adaptive modification of behavior.

Thus, with the exception of the emphasis on behavior, Jennings' comparative psychology stood in stark contrast to the mechanist viewpoint (see Table 9.1). It emphasized internal physiological causation, behavioral variability, progressive evolution of species diversity and complexity, and dynamic adaptation to a changing set of environmental conditions. Animal behavior, in Jennings' way of thinking, was the means to understanding the relationship between structure, function, and the hypothesis of continuity in mental evolution. For Loeb, on the other hand, animal psychology was useful in so far as it could reveal the ways in which external forces control behavior.

THE IMPACT OF THE TWO COMPARATIVE PSYCHOLOGIES

A series of articles and books appeared between 1890 and 1907 laying out the differences in the comparative psychologies of Jennings and Loeb. That they had a significant impact on the development of the field is evidenced by the fact that Washburn's *Animal Mind,* (1908), the most comprehensive review of the animal psychology literature of the time, contained more references to these two individuals than to any other two psychologists or biologists. But neither individual established a school in the sense that Structuralism, Functionalism, or Behaviorism were schools of thought among psychologists. Technically, both antici-

TABLE 9.1
The Comparative Psychologies of J. Loeb and H. S. Jennings

System Variables	Loeb's Emphasis	Jennings' Emphasis
Motivating force	External forces (stimulus control)	Internal forces (physiological processes)
Behavior emphasis	Reflex activities	Adaptive behavior (trial and error)
View of the response	Stereotypy	Plasticity
Species differences	Discontinuity	Continuity
Analysis of the organism	Mechanistic	Dynamic
Purpose of CP	To reveal ways in which external forces can be manipulated to control behavior	To understand the nature of progressive mental evolution and the relationship of structure and function to consciousness

pated Behaviorism, although Watson's (1907) review of *Behavior of the Lower Organisms* criticized Jennings for not going far enough in his behavioral analysis. Gradually, however, Loeb and Jennings began to shift their own interests to other areas. Loeb became attracted to the problem of artificial parthenogenesis and Jennings turned to the study of genetics.

Without a sustained program of research and a cadre of proteges to promote their ideas, the influence of the two comparative psychologies can only be determined from subtle trends. We may ask what sort of impact the students of Jennings and Loeb had on comparative psychology, or what features of their research programs continued into the next generation of psychological studies. We can ask which orientation was reflected in the journal articles and textbooks that were published, and in the research philosophy of the laboratory directors, teachers, and editors of journals in comparative psychology. And finally, we can ask how the fundamental distinctions between these two psychologies have stood the test of time, that is how closely each comes to characterizing the current image of comparative psychology.

The Students of Jennings and Loeb

Though Jennings and Loeb were biologists, several of their students did leave their mark on psychology, even though they did not promote the tropism theory or psycho-physiological evolutionism. Jennings' principle disciple was S. O. Mast, who continued to do studies on invertebrate behavior well into the 1920s.

But it was Karl Lashley who was to play the more important role in the development of comparative, and especially physiological psychology. Trained in zoology at Hopkins under Jennings, he obtained his PhD in 1914. While there he collaborated on several projects with John Watson. At this time Watson was just publishing his *Introduction to Comparative Psychology* (1914), in which Lashley wrote a chapter on learning, and he had recently completed his first foray into Behaviorism (Watson, 1913). In his autobiography, Watson (1961) notes, "Lashley, who came to me a well-trained biologist from Jennings, contributed to my point of view more than his own modesty will allow him to say" (p. 277). It has even been suggested that Lashley showed Watson the importance of Pavlov's work at precisely the time that Watson was developing his radical position (Herrnstein, 1969). But despite his behaviorist orientation, Lashley never quite dismissed the notions of insight, intelligence (Lashley, 1929), and consciousness (Lashley, 1923) that characterized the point of view of his teacher Jennings. He would never become a convert to Watson's radical brand of behaviorism. Hebb (1963) stated: "Unlike some other behaviorists, he was not afraid to use the word mind, and it was the problem of *mind* that he wanted to solve" (p. ix).

Like Jennings, Lashley's behaviorism was operational and objective, and lightly sprinkled with psychological terminology. He also continued Jennings' emphasis on internal physiological causation and adaptive modification of behavior. However, he never became particularly interested in the progressive evolution of mental activity, or in species diversity in behavior. In fact, he frequently emphasized that his lesion experiments with rats were quite compatible with the neuropathology reported in the human clinical literature. Although he was later to write a paper on instinct (Lashley, 1938) that very closely paralleled Lorenz's position and that Thorpe (1979) has characterized as representing the ethological perspective, he was not an evolutionist.

Quite different in his treatment of mental evolution was Robert M. Yerkes. Although not a student of Jennings, he nevertheless developed from the same academic mold. Both Jennings and Yerkes attended Harvard in the late 1890s majoring in zoology, though Jennings was leaving just as Yerkes arrived. Both studied under C. B. Davenport, a devotee of Loeb's tropism theory and an important figure in the genetics movement and in several influential scientific circles. Like Jennings, Yerkes found the new experimental biology to be a welcome addition to the study of mental evolution. He also viewed the mental life and behavior of animals as functional, adaptive activities that needed to be systematically related to their evolutionary history and neural machinery. And finally, like Jennings, he was strongly influenced by the revival that was taking place in the study of heredity, and he came to assume the existence of inherited consciousness in animals. Where Yerkes differed from Jennings was his acceptance of Loeb's tropism theory. For Jennings, the tropism model was misleading at best; for Yerkes it provided an objective and precise way to examine the role of heredity and the role of consciousness in the evolution of life (Cravens, 1978), although he accepted it with reservations (Yerkes, 1961).

Yerkes' early career was given over to the study of tropisms, or what he called "organic receptivity." He began by studying these innate traits in invertebrates as a student of Davenport in zoology. When his mentor moved to the University of Chicago in 1899, Yerkes migrated to the Harvard psychology department, where he came under the influence of Hugo Munsterberg (Cravens, 1978). Munsterberg encouraged his young protege to apply mental measurement techniques to animals, and his 1902 dissertation on the orientation reaction of jellyfish to light marked the beginning of a systematic program in which the vigorous methods of experimental biology were used to answer questions about the evolution of mind (Reed, 1981). His initial research was dominated by issues central to the Loeb–Jennings debate (Yerkes, 1906), but he soon shifted his research interest to "organic adaptivity," better known as habit formation, and with this change came an interest in "higher" organisms. Boring (1950) is most colorful in describing this shift: "He might almost be said to have climbed steadily up the evolutionary scale in his researchers, for from 1900 on he worked successively on various lower animal forms, then on the crab, the turtle, the frog, the dancing mouse, the rat, the worm, the crow, the dove, the pig, the monkey and man" (p. 628). In all these studies, however, Yerkes reinforced his committment to what he liked to refer to as the psychobiological approach, i.e., an integration of structure and function. This was the reason for his abiding interest in heredity and behavior, and the force behind his organizational efforts to link comparative neurology and psychology. His approach as a comparative psychologist was to establish a natural history of mental life using a broad, multidisciplinary approach. In contrast to Loeb and Davenport, he rejected a rigid reductionism, retaining a respect for philosophical categories of thought. Like Jennings, he emphasized internal physiological causes as well as adaption to changing conditions, and he believed in the diversity and continuity of species differences. He was never able to sympathize unreservedly with the extreme objectivism of Loeb and the mechanistic school, and in later years he came to realize that his differences with Watsonian Behaviorism were no less fundamental (Cravens, 1978; Yerkes, 1961). For both Jennings and Yerkes, the most fascinating and important problem in biology was the nature and evolutionary relationship of consciousness.

Loeb's influence on psychology through his students is a bit more obscure. Never having approved of psychology, it is quite understandable that his students would generally share this distaste. However, when Loeb came to America in 1891, assuming a position at the University of Chicago from 1892–1906, one of his students in biology, and again in physiology, was John Watson. In his autobiography, Watson (1961) noted that Loeb was interested in supervising his dissertation, but when it was discussed with J. R. Angell and H. H. Donaldson,

Watson was talked out of it. What exactly Loeb had in mind as a thesis topic we are not in a position to know, but the topic Watson finally settled upon, i.e., the neurological and psychological maturation of the white rat, would have been as important to Loeb's way of thinking as was his invertebrate research (cf. Loeb, 1900). Watson, in turn, was equally impressed with Loeb's tropism hypothesis. Even in later years, when Loeb was regularly attacking the comparative psychologist in print, Watson (1906a) continued to appreciate this work: "The value of Loeb's contribution to comparative psychology must not be underrated even if later investigations have thrown certain of his results into disfavor. In addition to the intrinsic value of his work, we can trace back many contributory investigations in this field either directly or indirectly to his stimulating influence" (p. 159). Whether we can credit Loeb as being the chief influence on Watson's thinking, or just one of his many inspirations, it is clear that with the exception of the focus on physico-chemical processes, Watson's Behaviorism incorporated the same general orientation as the mechanistic school. He emphasized the objective description of external forces (stimuli) influencing reflexive units of behavior (response) under controlled experimental conditions, and he minimized the significance of phylogenetic comparison and sensory physiology. The purpose of Watson's program of research, like that of Loeb's, was to produce a technology of behavioral control.

What makes this story complicated, however, is that Watson did not develop his brand of behaviorism at Chicago under Loeb's direct influence. In fact, Watsonian Behaviorism was not formulated for another decade, and his radical Behaviorism took still longer. First at Chicago and then in his early years at Hopkins, he taught a rather traditional Jamesian type of general psychology, and he relied on Titchener's laboratory manuals in his experimental courses (Watson, 1961). He also aligned himself with the evolutionary school at this time in his professional affiliations and in some of his writing. For example, in 1906 he published an article on the importance of a field station for studies of animal behavior (Watson, 1906b) "which will give to the animals naturalness in environment and to the investigator ample space for experimentation" (p. 155). He concluded this article by stressing that: "the need to the psychologist of an experimental station for the study of the evolution of the mind is as great as is the need to the biologist of an experimental station for the study of the evolution of the body and its functions" (p. 156).

Soon after moving to Hopkins in 1908, Watson took Jennings' courses on evolution and his lab work on lower organisms (Herrnstein, 1969). The link to the evolutionists was further strengthened when he joined Jennings and Robert Yerkes as editor of the *Journal of Comparative Neurology and Psychology*—a journal dedicated to the "development of the comparative method . . . (to) show what is meant by the evolution of action" (Herrick, 1904, p. 271). And he frequently reviewed articles in the comparative psychology sections of the *Psychological Review* and the *Psychological Bulletin* that were concerned with the origins of consciousness and the hierarchy of mental processes. It is noteworthy that, in several of these reviews (Watson, 1906a, 1907), he strongly criticized Loeb's misunderstanding of psychology and the belief that physico-chemical explanations can take the place of psychological explanations. Watson also corresponded frequently with Yerkes and asked his advice about doing field studies on a Carnegie Institute grant in the Tortugas (Cravens, 1978). He eventually produced some fine studies on nesting, the behavioral development of young birds, and the homing instinct in Terns (Watson, 1908), which were far better than the vast majority of field studies done at that time, anticipating the experimental methods of von Frisch by 6 or 7 years and those of Tinbergen by 30. Thus, at this point in his life, evolutionary ideas were certainly on Watson's mind even though his research only occasionally reflected this. He had not ignored the theory of evolution as Loeb had done, but this was soon to change.

Throughout all this time Watson continued to emphasize behavioral control, reflexive actions, and external stimuli, the hallmark of Loeb's comparative psychology. By 1914, when he published *An Introduction to Comparative Psychology*, the prediction and control of behavior had taken priority over the ontogeny and phylogeny of mental activity, and by 1924 it replaced them altogether. Herrnstein (1969) stated: "the concept of conditioning had taken its place at the very center of Watson's system, leaving room for little else. Instincts, emotions, thought, feelings, temperament, personality, intelligence, all the old and new preoccupations of psychology were either explained away by the conditioned reflex or repudiated altogether" (p. 64).

Textbooks in Comparative Psychology

Watson's *Introduction to Comparative Psychology* brought to the study of animal behavior a straightforward and objective methodology, but it also eliminated the very questions that formed the basis of an evolutionary comparative psychology, that is, the problem of the origins, distribution, and development of mind. He stressed the need for objective description of external conditions and experimental control. This was the legacy of Loeb and his mechanists, and it became the accepted version of comparative psychology after 1910. Why this is so would require another chapter, but some of the deciding factors seem to be the positivist character of science at the time, the lure of methodological rigor and experimental control, the devaluation of speculative metaphysics and the rise of operationism, fact finding, and data collection (Mackenzie, 1976; O'Donnell, 1979). To this list we might also add the fact that Watson's gradual transformation from functionalism at Chicago, to a moderate form of behaviorism at Hopkins, to the radical position his books began to take after 1915 fit the development of general psychology perfectly. His early years were entirely consistent with the functionalist ideology spreading throughout America, and his *Comparative Psychology* was "on the whole critical, careful, conservative, and free from dogmatism" (Carr, 1915, p. 309). Herrnstein (1969) has argued that the reaction to the book was positive because this was already the prevailing trend in the psychological community, and Cravens (1978) has argued that the trend itself was due to a purge by the younger psychologists to deliver the discipline of psychology from philosophy and to establish it as a natural science. Cravens (1978) commented: "These post-1900 psychologists considered themselves experimental psychologists, not merely advocates of experimental methods" (p. 192). It received praise from Carr (1915) and Thorndike (1915), and was adopted even by people who could not identify themselves with any form of behaviorism. Jastrow (1961) commented:

> When I began [my course in Comparative Psychology], the older view of animal intelligence still prevailed. I could find no more suitable text than Romanes' account of *Animal Intelligence,* full though it was of questionable anecdotes and uncertain conclusions. T. Wesley Mills at Montreal offered a more scientific survey, and with the appearance of Lloyd Morgan's *Comparative Psychology* it was at least possible to indicate the bearing of the analysis of animal behavior upon human psychology . . . When in 1914, Professor John B. Watson published his book on *Behavior: An Introduction to Comparative Psychology,* I at once adopted it as a text for my course in that subject. Though I could not fully endorse his claim that the whole of psychology could be pursued by the method he so well applied to the "primitive" objective phases of response, I found the statement that psychology must proceed as a "natural science" with the emphasis on (functional) behavior wholly in accord with my own formulation. (p. 143, 153)

Jastrow went on to point out that the next stage in Watson's evolution was too much for him to stomach, and that the change from "Behavior" to "Behaviorism" transformed a promising science into a confusing cult. But by now Watsonian comparative psychology, derived from Loeb and fostered by the Behaviorists of the 1920s and 1930s, had become synonomous with all of comparative psychology. Even Boring (1929) had said so.

Watson's book was not the only text in comparative psychology, of course, and it is instructive to examine the others available at the time. The list in Table 9.2 is necessarily selective, but I tried to restrict myself to the works that would have appealed to the various teachers of comparative psychology at that time. I did not include, for example, C. J. Herrick's (1924) *Neurological Foundations of Animal Behavior* because this was primarily a textbook in physiological psychology. Similarly, I omitted C. O. Whitman's (1919) *The Behavior of Pigeons,* and several works by Yerkes, despite their consideration of many of the conceptual problems in comparative psychology, because of their limited focus on one taxonomic group.

Romanes' book has already been discussed. It was perhaps the first compendium of animal behavior relying principally on carefully selected anecdotes purported to show instances of animal intelligence and purposive action in sup-

TABLE 9.2
Textbooks in Comparative Psychology

Author	Title	Publication Date
G. J. Romanes	Animal Intelligence	1882
C. L. Morgan	An Introduction to Comparative Psychology	1894
W. Wundt	Lectures on Human and Animal Psychology (Trans.)	1894
T. Wesley Mills	The Nature and Development of Animal Intelligence	1898
J. Loeb	Comparative Physiology of The Brain and Comparative Psychology	1900
C. L. Morgan	Animal Behaviour	1900
L. T. Hobhouse	Mind in Evolution	1902, 1915
H. S. Jennings	Behavior of the Lower Organisms	1906
M. F. Washburn	Animal Mind	1908, 1917, 1926, 1936
E. L. Thorndike	Animal Intelligence	1911
J. B. Watson	Behavior: An Introduction to Comparative Psychology	1914
S. J. Holmes	Studies in Animal Behavior	1916
F. A. Moss	Comparative Psychology	1934, 1942
C. Stone	Comparative Psychology	1934, 1942, 1951
M. R. F. Maier and T. C. Schneirla	Principles of Animal Psychology	1935, 1963
Warden, Jenkins, and Warner	Comparative Psychology (3 Vols.) 1. Principles and Methods 2. Plants and Invertebrates 3. Vertebrates	1935 1936 1940

port of mental continuity. Lloyd Morgan's text, in contrast, set the scene for a scientific comparative psychology based on behavior, in which consciousness and other psychological traits could be inferred only from direct observation, and then only when no simpler explanation of the observed behavior could be found. These were undoubtedly the books most often used in the first courses in comparative psychology (see Table 9.3), for they continued the historical connection that linked the problems of philosophy and psychology. Morgan's book was reviewed by G. H. Mead (1895) who favored the new experimental psychology

TABLE 9.3
Courses in Comparative Psychology

Institution	Earliest Course Date	Offered by	Present Course Hrs. Lect.	Hr. Lab.	Enrol- ment	Graduate, Under- graduate or Both
Barnard	1923	G. S. Gates	36	0	18	U
Bryn Mawr	1912	J. H. Leuba	45	0	21	U
[b]California U	1918	E. C. Tolman	36	108	—	B
Catholic U of Am	1925	C. J. Connolly	36	0	—	B
[b]Chicago U	1899	G. H. Mead	36	72	26	B
Clark U	1899	E. C. Sanford	36	36	9	B
Colorado U	1910	L. W. Cole	54	0	80	U
[b]Columbia U	1924	C. J. Warden	72	72	12	G
Cornell U	1909	I. M. Bentley	Dropped			
Drake U	1906	Florence Richardson	Dropped			
Emory U	1918	H. W. Martin	—	—	—	—
Geo. Washington U	1925	Wm. Middleton	54	0	35	B
[a]Harvard U	1902	R. M. Yerkes	54	0	—	B
[a]Idaho U	1916	H. B. Reed	54	0	—	U
Illinois U	1913	I. M. Bentley	36	108	10	B
Indiana U	1910	M. E. Haggerty	Dropped			
Iowa U	1902	M. C. Williams	Dropped			
Johns Hopkins U	1908	J. B. Watson	Dropped			
Kansas U	1912	F. C. Dockeray	36	36	8	B
[c]Michigan U	1909	J. F. Shepard	36	0	—	B
Minnesota U	1915	Jos. Peterson	36	210	9	B
Mt. Holyoke	1906	S. P. Hayes	Dropped			
New Mexico U	1925	B. F. Haught	54	0	—	—
[b]New York U	1924	P. D. Stout	54	36	40	U
No. Carolina U	1920	J. F. Dashiell	54	36	4	B
Oberlin	1910	R. H. Stetson	54	0	20	B
[a]Ohio State U	1907	T. H. Haines	72	0	9	B
Ohio Wesleyan U	1921	E. B. Skaggs	36	18	6	B
Oklahoma U	1907	L. W. Cole	54	54	11	B
Pittsburgh U	1912	J. H. White	Dropped			
[a]Radcliffe	1913	R. M. Yerkes	54	0	—	U
Smith	1918	Ruth Clark	30	18	26	B
Southern Calif. U.	1921	K. T. Waugh	—	—	—	—
[c]Stanford	1916	J. E. DeCamp	36	0	21	U
Texas U	1908	C. S. Yoakum	Dropped			
Vassar	1918	M. F. Washburn	54	0	6	U
Washington State Col	1922	C. I. Erickson	36	0	7	B
Washington U. (Seattle)	1913	Stevenson Smith	36	0	42	B
Wisconsin U	1911	Joseph Jastrow	36	—	45	B

[a]Irregular, usually in alternate years.
[b]Course offered in summer session also.
[c]Offer an additional laboratory course.
Note: Adapted from Warden & Warner (1927).

of Wundt, and in fact initiated the first comparative psychology course at Chicago. But although he praised Morgan for attempting to drag this science out of its anthropomorphic, mentalistic beginnings, Mead also criticized him for his tendency to reason by analogy, saying that it is at best a superficial account, and that such an orientation is rift with errors. Morgan's second book on this list, *Animal Behaviour*, was also reviewed in the psychological literature (Mills, 1901), but this time he was very favorably received, although with some reservations. In fact, Mead would probably have been more comfortable with Wundt's *Lectures on Human and Animal Psychology*, and Mills with his own *Nature and Development of Animal Intelligence*, but it is clear that both books represented a direction in research that comparative psychology was moving away from.

Wundt's textbook was an uneasy marriage between Structuralism and the instinct doctrine, and it was criticized for being a "product of Wundt's own imagination" (Peckham & Peckham, 1894). The volume by T. Wesley Mills, on the other hand, is a treatise to the primacy of detailed observation and getting to know your subjects and the conditions under which they develop. Mills was frequently at odds with people like Morgan, James Mark Baldwin, and E. L. Thorndike for their lack of first-hand knowledge of the behavior of their animals (cf. the exchange of letters in *Science* in 1896, and *Psychological Review* in 1899). Although he seemed to have presented a broader picture of the importance of complete observation and detailed developmental analysis in comparative psychology, Mills continued to resort to anthropomorphic statements about the mental life of these organisms at a time when the behaviorist predilection was beginning to take hold. As the previous statement by Joseph Jastrow would indicate, Mills' book was probably used more as a supplement than as the focal point in these early courses in comparative psychology.

Margaret Washburn's *Animal Mind* was perhaps the most popular book in the field, having gone through four editions between 1908 and 1936. It was a truly encyclopedic collection of theoretical issues and research totaling 1683 reference titles by the final edition. To Boring (1929), this was the mark of maturity of comparative psychology "A movement in a field of research can hardly be said to have passed adolescence until there is a compendium that represents it, and Washburn's book constitutes just such a symbol of self-conscious unity and also a history of the movement" (p. 561). A scholarly review, the topics were arranged hierarchically from simple sensations to higher mental processes and emotion. Within the relevant chapters, the discussion of species was arranged taxonomically. But other than this suggestion of an evolutionary framework, there was no sustained emphasis on the process of mental evolution apart from an historical reference in the first chapter. Like Lloyd Morgan, Washburn argued that consciousness might be attributed to those animals that have a physiological structure similar to humans and readily adapt to experience, but she did not dwell on evolutionary issues. Instead, most of the book was concerned with providing experimental evidence of the existence of simple and complex mental processes in animals (Scarborough-Goodman, 1981). As she indicated in the preface to the first edition, the book was more a compendium of facts than a treatise on the nature of mental evolution.

The Animal Mind took a position at odds with Watson's *Introduction to Comparative Psychology* at a time when Behaviorism was on the rise. Washburn's book was a mixture of structuralist interpretations on functionally arranged topics generated from a mountain of objective descriptions of behavior. It was decidedly eclectic and experimental in its emphasis and this plus the sheer volume of material incorporated into the book made it an invaluable reference. It received excellent reviews (Carr, 1918; Gard, 1908) and was adopted by numerous instructors of comparative psychology. Yerkes, for example, used it as a text for his class at Harvard and emphasized that comparative psychology should study conscious behavior "after the manner of Jennings and Washburn" (Scarborough-Goodman, 1981). Otto Klineberg, a graduate of McGill in 1919, wrote in his autobiography that his professor of psychology, a philosopher whose knowledge of the new psychology was limited, would read long passages from Washburn's book in the course on comparative psychology (cf. Ferguson, 1982). The fact is, however, that the *Animal Mind* marked the end of an era in animal psychology. After it, no other text would use the approach of inferring mental states from behavior. The questions that had interested Spencer, Lloyd Morgan, Jennings, and Yerkes went out of fashion and mostly disappeared from the literature. Almost all subsequent textbooks in the field were behaviorist in orientation, and primarily concerned the issues and problems of learning (e.g., Moss, 1934; Stone, 1934, 1941, 1951; Thorndike, 1911; Watson, 1914).

The books by our two principles, Loeb's *Comparative Psychology of the Brain and Comparative Psychology* (1900), and Jennings' response to Loeb in *The Behavior of the Lower Organisms* (1906), were precisely what the behaviorist approach was all about. As I have argued here, they were immensely important to the development of an objective comparative psychology. As textbooks, however, they presented a rather limited perspective. Loeb's book, for example, was largely an introduction to the comparative physiology of the brain. Given its antimetaphysical nature, one might imagine that it would have been difficult for philosophically trained psychologists dominating the academic scene at the turn of the century to relate to this work. The fact is, however, that Loeb repeatedly made the connection between what others referred to as psychic or conscious phenomena and physiological processes. But the fact that most of the book was concerned with the orientation responses of invertebrates, and little was said about the processes more commonly called attention, perception, discrimination, association, and choice in "higher organisms," meant that most of the really interesting psychological questions were left unanswered. Loeb implied that the tropism theory could account for these, but he was never able to adequately demonstrate this in vertebrates. Jennings' book, in fact, brought these issues to a head by directly showing how Loeb's position was unsatisfactory.

Unfortunately, by limiting his treatment to the "lower organisms," Jennings also guaranteed the limited usefulness of his work as a comprehensive textbook in animal psychology.

In contrast, *Mind in Evolution* (1902) by the British psychologist L. T. Hobhouse presented the most complete evolutionary systematization of learning, perception, and thinking to date. This was a well-used book, going into a second edition in 1915, and it raised significant questions about some of the interpretations that the early behaviorists like Thorndike were making about their research. For example, Hobhouse presented some of his own experiments, not unlike Köhler's (1917) later work on insight, and concluded that cats and animals other than primates are capable of "practical ideas," though not "articulate ideas." At McGill in 1908, Hobhouse was required reading in a course called "Problems of Comparative Psychology," which included some lectures on child psychology (Ferguson, 1982). The students were also asked to read Romanes, Lloyd Morgan, and James Mark Baldwin's *Mental Development in the Child and the Race*. However, despite its evolutionary framework and comprehensive theoretical nature, this book did not become the standard for comparative psychology in America. Perhaps this is due to the fact that Hobhouse did not meet regularly with the American psychologists, or perhaps his failure to incorporate a behaviorist model is at fault. In either case, American comparative psychology after 1910 appeared to develop without much attention to the evolutionary viewpoint.

There is one important exception to this generalization and it represents a different slant on history that is often overlooked. In 1916, S. J. Holmes published a little book called *Studies in Animal Behavior,* which was largely devoted to topics that directly concerned evolutionary biology, including the issues that Loeb and Jennings debated, the controversy over trial and error learning, and a well thought out review of the question of the evolution of intelligence. There were also chapters on topics that have a more modern ring; e.g., the evolution of parental care, the role of sex in the evolution of mind, and the significance of death-feigning strategies in predator avoidance. Holmes (1916) took two approaches to the topics he discussed, the "mechanistic" (i.e., behavioristic), and the "genetic," by which he meant evolutionary history. He remarked: "These two methods of attack are not opposed or mutually exclusive, as is sometimes implied, but complementary. We cannot obtain a complete explanation of behavior by an analysis of the activities of the individual alone; it is necessary to know also the evolutionary history of the species, and the various steps by which its present behavior has been acquired" (p. 3). This was not the only source of evolutionary ideas. In 1912, Walter B. Pillsbury stated American psychology's central thesis: "The very general acceptance in recent times of the doctrine of evolution has forced us to read the story of mind in light of the development of the human organism from the lower forms of life" (p. 10–11). And Thorndike (1900), in a review of C. O. Whitman's (1899) lectures on animal behavior delivered at Wood's Hole, noted that the comparative psychologist could no longer stop at enumerating and describing animal instincts, but he must also try to demonstrate how and why they evolved. Thus the evolutionary approach in comparative psychology had not disappeared, it was simply developing along different lines among a "tiny band of hardy souls," as Beach (1950) was later to call them. Along with Beach and Holmes belong the names of Carpenter, Schneirla, and Scott, as well as Aronson, the Brelands, the Herrick brothers, Hess, Lehrman, Nissen, and many others. The point is that the comparative psychology of Loeb and Watson did not become the all-inclusive, unfettered force in America, although this is what most of our historians from Boring on down would have us believe. There is a tendency to lose sight of the fact that comparative psychology has too often been associated with learning theory and too infrequently associated with its evolutionary, developmental, and psycho-biological influences. The historical links to Spencer, Jennings, Yerkes, and Holmes have always been there, we just have not looked very hard.

The Research Orientation and Development of Professional Journals

For various reasons, American psychologists have always tended to be preoccupied by analysis more than synthesis. Focused on the more narrowly analytical problems of mind, Darwinism had little immediate significance (Angell, 1909). One way in which this is reflected is in the choice of species studied. A mechanistic approach is concerned with the analysis of general phenomena and, consequently, species diversity and variability are treated as forces to be controlled and minimized. An evolutionary approach, in contrast, focuses on species diversity and variability. This being the case, there is an irony in the fact that American comparative psychologists lost interest in the behavior of lower organisms soon after Jennings' book was published. One would have predicted the opposite, and in fact Watson (1905) did:

> As long as experiments seemed to prove the machine-like character of the reactions of lower organisms, the psychologist preferred to turn his attention to the behavior of animals in whose reactions variability is a clearly recognized factor. Removing the barrier of "uniformity" (and Professor Jennings had done this, at least in the eyes of the reviewer) the behavior of the whole animal series from amoeba to man, claims the attention of psychologists. (p. 145)

The investigation of primitive life forms was supposed to provide a foundation for understanding the embryonic and phylogenetic processes whereby mental life originated, but by the end of the first decade of the 20th century comparative psychologists were no longer interested in simple organisms. Naturalists continued to provide descriptions of insect behavior, and cell physiologists continued to experiment on the neural and molecular correlates of invertebrate responses, but the substantive problems of mental evolution in simple organisms were all but forgotten.

In fact, this trend away from wide phylogenetic analysis had already begun while the Loeb–Jennings controversy was just heating up (Morgan, 1905). As the Darwinian conception of evolution became established in the minds of most people, and mental continuity had taken its place within this scheme, the emphasis shifted from broad phylogenetic analysis to a more comprehensive analysis of circumscribed problems in "higher" organisms, typically white rats. This trend has been demonstrated by several people over the years using frequency counts of the different species studied in published journal articles (Beach, 1950; Dore & Kirouac, 1983; Lown, 1975), but the evidence is there in the very first issues of the new comparative psychology journals, and in the research orientation of the first comparative psychologists.

Specialists in natural history had made the *American Naturalist* the major national publication for behavioral and other natural history studies in the late 1800s. By the 1890s, however, there was insufficient space to accomodate the growing number of articles generated by the new experimental biology. In 1891 a group of experimental neurologists and zoologists established the *Journal of Comparative Neurology and Zoology*, which was subsequently shortened to the *Journal of Comparative Neurology*. In 1904 the title was again changed, this time to the *Journal of Comparative Neurology and Psychology*, and Yerkes was made an editor joining the Herrick brothers with Jennings as an associate. The first volume contained seven behavior articles, four concerning invertebrate tropisms, and one each on the frog, the tortoise, and guinea pig behavior. The following year the journal published five articles, only one of which concerned invertebrates, and one by Watson on white rats. In each of the next 3 years, there were three mammal studies and three reports of invertebrate behavior. In almost all cases the invertebrate experiments concerned orientation reactions to various external stimuli, whereas the mammal studies involved some form of learning. Watson was formally added to the editorial board in 1908, and in 1911 the journal was split with Yerkes, Jennings, and Watson continuing as editors of the comparative psychology publication, now named the *Journal of Animal Behavior* (JAB). Also in 1911, the first volume of *Behavior Monographs* appeared under Watson's sole jurisdiction. Volume 1 contained two invertebrate studies, one rat study, and two studies using birds, one of which was the massive collaboration between Yerkes and Watson (1911) on methods of studying vision in animals. In the next three volumes, however, more than half the experiments were conducted with rodents. Only one invertebrate experiment was included, and *all* the studies in these volumes concerned learning of one sort or another. The *Journal of Animal Behavior* ceased publication in 1917 because of WWI, but it was replaced by *Psychobiology*, edited by Knight Dunlap. The 37 papers included in this two-volume collection contained only three papers using invertebrates and the remainder were concerned almost entirely with rat learning or human reaction time. In 1921 *Psychobiology* and *JAB* were officially consolidated to form the *Journal of Comparative Psychology* under the joint editorship of Dunlap and Yerkes, who by now was working in the mental testing field. In the same year, Dunlap took over the editorial chores of *Behavior Monographs,* which then became the *Comparative Psychology Monographs.* Needless to say, rats and humans dominated the species studied in both publications. Strange but perhaps significant is the fact that Knight Dunlap (1961) edited three of the first comparative psychology journals, and yet in his autobiography he denies any allegiance to comparative psychology: "I am not a comparative psychologist . . . but there is a distinct advantage, at times, in having an editor who does not know much about the subject and has no particular bias" (p. 54). I would argue that, in this particular case, having an editor who did not know much about the field was detrimental to comparative psychology. Dunlap was decidedly a human behaviorist, uninterested in evolutionary psychology. In fact, he claims primacy for the ideas expressed in Watson's first Behaviorism (Dunlap, 1961), a view that Watson does not dispute (Watson, 1961). Yerkes, at this stage in his career, was preoccupied with the reports of his work on the Army intelligence testing program, and it shows in the types of articles that appeared in the first few volumes. The journal had no focus, and it was comparative only in the trivial sense that many different sorts of studies were included, from tropisms in land snails to aviation research (human), and the effects of cigar smoking on dart throwing. No wonder people in the field developed an identity crisis!

The Research Orientation of the First American Comparative Psychologists

We see the same trend in the research interests of the people who taught the first courses in comparative psychology in this country (see Table 9.3). This list was compiled by Warden and Warner (1927) from a questionnaire survey sent to 100 colleges and universities in the United States, and from a search of college catalog files at several New York libraries. Searching the *Psychological Abstracts,* I found that over one third of the individuals listed in this table specialized in research on rats, and in each case their primary interest was in establishing some principle of learning or motivation. The species studied appeared to be incidental. Another third of the people on this list did not publish any experimental research in comparative psychology; some because they were primarily philosophers, and others because they were employed at an institution that for one reason or another did not encourage research. This was especially true of new PhDs in psychology after 1900, because the only positions available were at small denominational colleges, normal schools, and land-grant colleges. Take the case of Thomas H. Haines who taught the earliest course in comparative psychology offered by Ohio State in 1907. Having completed his doctorate under Yerkes at Harvard in 1901, he obtained an appointment as the only psychologist in the department of philosophy at Ohio State. Although he believed that his animal studies in graduate school possessed significant implications for understanding the causes of the evolution of mind, his efforts to continue the work in Ohio were stymied because of lack of space, lack of funds, and because the monist philosophy that he adopted appalled his dualist colleagues. Believing in a fundamental distinction between man and brute, the philosophers and the university officials were not particularly sympathetic to Haines' needs. He eventually did get his laboratory in 1908, and psychology at Ohio State prospered in later years (Cravens, 1978).

Of the remaining 30% of the names on this list, half were psychologists of the old school who had an abiding interest in the evolutionary point of view (e.g., G. H. Mead at Chicago; F. C. Dockeray at Kansas; J. Jastrow at Wisconsin), and only about six could be classified as comparative psychologists in the sense that they studied more than one species during their careers. This includes L. W. Cole at Colorado, I. Bentley at Cornell (and Illinois), R. Yerkes at Harvard (and Radcliffe), J. Watson at Hopkins, M. F. Washburn at Vassar, and C. J. Warden at Columbia. Some people may argue that Tolman, or Dashiell, or Shepard should be added to the list, but my point is that the major portion of the instructors in the first comparative psychology courses in the United States were not, in fact, involved in comparative research or concerned about evolutionary issues. And this did not appear to be any less true in Canada. At McGill, a philosopher, J. W. A. Hickson taught the comparative course despite the fact that he knew little about the field (Ferguson, 1982). At Alberta, John MacEachran, one of the founders of the Canadian Psychological Association, taught a course that was described as comparative psychology including animal evolution, child psychology, and racial psychology (Nelson, 1982). MacEachran, however, was more interested in philosophy than psychology, and comparative had very little significance for him. Even the people who shared an interest in animal studies, like J. Mark Baldwin at Toronto in the 1890s and T. Wesley Mills at McGill, did not agree on how evolution and mental activity are related, and consequently the evolutionary brand of comparative psychology drew a limited audience. The Loeb–Watson comparative psychology on the other hand, appealed to the analytically oriented experimentalists that came to dominate animal psychology in the 1920s and 1930s. Hence the belief that "comparative psychology led directly into behaviorism" (Boring, 1950, p. 631).

By 1910 there were at least eight laboratories of comparative psychology in the United States and almost a score of universities offering courses. Clark and Harvard organized the first labs, both in 1899, under the direction of E. C. Sanford and R. Yerkes, respectively. Chicago came next in 1903 under the direction of J. B. Watson. Warden and Warner (1927) have provided us with a list of these first comparative research laboratories (see Table 9.4), and we see many of the same names here as on the list of teachers of the first course in comparative psychology. One observation that immediately becomes apparent

TABLE 9.4
Research Laboratories

| Institution | Earliest Laboratory | | Present Laboratory | |
	Date	Directed by	Rooms	Square Feet
California U.	1918	E. S. Tolman	6	—
Chicago U.	1903	J. B. Watson	9	—
Clark U.	1899	E. C. Sanford	5	810
Colorado U.	1910	L. W. Cole	2	100
ªColumbia U.	1924	C. J. Warden	4	1,200
Cornell U.	1909	I. M. Bentley	Dropped	
Harvard U.	1899	R. M. Yerkes	—	—
Illinois U.	1913	I. M. Bentley	2	2,400
Johns Hopkins U.	1908	J. B. Watson	Dropped	
Kansas U.	1912	J. C. Dockeray	2	1,600
Michigan U.	1909	J. F. Shepard	6	—
Minnesota U.	1917	K. S. Lashley	8	1,600
New York U.	1926	L. H. Warner	1	—
No. Carolina U.	1920	J. F. Dashiell	1	200
Ohio State U.	1926	H. E. Burtt	2	800
Ohio Wesleyan U.	1921	E. B. Skaggs	2	125
Princeton U.	1925	H. S. Langfeld	3	500
Smith	1924	M. Wooster	1	—
ªStanford U.	1916	J. E. DeCamp	1	1,500
Texas U.	1908	C. S. Yoakum	Dropped	
Washington U. (Seattle)	1913	Stevenson Smith	2	300
Wisconsin U.	1923	C. J. Warden	9	2,000
ᵇYale U.	1923	J. E. Anderson	3	700

ªResearch course offered in addition to regular laboratory work and individual research.

ᵇIn addition, both course work and research are now carried on at the Institute of Psychology at Yale under the direction of Prof. Yerkes.

Note: Adapted from Warden & Warner (1927).

from this list is that all the laboratories established after 1915 were devoted to rat-learning experiments. Whether other species were also studied or used for demonstration purposes in connection with the comparative course, it is difficult to say, but certainly from the point of view of the director's publication record comparative psychology before and after 1915 takes on a different appearance. There are also some anomalies about this list. E. C. Sanford at Clark and F. C. Dockeray at Kansas are listed as the directors of their laboratories, but they never published animal research. And it is evident from the T. H. Haines case just discussed that an animal laboratory was established at Ohio State 18 years before H. E. Burtt took over as director. A similar situation exists with the Wisconsin entry because Jastrow (1890) has indicated that the advanced psychology course included laboratory demonstrations and exercises in comparative psychology and attempts were made to "have several instinct studies going on" (p. 276).

Nevertheless, taking into consideration the trends in the research orientation of the laboratory directors and course instructors, and the type of articles that appeared in the journals devoted to comparative psychology, one is left with the overwhelming feeling that psychology was losing sight of its biological, evolutionary background. Research that went by the name of comparative psychology stressed mechanistic laws and environmental cues. It was Loeb's influence come to fruition.

The Current Status of Comparative Psychology

A few years ago (Demarest, 1980), I wrote that comparative psychologists had an identity crisis. There were a half-dozen other names that we could use to identify our scientific interests. Universities and Colleges were renaming their comparative programs every few years as these jargon fads came and went; the field was being attacked for being noncomparative and ignorant of evolutionary biology and jobs were becoming harder to find. Almost every critic pointed to the failure to incorporate evolutionary thinking into comparative psychology.

The identity problem has not changed much in the intervening years, and the job market has not gotten better. But some of us are beginning to realize that the solution to the problems is not going to be found in what we call ourselves or in the way we do our research. The issue, it seems to me, rests on the image that biologists and psychologists have of comparative psychology. Most psychologists schooled in the history of psychology after Boring (1950) were taught that evolutionary psychology disappeared with the emergence of Behaviorism. Even today a commonly held belief is that comparative psychology is synonymous with the study of rat behavior. In some respects this indictment is not inappropriate, for much psychological research with animals has been and continues to be limited to a few species. This is the mechanistic comparative psychology derived from Loeb and Watson. Its influence is still strong. But if we explore the texture of history instead of merely looking at the general pattern, we find another comparative psychology woven in the seams that is very modern by current standards. This is the evolutionary comparative psychology of Jennings, Yerkes, and Holmes. It has been there all the time, and it has an equally rich though somewhat more obscure history (Demarest, 1983). The current status of comparative psychology has returned to a point where a single focus no longer characterizes the field. There are still those who practice a Loeb–Watson brand of mechanistic animal psychology, and there are others whose interests embody the evolutionary ideas of Jennings and Yerkes and Holmes.

It is wrong to continue fostering a biased view of history. We pay a price for dealing in inaccuracies, no matter what our debt is to this field. The very least we lose is a sense of the past and how ideas change with time. The cost for those of us who work in the field of comparative psychology may be more substantial. We risk the complete demise of our discipline; undercut by the interests of behavioral biologists on one hand, and the lack of interest of anthropocentric psychologists on the other. If other psychologists see our contributions as invalid and unimportant for understanding human behavior, as a reading of Boring (1950), Hodos and Campbell (1969), and others would suggest, then we have an obligation to Boring to look at this field more closely, and we have an obligation to comparative psychology to challenge our positivistic typecasting. "The worst way to repay intellectual debts", said the historian Young, "is to repeat the findings of one's mentors rather than extending, amending, and deepening them" (Young, 1966, p. 10).

ACKNOWLEDGMENT

Preparation of this chapter was supported by a Faculty Grant-in-Aid from Monmouth College.

REFERENCES

Angell, J. R. (1909). The influence of Darwin on psychology. *Psychological Review, 16,* 152–169.
Baldwin, J. M. (1902). *Development and evolution.* New York: Macmillan.
Baldwin, J. M. (1961). Autobiography. In C. Murchison (Ed.), *A history of psychology in autobiography* (Vol. I) New York: Russell & Russell.
Beach, F. A. (1950). The snark was a boojum. *American Psychologist, 1950, 5,* 115–124.
Beer, T., Bethe, A., & von Uexkull, J. (1899). Vorschläge zu einer objektivierenden Nomenklatur in der Physiologie des Nervensystems. *Biologisches Zentralblatt, 19,* 517–521.
Bethe, A. (1898). Dürfen wir den Ameisen und Bienen psychische Qualitaten zuschreiben? *Arch. f.d. ges. Physiol.,* (Pflugers), *70,* 15–100.
Binet, A. (1894). *The psychic life of micro-organisms* (Trans.). Chicago: Open Court Publishing Co.
Boring, E. G. (1929). *A history of experimental psychology* New York: Century.
Boring, E. G. (1950). *A history of experimental psychology* (2nd ed.). New York: Appleton-Century-Crofts.
Calkins, M. (1905). The limits of genetic and of comparative psychology. *Journal of Psychology, 1,* 261–285.
Carmichael, L. (1968). Some historical roots of present-day animal psychology. In B. Wolman (Ed.), *Historical roots of contemporary psychology.* New York: Harper & Row.
Carr, H. (1915). Review of an introduction to comparative psychology by J. B. Watson. *Psychological Bulletin, 12,* 308–312.
Carr, H. (1918). Review of the animal mind (2nd ed.) by M. Washburn. *Psychological Bulletin, 15,* 288–290.
Claparede, E. (1901). Les animaux sont-ils conscients? *Review Philosophique, 51,* 24. (Trans. in *International Quarterly, 8,* 296).
Cravens, H. (1978). *The triumph of evolution.* Philadelphia: University of Pennsylvania Press.

Demarest, J. (1980). The current status of comparative psychology in the American Psychological Association. *American Psychologist, 35,* 980–990.

Demarest, J. (1983). The ideas of change, progress, and continuity in the comparative psychology of learning. In D. W. Rajecki (Ed.), Comparing behavior: Studying man studying animals. Lawrence Erlbaum Associates. NJ: Hillsdale.

Dore, F. Y., & Kirouac, G. (1983). The nature of ethology: Was the snark a boojum? *Comparative Psychology Newsletter, 3*(4), 1–4.

Dunlap, K. (1961). Autobiography. In C. Murchison (Ed.), *A History of psychology in autobiography* (Vol II) New York: Russell & Russell.

Ferguson, G. A. (1982). Psychology at McGill. In M. J. Wright & C. R. Myers (Eds.), *History of academic psychology in Canada.* Toronto: C. J. Hogrefe.

Forel, A. (1904). *Ants and some other insects* (Trans.). Chicago: Open Court Publishing Co.

Gard, W. L. (1908). Review of the animal mind by M. Washburn, *American Journal of Psychology, 19,* 279.

Gottlieb, G. (1979). Comparative psychology and ethology. In E. Hearst (Ed.), *The first century of experimental psychology.* Hillsdale, NJ: Lawrence Erlbaum Associates.

Hebb, D. O. (1963). Introduction to K. S. Lashley's *Brain mechanisms and intelligence.* New York: Dover.

Herrick, C. J. (1904). Editorial. *Journal of Comparative Neurology and Psychology, 14,* 271.

Herrick, C. J. (1924). *Neurological foundations of animal behavior.* New York: Holt.

Herrnstein, R. J. (1969). Behaviorism. In D. L. Krantz (Ed.), *Schools of psychology: A symposium.* New York: Appleton-Century-Crofts.

Hobhouse, L. T. (1902). *Mind in evolution.* London: Macmillan. (2nd ed., 1915).

Hodos, W., & Campbell, C. B. G. (1969). Scala naturae: Why there is no theory in comparative psychology. *Psychological Review, 76,* 337–350.

Holmes, S. J. (1916). *Studies in animal behavior.* Boston: Richard G. Badger.

Hyman, B. (1982). Reconstructing accounts of psychology's past. *Journal of Mind and Behavior, 3,* 55–66.

James, W. (1890). *The principles of psychology.* (2 vols.). New York: Holt.

Jastrow, J. (1890). Psychology at the University of Wisconsin. *American Journal of Psychology, 3,* 275–276.

Jastrow, J. (1961). Autobiography. In C. Murchison (Ed.), *A history of psychology in autobiography.* New York: Russell & Russell.

Jennings, H. S. (1906). *Behavior of the lower organisms.* New York: Macmillan.

Jennings, H. S. (1907). The interpretation of the behavior of the lower organisms. *Science, 27,* 698–710.

Köhler, W. (1917). *Intelligenzprüfungen an Menschenaffen.* Berlin: Springer. (*The Mentality of Apes.* London: Kegan & Paul, 1924).

Lashley, K. S. (1923). The behavioristic interpretation of consciousness. *Psychological Review, 30,* 237–272; 329–353.

Lashley, K. S. (1929). *Brain mechanisms and intelligence.* Chicago: University of Chicago Press.

Lashley, K. S. (1938). Experimental analysis of instinctive behavior. *Psychological Review, 1938, 45,* 445–471.

Loeb, J. (1890). Der Heliotropismus der Tiere und seine Uebereinstimmung mit dem Heliotropismus der Pflanzen (The heliotropism of animals and its identity with the heliotropism of plants). In J. Loeb, *Studies in general physiology.* Chicago: University Chicago Press, 1905.

Loeb, J. (1900). *Comparative physiology of the brain and comparative psychology.* New York: Putnam.

Lown, B. A. (1975). Comparative psychology 25 years after. *American Psychologist, 30,* 858–859.

Lubbock, J. (1882). *Ants, bees and wasps.* London: Kegan & Paul.

Mackenzie, B. (1976). Darwinism and positivism as methodological influences on the development of psychology. *Journal of the History of the Behavioral Sciences, 12,* 330–337.

Maier, M. R. F., & Schneirla, T. C. (1935). *Principles in animal psychology.* New York: McGraw-Hill. (Dover edition 1963)

Mead, G. H. (1895). Review of an introduction to comparative psychology by C. L. Morgan. *Psychological Review, 2,* 399–402.

Mills, T. Wesley (1898). *The nature and development of animal intelligence.* London: T. Fisher Unwin.

Mills, T. Wesley (1901). Review of animal behavior by C. L. Morgan. *Psychological Review, 8,* 299–304. .

Morgan, C. L. (1894). *An introduction to comparative psychology.* London: Walter Scott.

Morgan, C. L. (1900). *Animal behaviour.* London: Edward Arnold.

Morgan, C. L. (1905). Comparative and genetic psychology. *Psychological Review, 12,* 78–97.

Morgan, C. L. (1961). Autobiography. In C. Murchison (Ed.), *A history of psychology in autobiography* (Vol. II) New York: Russell & Russell.

Moss, F. A. (1934). *Comparative psychology.* New York: Prentice Hall. (2nd ed. 1942)

Nelson, T. M. (1982). Psychology at Alberta. In M. J. Wright & C. R. Myers (Eds.), *History of Academic Psychology in Canada.* Toronto: C. J. Hogrefe.

Nuel, J. P. (1904). LaVision. *Bibliotheque Internationale,* Paris.

O'Donnell, J. M. (1979). The crisis of experimentalism in the 1920s. *American Psychologist, 34,* 289–295.

Pauly, P. J. (1981). The Loeb–Jennings debate and the science of animal behavior. *Journal of the History of the Behavioral Sciences, 17,* 504–515.

Peckham, G. W., & Peckham, E. G. (1894). Review of lectures on human and animal psychology by W. Wundt. *Psychological Review, 2,* 179.

Pillsbury, W. B. (1912). *The essentials of psychology.* New York:

Reed, J. (1981, June). *Robert M. Yerkes: The psychobiologist as comparative psychologist.* Paper presented at the Cheiron Society Meetings, University of Wisconsin, River Falls.

Romanes, G. J. (1882). *Animal intelligence.* New York: Appleton.

Scarborough-Goodman, E. (1981, June). *Margaret Washburn, The Animal Mind, and comparative psychology.* Paper presented at the Cheiron Society Meetings, University of Wisconsin, River Falls.

Spencer, H. (1853). *The principles of psychology.* New York: Appleton.

Spencer, H. (1886). *The principles of psychology* (Vol. 1, 3rd ed.). New York: Appleton.

Stone, C. (1934). *Comparative psychology.* Englewood Cliffs, NJ: Prentice Hall.

Stone, C. (1941). *Comparative psychology* (2nd ed.). Englewood Cliffs, NJ: Prentice Hall.

Stone, C. (1951). *Comparative psychology.* (3rd ed.). Englewood Cliffs, NJ: Prentice–Hall.

Thorndike, E. L. (1900). Review of animal behavior by C. O. Whitman. *Psychological Review, 7,* 201–206.

Thorndike, E. L. (1911). *Animal intelligence.* New York: Macmillan.

Thorndike, E. L. (1915). Watson's Behavior. *Journal of Animal Behavior, 5,* 462–467.

Thorpe, W. H. (1979). *The origins and rise of ethology.* London: Praeger.

Verworn, M. (1894). Modern physiology. *Monist, 4,* 370–372.

von Uexkull, J. (1902). Psychologie und biologie in ihrer Stellung zur Tierseele. *Ergebnisse der Physiologie, 1,* 233.

Warden, C. J. (1927). The historical development of comparative psychology. *Psychological Review, 34,* 57–85; 135–168.

Warden, C.J. (1928). The development of modern comparative psychology. *Quarterly Review of Biology, 3,* 486–522.

Warden, C.J., Jenkins, T. N., & Warner, L. H. (1935, 1936, 1940). *Comparative Psychology* (3 Vols.). New York: The Ronald Press.

Warden, C. J., & Warner, L. H. (1927). The development of animal psychology during the last three decades. *Psychological Review, 34,* 200–201.

Washburn, M. F. (1908). *The Animal Mind.* New York: Macmillan. (2nd, 3rd & 4th eds, 1917, 1926, 1936)

Waters, R. H. (1934). The historical background of comparative psychology. In F. A. Moss (Ed.), *Comparative psychology.* New York: Prentice–Hall.

Watson, J. B. (1905). Review of contributions to the study of the behavior of lower organisms by H. S. Jennings. *Psychological Bulletin, 2,* 144–147.

Watson, J. B. (1906a). Review of the dynamics of living matter by J. Loeb. *Psychological Bulletin, 4,* 291–293.

Watson, J. B. (1906b). The need of an experimental station for the study of certain problems in animal behavior. *Psychological Bulletin, 3,* 149–156.

Watson, J. B. (1907). Review of behavior of the lower organisms by H. S. Jennings. *Psychological Bulletin, 4,* 288–291.

Watson, J. B. (1908). The behavior of noddy and sooty terns. *Carnegie Publication, 103,* Washington.

Watson, J. B. (1913). Psychology as a behaviorist views it. *Psychological Review, 20,* 158–177.

Watson, J. B. (1914). *Behavior: An introduction to comparative psychology.* New York: Henry Holt.

Watson, J. B. (1961). Autobiography. In C. Murchison (Ed.), *A history of psychology in autobiography* (Vol. III). New York: Russell & Russell.

Whitman, C. O. (1899). Animal behavior. *Biological Lectures from the Marine Biological Laboratory,* pp. 285–338. Woods Hole, MA.

Whitman, C. O. (1919). The behavior of pigeons. *Publication of the Carnegie Institute, 257,* 1–161.

Wundt, W. (1894). *Lectures on human and animal psychology* (Trans.). London: Macmillan.

Yarczower, M., & Hazlett, L. (1977). Evolutionary scales and anagenesis. *Psychological Bulletin, 84,* 1088–1097.

Yerkes, R. M. (1904). Editorial. *Journal of Comparative Neurology and Psychology, 14,* 63–64.

Yerkes, R. M. (1906). Objective nomenclature, comparative psychology and animal behavior. *Journal of Comparative Neurology and Psychology, 16,* 380–390.

Yerkes, R. M. (1961). Autobiography. In C. Murchison (Ed.), *A history of psychology in autobiography* (Vol. II). New York: Russell & Russell.

Yerkes, R. M., & Watson, J. B. (1911). Methods of studying vision in animals. *Behavior Monographs, 1,* whole No. 2.

Young, R. M. (1966). Scholarship and the history of the behavioural sciences. *History of Science, 5,* 1–51.

INTERNATIONAL STATUS OF COMPARATIVE PSYCHOLOGY

INTRODUCTION II:
Contemporary Status of
Comparative Psychology

Ethel Tobach
American Museum of Natural History, New York

Comparative psychologists from many countries who had been invited to attend
the founding meeting of the International Society for Comparative Psychology
were unable to attend, or if they were able to attend did not make any presenta-
tions. However, subsequent to the Toronto meeting, chapters were solicited and
these are presented in the second section of this volume.

The picture of comparative psychology presented in these chapters reflects the
historic development of science, and in particular, psychology in the various
nations. The relative eminence of the study of behavior in the academic institutions is an index of the sociopolitical priorities of the nation. Insofar as these
affected the life and development of the academic institutions, these were organized as centers for study in science, technology, or the humanities. Further,
within those institutions, the development of behavioral studies in relation to
philosophy, physiology, biology, or experimental psychology in each country
reflected international processes of exchange of knowledge dependent on the
ease with which the scholars of one nation interacted with other scholars and
scientists. These conditions created or did not create institutions in which students could become interested in problems of evolution, or in which students
could discover that the study of animal behavior was as much in the province of
psychology as in the territory of biology, or zoology.

The significance of this history is clearly evident in the chapter by Ardila who
speaks for many of the countries that have been the areas for scientific studies by
people from the United States and Europe. This has been accompanied by a too
frequent lack of collaborative work between North American and European
scientists and the scientists of the countries in which the research was being
carried out, and it has equally kept many of us in ignorance of the rich history of

those countries and their early interest in evolution; the chapter by Papini illustrates how much is to be known.

The historical development of science and academia in the European countries (Italy), The Netherlands, United Kingdom, The Soviet Union) and in Japan lead to different problems than those in the Latin American countries represented. Nonetheless, the similarity of the status, or one might say, marginal existence, of comparative psychology in all the chapters presented in this volume indicates the need for futher examination of the problem and the anticipation of growth and change in a constructive direction.

10 Comparative Psychology in Latin America

Rubén Ardila
National University of Colombia

INTRODUCTION

When the first scientific work on "comparative" psychology was conducted during the last decades of the 19th century all people concerned with this type of research were expecting results relevant to human behavior, aside from results that were useful for the study of psychological processes in animals. Work on learning, perception, memory, problem solving, social behavior, sexual behavior, and even psychopathology and communication, was supposed to throw light on very basic psychological factors, common both to humans and to other animals. No one attempted to extrapolate the results obtained in cats, rats, chickens, dogs, or monkeys to humans. Actually, the reverse process was more common, to extrapolate human behavior to animals different from men (anthropomorphism).

All investigators knew very well that "evolutionary level" makes a difference, related to cerebral cortex, capacity for complex behavior and problem solving, and for that modification of the environment that came to be called "culture." In other words, we were the only animal able to produce culture, to talk, to communicate abstract ideas, and so forth. Psychological research in animals was very important, both for its own sake and because of its relevance to human behavior. If we were going to understand color vision, or maternal behavior, or the role of hormones in sexuality, a study of animal conduct was very relevant. However, in the last two decades, comparative psychology has been attacked and practically reduced to a branch of pure science, interesting in itself but with very little relevance for understanding "important" psychological issues. Why did this happen? Why did human psychology and animal psychology become so dissociated? Was it affected by the intellectual environment in different parts of the world, or only in the USA and Europe? What is the current situation in Latin America? These questions are discussed in this chapter, and a general description of the contemporary study of animal behavior in Latin America is presented.

Comparative psychology owes a lot to Pavlov and Thorndike, but certainly much more to Darwin. In Darwin's books (1859, 1871, 1872) there are many psychological observations, many more than one would expect. Darwin was very interested in psychological problems, and he included among them aesthetic perception in birds, sexual behavior, aggression, cooperation, problem solving, and some other areas that comparative psychologists have not dealt with very much. But the general inspirer of comparative psychology is Darwin. Without him, Thorndike probably (1898, 1911), would not have placed his cats in the puzzle box, nor would Pavlov (1927) have done his experiments on salivation in dogs and other species.

The study of nonhuman animals has been a topic of central interest to psychologists for more than 70 years, and this is a long part of our 100-year history.

In the history of comparative psychology (see Ardila, 1968a, Dewsbury, 1984) some basic questions were asked. One concerned the role of understanding in problem-solving behavior in animals. Everyone believed, because of the anecdotal "evidence" provided by people like Romanes (1882) that animals really understood what they were doing. Thorndike believed otherwise, that is just pure trial and error and no understanding was involved in solving puzzle problems in the behavior of his animals. Only the more or less gradual formation of the practical associations between sensory and motor systems as a function in some degree of frequency of occurrence (Law of Exercise) and as a function of rewarding consequences (Law of Effect), was involved . . . no understanding, just practice and rewarding or punishing consequences.

The commonality or the divergence of learning mechanisms was very much at issue in those early experiments. Are there differences among the species concerning psychological processes? Could we say that apes solve their problems by "understanding" whereas cats in puzzle boxes to it just by "trial and error"? A different issue was sensory-sensory (S–S) association, versus sensory-motor (S–R) association. After two neutral stimuli have been paired repeatedly, the animal is trained to make some new response to one of them, and then we ask whether the other stimulus will evoke the same response.

The role of reward and punishment on learning was of central importance to comparative psychology. Because Thorndike's law of effect aroused much controversy and gave origin to so many experiments, we can say that that law was one of the most important laws in comparative psychology, and no doubt, in the whole of psychology, animal and human. The role of reward and punishment in learning can be evaluated by reading some of the contemporary works (see

Bitterman, 1960, 1965, 1975; Dewsbury, 1984; Mackintosh, 1974; Tobach, 1971; Tobach, Adler, & Adler, 1973).

The study of psychological processes in animals is a very important field if we are going to understand human behavior, evolution, and preserve our environment. It has a long history as an area of interest, but a short path of scientific development.

In Latin America, comparative psychology is not one of the strongest areas of psychology. In previous works, I have presented the state of psychology in Latin America to an English-speaking audience (Ardila, 1968b through 1987) and it is not necessary to repeat here what was previously said. Psychology is a well-developed science in Latin America, particularly in Mexico and Brazil, and to a lesser extent in Columbia, Chile, Venezuela, Cuba, and other nations. There are psychology training programs in practically all countries, and psychology as a profession is beginning to have a social impact. The level of development is very uneven. In some nations psychology has reached a situation similar to some European countries; in other nations psychology is identified with magic, astrology, and so forth. In this heterogeneous environment it is difficult to make a clear picture of comparative psychology and its role in the preservation of endangered species. The ideas presented here should be considered preliminary because a complete picture of comparative psychology in Latin America cannot be presented yet (see also Ardila, 1964, 1967, 1968a, 1971b, 1984).

PHILOSOPHICAL FOUNDATIONS

The philosophical framework of Latin America in the mid 19th century, when the majority of the countries became independent from Spain and Portugal, was scholasticism. The ideas of Aristotle and St. Thomas predominated in Latin American universities and were taught to students in the schools of philosophy and medicine. The "soul" was a unique characteristic of human beings, and animals did not have it. To study the psychology of animals would have been a logical impossibility. Animals did not have "souls," and because psychology was the study of the soul, animal psychology did not exist.

Some countries decided, when they obtained independence, that positivism was the most appropriate system for education and for being really independent, intellectually and practically. Positivism became the predominant philosophy in Argentina, Chile, and Mexico during the last decades of the 19th century and the beginning of the 20th century, Positivism, in Comte's sense, was promising, a new Renaissance, and a return to human values in contrast to religious values. Some of the basic psychological ideas developed within the frame of reference of positivism. In Argentina, José Ingenieros (1877–1925) was a leading psychologist and philosopher, whose ideas were centered on positivism, and who was concerned with the study of psychological processes of animals, aside from being a very important thinker and social philosopher (see Ardila, 1971c,; Papini, 1985).

Due to the influence of religion, Darwin's ideas arrived late in Latin America, but were enthusiastically received by scientists and by progressive people. Darwin's ideas caused a revolution not only in biology but also in the conceptualization of humans and their place in the world. Evolution was attacked by the "establishment" and became the symbol of progress, the symbol of science, the symbol of the new order. A synthesis of positivism and Darwinism was considered but was not successful. Little by little, evolution became part of the mainstream of biology and influenced the daily life of people in Latin America, as had previously happened in Europe and in the United States.

In Darwin's conceptualization, the psychology of animals was a very important topic (see Darwin, 1859, 1871, 1872).

Some of his observations were just common sense, others were based on scientific data. At the beginning Darwin was not sure whether to include people in the evolutionary process, but later on he determined that human beings belonged to the same family as infrahuman animals, and that evolution included all living beings, from the most simple to the most complex (and what were simplicity and complexity anyway?).

Darwinism has always been considered as one of the central influences in the world development of comparative psychology. After a kind of "eclipse" at the turn of the century, Darwinism was reshaped into the Synthetic Theory of Evolution by Fisher, Haldane, and Wright. Later on Dobzhansky, Mayr, and Simpson refined the whole picture, and today we have a theory of evolution in which adaptation is emphasized, and a number of environmental and genetic factors have entered into the picture.

This is the standard story, but it is not what happened in Latin America. Darwinism in the classical sense was more important in this part of the world that the new Synthetic Theory of Evolution. The role of adaptation to the environment was given central importance in Latin American science.

The reception of Darwin's ideas in Argentina has been documented (see De Vega, 1984) and it was probably similar in other Latin American countries. At the beginning, the establishment was against them due to the atheistic overtones and the attacks on the established order. Religion felt threatened by Darwinism in Latin America, as had been the case in England and continental Europe some decades earlier. Biologists, on the other hand, were receptive to Darwinism, and the whole system became part of the new establishment, a new system to explain adaptation, change, modification, and animal behavior.

Psychologists were also interested in Darwinism and in some early writings we find a positive evaluation of Darwin's ideas. In Latin America we probably cannot find a Thorndike who was so well informed about Darwinism and the great impact it could have on psychology, but in spite of that, Latin American psychologists realized the role that Darwin's ideas would have in psychology as a science.

ANIMAL BEHAVIOR AND PSYCHOLOGY

As I have indicated (Ardila, 1968b, 1970a) psychology defined as the study of behavior is relatively recent in Latin America. For a long time psychology was defined as the study of soul, mind, mental processes, psychic processes, and so forth. The study of animals and the comparison of the psychological processes of several species, including humans, was not a relevant work to be done.

But some investigators defined psychology as the science of behavior, even in Latin America, and were interested in the study of animals. José Ingenieros, the Argentinian psychologist, was one of the first authors to define psychology as the study of behavior. He proposed a psychological "system" or a psychological "school" called genetic psychology, that wanted to include many methods and to study psychology within the realm of natural sciences (see Ingenieros, 1911).

After Ingenieros' studies, several decades passed before comparative psychology, in the real sense, started. A great number of investigators, from Europe and the USA came to Latin America to study species of animals that existed only in this part of the world. They performed careful observations and controlled studies of monkeys, ants, fish, birds, and many other species. These observations have given rise to important systematizations and to large research programs. To a certain extent, contemporary comparative psychology could not be understood without the work done *in Latin America* (a similar statement could be made concerning work done in Africa). The problem was that native investigators were not included and were not even informed of the results obtained. Latin America served only as a place to collect data concerning the behavior of animals in the natural environment. To a certain extent this trend continues (see Terborgh, 1984) in spite of the fact that psychology is a developed science in Latin America, and comparative psychology is a topic taught practically in all the schools of psychology from Mexico to Argentina, as well as in the Caribbean. We hope to see some changes in the near future.

In Latin America the promise of comparative psychology, of understanding psychological processes using animal models, was received with uneasiness. It did not fit well in the general intellectual environment, idealistic and rationalistic. Nobody there expected that the comparison of psychological processes in different species of animals could help to solve the problems in the Third World. But with the passage of time, when the importance of Pavlov's work on experimental neuroses, of Thorndike's research on the Law of Effect, and of Skinner's experimental analysis of behavior came to be taken into consideration, the situation changed.

A typical course of comparative psychology in Latin America is a semester course that uses as a text a translated book or one in English (for instance, Fox, 1968; Hinde, 1970; Maier & Schneirla, 1964; Ratner & Denny, 1970; Roe & Simpson, 1958; Tinbergen, 1951; Waters, Rethlingshafer, & Caldwell, 1960). In the majority of cases, it is a theoretical course. Although there are psychological laboratories with animal subjects used for other courses (psychology of learning, perception, physiological psychology), the comparative psychology course is mainly theoretical. A large part of the course is usually devoted to the introductory part that tries to justify the use of animals in psychology. Philosophical foundations, the comparisons of humans and other animals, the differences between comparative psychology and ethology, are given great attention; as a consequence, in many universities the course is called "Comparative Psychology and Ethology" and not only Comparative Psychology. Animal classification, evolution, the physiological bases of animal behavior, perception, instinct, learning, motivation, social behavior, communication, abnormal behavior, and other important topics are studied. But no practical observations of animals in the field are usually done, and no laboratory experiments are performed in the majority of the cases. However, because in other courses experiments are performed using animals, it is unusual that psychology students can get their degrees in psychology without having done experiments with animals. Their relevance is not always discussed, but in the long run it is recognized by the profession and in some cases even by the public at large.

There are many species worth being studied in Latin America, in the Amazon jungle, in the Andes mountains, in the Argentinian pampas, in the big rivers, in the deserts of Chile and Peru, that it is surprising not much more work is done in comparative psychology in Latin America.

Some politically oriented Faculties of Psychology, attacked this course as being behavioristic, forgetting that behaviorism was not too interested in the comparison of psychological processes among different species. In any case, it is not a very popular course. It is included in the experimental psychology sequence, as a basic course, very theoretical and not considered too relevant for the study of big issues in psychology, particularly in the developing part of the world.

The large Faculties of Psychology are different. Their professors have a better level of information and more interest in scientific problems. In countries such as Mexico and Brazil, and to a lesser extent Venezuela, Colombia, Argentina, and Chile, work is done that could be considered as comparative psychology.

In some schools, biology courses on "Ethology" are offered and are very popular among biology students. Some of the research done in comparative psychology by Latin American investigators has been done by biologists.

The level of information is adequate. A psychologist has some information about evolution, about the criticisms made by Hodos and Campbell (1969) of the concept of the phylogenetic scale; about the nature–nurture controversy; the difference between ethology, comparative psychology, and animal behavior; the main names and books in the area, the problems of working with few species (rats, pigeons, monkeys, dogs, cats, humans). They are familiar with the work done by Bitterman, by Schneirla, and by Harlow. The problem of reward, the problem of rearing, the problem of sensory ability, are among the issues discussed in Latin America, as is the case in other psychological centers of the world.

Sociobiology (Wilson, 1975) has not been taken seriously by Latin American psychologists or biologists. There has not been much discussion concerning this area. Because of its broad implications, to a small extent scientific, and to a greater extent, philosophical, sociobiology could be an area of great interest in the future in this part of the world. But it has not been up to now. Few Latin Americans have worked in sociobiology nor considered seriously its implications for animal and human behavior.

ETHOLOGY AND COMPARATIVE PSYCHOLOGY

Latin America has been more interested in "absolute" systems, in extremistic concepts than in points of convergence among different frames of reference. A number of years after the arrival of Darwinism in biology, a new movement, ethology, was accepted with enthusiasm in this part of the world. Darwin had pointed out the importance of studying animal behavior in order to understand basic processes. Now ethology, also coming from a biological viewpoint, insisted on the need to investigate animal behavior in the natural environment. As a consequence, comparative psychology (not yet developed in Latin America at that time) was attacked because of its laboratory orientation and its association with the psychology of learning, particularly with regard to Skinnerianism. In the early polemic between field and laboratory approaches as the best alternative to study behavioral processes in animals, Latin Americans enthusiastically endorsed field observation.

One of the consequences of this interest in ethology by Latin American biologists and psychologists was to turn to the environment and to discover the enormous wealth of species that can be found in Latin America. Monkeys, birds, fish, different species of mammals, insects, are part of the daily life in many countries. The variety is broad and in many cases those animals have not been studied at all. For some species, even the taxonomic classification is debatable and their behavior is practically unknown. What do we know about the psychological processes of some species of monkeys of Brazil and Colombia, that are at very high levels of evolution? What do we know about the social organization of ants in Panama? What investigations have been carried out in the finches and the tortoises of the Galapagos Islands (Ecuador) exactly the place in which Darwin found many of the proofs for his theory of evolution? The richness, the variety is very great. And also is our ignorance.

As said before, a number of foreign scientists, from the USA and Europe, came to Latin America to work with those species of animals. Many important observations and investigations were done that today are classics of comparative psychology (see for instance Carpenter, 1934; Schneirla, 1929; also Brown, 1970; Mason, 1974).

The flow of scientists has continued, and Latin America has been very appropriate as a working place for comparative psychologists and ethologists. However, few native scientists have participated in the enterprise. In some cases only the results are known in Latin America. In the large majority of the research projects, Latin America serves only as a place to collect data on animal behavior that is analyzed elsewhere and published in the USA and Europe. In journals such as *Animal Behaviour, Journal of Comparative and Physiological Psychology* (now divided into two periodicals), *Journal of Experimental Psychology: Animal Behavior Processes, Behaviour, Primates,* and many others, it is possible to find works based on data collected in Latin America.

This contribution could be increased if native investigators were involved in the research projects, and if the data were sent back to this part of the world. If science is going to form an international network (see Ardila, 1982a), this method of doing research on animal behavior in Latin America should give way to a collaboration on equal terms.

In Latin America there is some comparative psychology research done by Latin American Investigators. We can mention Ades, Bueno, and Bock (1976); Agudelo, Ardila, and Guerrero (1976); Ardila (1970b, 1974, 1975, 1976b); Ardila, Rezk, Polanco, and Pereira (1977); Correa and Ardila (1975); Florez Beltrán and Ardila (1981); Papini (1984); Pereira, Ardila, and Figueroa (1980); Sabogal, Otero, and Ardila (1975).

These are just samples of research in comparative psychology, and not a full presentation of the work done by native investigators.

ENDANGERED SPECIES

The great wealth of zoological variation of Latin American jungles and prairies is in danger. Due to the processes of industrialization and development, to the construction of roads in the forest, the destruction of jungles, and so forth, the habitat of many animals has been disturbed. However, nobody would propose that industriazation be stopped, that roads not enter the jungles, just because animals can be disturbed. The problems of industrialization versus environmental preservation is very complex. Modernization implies changes in the environment in order to adapt it to human needs. According to new developmental programs, a number of changes must be made, and in many cases there is not enough respect for the environment. To respect the environment or to develop the country is a difficult decision to make. This has been made clear in many Latin American nations, particularly in the Amazon region. New human settlements in regions previously unpopulated imply the destruction of the jungle. The industrialized countries did that several decades ago, and now they are asking us in the developing world to respect the environment and not to develop or get industrialized. It is clear that politics enter the picture, and ecological considerations are not given enough importance. Previously, some areas of Latin America had a "prosperous" market in the exporation of animals to the USA and Europe, for scientific research. Monkeys, birds, fish, were sent to laboratories and breeding centers. In many cases the fauna was severely diminished; some species of monkeys almost disappeared due to this trade. The situation changed when laws were passed in all countries to protect the fauna and flora. At the present time it is very difficult to export animals or plants, and the laws are strictly enforced. The exportation of animals, with no control and no respect for the ecological equilibrium, is a matter of the past.

In the meantime, due to developmental pressures, economical considerations, simple ignorance, and lack of care, a large number of species are in the process of extinction. In some cases there are only a few hundred animals left. In others, the zoos have taken responsibility for the preservation of endangered species. The large majority of the countries are aware of the situation and have devoted special areas and parks for the animals in danger. There are, at the national level, institutions for the preservation of natural resources that are in charge of reforestation, breeding of animals, giving norms for the zoos to insure the proper care of the animals, and so forth.

One of the species close to extinction is the Andean condor, which is the symbol of several nations of the Andean mountains. The condor has almost disappeared, and probably very few remain in the wild. Zoos in Latin America, in Europe, and in the USA have recently taken proper care of this bird. In this problem, of the preservations of endangered species, the Frankfurt Zoo is one of the most conscious, best-equiped zoos that have taken the problem of endangered species more seriously. Frankfurt will help several species to survive, among them the Andean condor.

In the Galapagos Islands (Ecuador) there is scientific research going on at the Darwin Foundation. Important information has been obtained that relates specifically to this problem of endangered species. Tortoises are in serious danger, and it was necessary to prohibit the sale of tortoises. At the present time Haiti is probably the only country in which one could get tortoise in a restaurant; 15 years ago, it was a common dish in the majority of Latin American countries. Similar considerations could be made concerning other species of reptiles, mammals, birds, and fish.

We are living in a world in which many living species are disappearing in front of our eyes. Jungles are becoming deserts because of human destructiveness. Habitats are changed drastically, and the ecological chains are disturbed. Very little consideration for ecology existed until a few years ago; it was thought that animals were to be "used," not to share the world with us.

Information about animal behavior is very relevant to this problem. Comparative psychology and ethology have done its part in the process of preservation of endangered species. Now that people and governments are aware of the problem, what is needed is more research. In many cases our level of information is very low concerning a number of species of animals. When we know more about behavior patterns of animals we can help them to survive in their natural habitats and to help ourselves as an animal species with many risks. The human being is an endangered species, and helping other animals to survive will, in the long run, help us and contribute to our own survival.

REFERENCES

Ades, C., Bueno, J. L. O., & Bock, A. M. B. (1976). Estimulação aversiva e exploração dirigida no rato. *Revista Latinoamericana de Psicología, 8,* 295–302.

Agudelo, R., Ardila, R., & Guerrero, J. (1976). Efectos del carbonato de litio sobre la ejecución bajo un programa de refuerzo múltiple IV 19'' RV$_7$. *Revista Latinoamericana de Psicología, 8,* 199–236.

Ardila, R. (1964). La motivación en la conducta animal. *Revista de Psicología, 9,* 115–119.

Ardila, R. (1967). Trabajos experimentales sobre los efectos de las experiencias tempranas en la conducta posterior. *Revista de Psicología, 12,* 75–84.

Ardila, R. (1968a). *Historia de la psicología comparada.* Lima: Universidad de San Marcos.

Ardila, R. (1968b). Psychology in Latin America. *American Psychologist, 23,* 567–574.

Ardila, R. (1970a). Landmarks in the history of Latin American psychology, *Journal of the History of the Behavioral Sciences, 6,* 140–146.

Ardila, R. (1970b). *Psicología del áprendizaje.* Mexico: Siglo XXI.

Ardila, R. (1971a). Professional problems of psychology in Latin America. *Revista Interamericana de Psicología, 5,* 53–58.

Ardila, R. (1971b). The great importante of comparative psychology in the training of psychologists. *American Psychologist, 26,* 1035–1036.

Ardila, R. (1971c). *Los pioneros de la psicología.* Buenos Aires: Paidós.

Ardila, R. (1973). The Interamerican Society of Psychology. *American Psychologist, 28,* 1137–1138.

Ardila, R. (1974). The effects of time, distance, and type of discrimination on transposition in rats. *Interamerican Journal of Psychology, 8,* 155–171.

Ardila, R. (1975). Imprinting sexual. *Revista Latinoamericana de Psicología, 7,* 289–297.

Ardila, R. (1976a). Latin America. In V. S. Sexton & H. Misiak (Eds.), *Psychology around the world* (pp. 259–279). Monterey, CA: Brooks/Cole.

Ardila, R. (1976b). Effects of verbal labeling on reproduction of visually perceived forms as a function of instructions, delay of reproduction, and age. *Psychological Reports, 38,* 259–265.

Ardila, R. (1977). Latin America: Psychology. In B. B. Wolman (Ed.), *International encyclopedia of psychiatry, psychology, psychoanalysis & neurology* (Vol. 6, pp. 353–335). New York: Aesculapius–Van Nostrand.

Ardila, R. (1978). Behavior modification in Latin America. In M. Hersen, R. M. Eisler, & P. M. Miller (Eds.), *Progress in behavior modification* (Vol. 6, pp. 123–142). New York: Academic Press.

Ardila, R. (1980). Historiography of Latin American psychology. In J. Brozek & L. J. Pongratz (Eds.), *Historiography of modern psychology* (pp. 111–118). Toronto: Hogrefe.

Ardila, R. (1981). The evolution of psychology in Latin America. *Spanish-Language Psychology, 1,* 337–346.

Ardila, R. (1982a). International psychology, *American Psychologist, 37,* 323–329.

Ardila, R. (1982b). Psychology in Latin America today. *Annual Review of Psychology, 33*, 103–122.

Ardila, R. (1984). Contemporary aspects of psychological experimentation. In V. Sarris & A. Parducci (Eds.), *Perspectives in psychological experimentation: Toward the year 2000* (pp. 43–56). Hillsdale, NJ: Lawrence Erlbaum Associates.

Ardila, R. (1987). Contemporary psychology in Colombia. In A. R. Gilgen & C. Gilgen (Eds.), *International handbook of psychology*. Westport: Greenwood Press.

Ardila, R., Rezk, M., Polanco, R., & Pereira, F. (1977). Early handling, electric shock, and environmental complexity: Effects on exploratory behavior, "emotionality" and body weight. *Psychological Record, 22*, 219–224.

Bitterman, M. E. (1960). Toward a comparative psychology of learning. *American Psychologist, 15*, 704–712.

Bitterman, M. E. (1965). Philetic differences in learning. *American Psychologist, 20*, 396–410.

Bitterman, M. E. (1975). The comparative analysis of learning. *Science, 188*, 699–709.

Brown, J. L. (1970). Cooperative breeding and altruistic behavior in the Mexican jay, *Aphelocoma Ultramarina*. *Animal Behaviour, 18*, 366–378.

Carpenter, C. R. (1934). A field study of the behavior and social relations of howler monkeys. *Alouatta palliata. Comparative Psychology Monographs, 10*, (2).

Correa, E., & Ardila, R. (1975). Efectos del fármaco tranquilizante Diazepán y del control de la locomoción sobre la adquisición de la respuesta de seguimiento en el troquelado (imprinting). *Revista Latinoamericana de Psicología 7*, 305–320.

Darwin, C. R. (1859). *The origin of species*. London.

Darwin, C. R. (1871). *The descent of man*. London.

Darwin, C. R. (1872). *The expression of the emotions in man and animals*. London.

De Vega, E. P. (1984). Darwin en la Argentina. *Quipu. Revista Latinoamericana de Historia de las Ciencias y la Tecnología, 1*, 119–132.

Dewsbury, D. A. (1984). *Comparative psychology in the twentieth century*. Stroudsburg, PA: Van Nostrand Reinhold.

Flórez Beltrán, H., & Ardila, R. (1981). Cáncer y comportamiento: Efectos conjugados de la metilnitrosoúrea (MNH) y de la respuesta emocional condicionada (CER) sobre la ejecución de un programa de intervalo variable (IV) y sobre el desarrollo de neoplasias en ratas. *Revista Latinoamericana de Psicología, 13*, 375–401.

Fox, M. W. (Ed.). (1968). *Abnormal behavior in animals*. Philadelphia: Saunders.

Hinde, R. A. (1970). *Animal behavior*. New York: McGraw–Hill.

Hodos, W., & Campbell, C. B. (1969). Scala Naturae: Why there is no theory in comparative psychology? *Psychological Review, 76*, 337–350.

Ingenieros, J. (1911). *Psicología genética*. Buenos Aires.

Mackintosh, N. J. (1974). *The psychology of animal learning*. London: Academic Press.

Maier, N. R. F., & Schneirla, T. C. (1964). *Principles of animal psychology*, New York: Dover.

Mason, W. A. (1974). Differential grouping patterns in two species of South American monkeys. In N. F. White (Ed.), *Ethology and psychiatry* (pp. 153–169). Toronto: University of Toronto Press.

Papini, M. R. (1984). Procedimiento para el estudio de la adquisición de cadenas de conductas en el laberinto. *Revista Latinoamericana de Psicología, 16*, 235–246.

Papini, M. R. (1985). La concepción de la psicología comparada de José Ingenieros. *Revista de Historia de la Psicología, 6*, 61–78.

Pavlov, I. P. (1927). *Conditioned reflexes*. Oxford: Oxford University Press.

Pereira, F., Ardila, R., & Figueroa, M. (1980). Efectos del stress antes del embarazo y a los ocho días de preñez, sobre la exploración, la defecación y el peso corporal de las crías de ratones. *Revista Latinoamericana de Psicología, 12*, 487–494.

Ratner, S. C., & Denny, M. R. (1970). *Comparative psychology*. Homewood, IL: Dorsey Press.

Roe, A., & Simpson, G. G. (Eds.). (1958). *Behavior and evolution*. New Haven: Yale University Press.

Romanes, G. J. (1882). *Animal intelligence*. London: Kegan Paul.

Sabogal, F., Otero, R., & Ardila, R. (1975). Efecto de las diferencias en la estimulación visual temprana sobre el aprendizaje de discriminación simple y compleja en ratones. *Revista Latinoamericana de Psicología, 7,* 65–76.

Schneirla, T. C. (1929). Learning and orientation in ants. *Comparative Psychology Monographs, 6.*

Terborgh, J. (1984). *Five new world primates*. Princeton: Princeton University Press.

Thorndike, E. L. (1898). Animal intelligence: An experimental study of the associative processes in animals. *Psychological Monographs, 2,* (4, Whole No. 8).

Thorndike, E. L. (1911). *Animal intelligence*. New York: MacMillan.

Tinbergen, N. (1951). *The study of instinct*. Oxford: Oxford University Press.

Tobach, E. (Ed.). (1971). *Biopsychology of development*. New York: Academic Press.

Tobach, E., Adler, H. E., & Adler, L. L. (Eds.). (1973). Comparative psychology at issue. *Annals of the New York Academy of Sciences, 223.*

Waters, R. H., Rethlingshafer, D. A., & Caldwell, W. E. (Eds.). (1960). *Comparative psychology*. New York: McGraw–Hill.

Wilson, E. O. (1975). *Sociobiology: The new synthesis*. Cambridge, MA: Harvard University Press.

11 The Study of Animal Behavior in Argentina

Mauricio R. Papini[1]
Instituto de Biología y Medicina Experimental and Universidad de Buenos Aires, Argentina.

INTRODUCTION

In Argentina, as in other countries, the study of animal behavior is carried out by researchers who have received training in different disciplines. Ecologists, physiologists, psychologists, etc. are participating in a variety of projects with different goals, methodologies, theoretical frameworks, and so forth. As a consequence, they tend to see their respective activities as not very related and, presumably, tend to develop different definitions of what should be meant by animal behavior. This state of affairs is reinforced by the absence of societies, journals, periodical meetings, or any other communication channel open to interchange of ideas and information. In addition to different personal histories and the lack of fluid communication, they also are sensitive to current controversies characterizing the field of animal behavior (Snowdon, 1983).

Many disciplines claim for themselves behavior as their object of study, such as comparative psychology, ethology, sociobiology, behavioral ecology, etc. Although there are important historical reasons for this multiple creation of "sciences" they seem to differ mainly in their approaches and theoretical frameworks. I doubt that these differences are relevant enough to support the existence of such a variety of disciplines and would like to suggest that all of them are fundamentally unified by their common purpose of explaining behavior (at different levels of analysis) using conventional scientific methodologies. Therefore, I review in this chapter the contribution of a series of researchers to the area of

[1]Preparation of this paper was supported by the Consejo Nacional de Investigaciones Científicas y Técnicas, Argentina.

animal behavior as a whole, without discrimination in terms of disciplines or type of studies.

Before getting into the historical background I would like to warn the reader not to expect a critical review of the history and contemporary features of animal behavior studies in Argentina. I will feel satisfied if this chapter shows some of the important past and present events and, mainly, if it contributes to strengthen the idea that Argentina researchers in animal behavior have a unique opportunity to contribute to the field if they focus their studies on the peculiar group of species forming the neotropical fauna.

HISTORICAL PERSPECTIVE

The interest in the study of behavior can be traced to the colonial period starting in the 16th century. Not commonly recognized is the role of many Spanish naturalists who came to America, and particularly to what is now Argentina, in the development of the general biology of the new fauna discovered here. Some of them had not even studied natural science but were theologians or philosophers who realized the uniqueness of the new fauna (Furlong, 1943). Behavioral observations are not scanty in the writings of these naturalists although none of them were exclusively dedicated to this purpose. In general, they shared a creationist hypothesis about the origin of species and rejected the idea that animals are machines without soul, as Descartes had proposed. These two aspects are present in the writings of José Sánchez Labrador, such as his *Paraguay Natural* written between 1771 and 1776. Interestingly enough, he rejected the view that fish are imperfect living beings (i.e., with no soul) by suggesting that they showed evidence of memory. He observed that *pacús (Colossoma mitrei)* returned year after year to the same places where certain sweet fruits fell into the water; he also suggested that fish remember where and when to find their food, where to hide for protection, and how to find the way back to their dwelling (Sánchez Labrador, 1968, p. 45). Similar ideas seem to have been developed by Joaquín Millás, who in his book *Instituciones Psicológicas,* published in 1797, discussed the existince of soul in animals (Horas, 1960).

The works of Félix de Azara represent another important contribution to the natural sciences. Among other things, Azara developed a series of ideas that can be considered an important prolegomenon to evolutionary biology (Alvarez López, 1934) and could have had some influence on Darwin, who made explicit reference to Azara's observations. His books on birds and mammals, where most of his biological thinking developed, were published in 1802. Azara's most important ideas are related to the observation that domestication produces increments in variability, that people can artificially pair animals with the conscious purpose of producing improvements in form or organs, that stronger species can produce the extinction of weaker ones and, perhaps most important of all, that on several grounds (i.e., biogeographical, predator–prey relationships) he considered it absolutely impossible to explain the existence of living species by a strictly creationist hypothesis and proposed separated geographical and temporal origins for different groups. For example, prey should have arisen before predators or otherwise the latter could cause the extinction of the former; also, some species of the American fauna should have originated locally because migration from other continents was prevented by natural barriers. Azara (1934) wrote on the relation between form and habit and suggested that although sometimes it is possible to predict some behaviors knowing the structural or morphological characters, this relation is in no way exact, as it happens with some birds of prey that have morphological adaptations in accordance to one type of food but also feed on insects.

Francisco J. Muñiz also contributed to the field of animal behavior during the 19th century. In 1848 he published a monograph on the *ñandú* (*Rhea americana*), a large flightless bird characteristic of the Pampas. Muñiz (1916) first pointed out the interesting mating system of the *ñandú,* which exemplifies a case of polyandry-polygyny. He carefully described the composition of flocks during the breeding season, agonistic behavior, sexual behavior, courtship by females, construction of the nest, and parental care by males.

Toward the end of the last century there was an important change in Argentina's intellectual environment. Positivism and evolutionism were accepted by an increasing number of educators and naturalists. Psychology was defined as a natural science and attempts at providing coherent views of this science appeared during the beginning of the present century. The first laboratory of psychology was created in 1891 by Víctor Mercante, an educational psychologist, and a few years later there were numerous laboratories in schools and universities (Papini, 1976). One of the leaders of this experimentalist movement in psychology was José Ingenieros. In his book *Principios de Psicología* (Ingenieros, 1919), initially published in 1910 and translated into French and German, Ingenieros developed the idea that the only way of studying psychological functions is through the evolution of species (comparative psychology), human societies (social psychology), and human ontogeny (developmental psychology). He defined a psychological function as a biologically acquired trait that serves to progressively adapt the organism to its environment. In his system, psychologists should incorporate an evolutionary approach in their studies, and in the case of comparative psychologists he discarded introspection and explictly favored behavior as their object of study. Behavior was defined as the way of expression of psychological functions (Ingenieros, 1919, p. 301).

Although Ingenieros had a profound influence on a generation of Argentine psychologists, this did not develop comparative psychology to the extent that its position within Ingenieros' psychological system would suggest. Clemente Onelli was one of the few interested in animal behavior and perhaps the first to use the term "comparative psychology" in relation to his empirical research

(Onelli, 1909). Onelli was director of the Zoological Garden of Buenos Aires and editor of the journal of this zoo in which many papers dealing with "animal habits" were published. He was predominantly an observer more than a person interested in testing or developing theories and therefore his writings have an anecdotal style. Between 1905 and 1922 he published a series of 64 papers in this journal with an amazing number of casual observations on the behavior of a variety of species that inhabited the zoo. Onelli also wrote in collaboration with Christofredo Jacob, a neurobiologist, the *Atlas del Cerebro de los Mamíferos de la República Argentina* (Jacob & Onelli, 1913), with general observations on the behavior of 41 mammals.

Although Onelli referred to some of his papers as examples of comparative psychology, he cannot be considered a full-time animal behaviorist because of the broad scope of his writings and activities. The same is true of other biologists who occasionally carried out behavioral observations. Among others, Angel Gallardo should be mentioned because he contributed to our understanding of social insects, particularly ants (Gallardo, 1907).

As far as I know, there has never been a journal fully dedicated to animal behavior in Argentina. Two journals that sporadically published articles were: *Revista del Jardín Zoológico de Buenos Aires*, which appeared in a first period between 1893 and 1895 edited by Eduardo L. Holmberg, and in a second period between 1905 and 1922 edited by Clemente Onelli; and *Physis*, the journal of the Argentine Society of Natural Sciences, published since 1912. A survey of *Physis'* 41 volumes (from 1912 to 1982) where 2483 articles were published, reveals that only 57 (2.3%) concerned behavioral problems, many at a descriptive level. The fact that 43 (75.4%) of these papers were published between 1960 and 1982 shows that the interest in animal behavior studies is increasing. Three taxonomic groups attracted most attention: Hymenoptera (16 papers), Amphibia (14 papers), and Mammalia (16 papers).

Finally, the only book entirely dedicated to animal behavior seems to be that by José Barbanza (1944), *La Psicología Animal.* This book briefly reviews problems such as orientation, drives, instincts, social behavior, and learning.

RECENT DEVELOPMENTS

As previously noted, most research has been carried out relatively recently. In this section I review works that have been published since the mid 1960s.

Several research groups contributed to the study of the physiological basis of behavior using a variety of species as models. Segura and his collaborators (Colombo & Segura, 1972; Segura, de Juán, Colombo, & Kacelnik, 1971) studied a variety of aspects related to reproduction and sexual behavior in the toad *Bufo arenarum.* Segura called attention to how little is known about the role of some brain structures, such as the reticular formation, in the control of behavior in amphibians. Segura et al. (1971) showed that several lesions at different levels of the neuraxis produced effects on postural reflexes, locomotion, clasping reflex, and swimming behavior.

A series of studies on the electrophysiological basis of sleep in marsupials, edentates, and rodents were carried out by Affanni, García Samartino, and colaborators (Affanni, 1972). Among other things, they described activity cycles in the armadillo *Chaetophractus villosus* with special reference to fast and slow sleep and a variety of behavioral patterns associated with these phases (García Samartino, Scaravilli, Affanni, & Cinto, 1974). In a different vein, Affanni also contributed to the understanding of the effects of olfactory peduncle transections on a variety of behavioral aspects such as the retention of a visual discrimination, general activity, and emotionality (Affanni, Papini, Filipello, & Mustaca, 1981).

Others that contributed to the area of physiology and behavior are Leonor Barán and Juán Izquierdo, both working on electrophysiological and pharmacological aspects of learning, and Enrique Caviedes Codelia (Caviedes Codelia, Caviedes Vidal, & Alcalá, 1983) who is working in physiological and behavioral aspects of thermoregulation in rodents of the genus *Ctenomys,* which are adapted to an underground mode of life.

Some studies have dealt with motivation and learning. Néstor A. Schmajuk published a series of papers on maintenance of water balance in *Bufo arenarum* (Schmajuk & Segura, 1982), and on appetitive instrumental learning (Schmajuk, Segura, & Reboreda, 1980) and reward downshifts (Schmajuk, Segura, & Ruidiaz, 1981) using access to water as reinforcement. The absence of successive negative contrast in this toad (Schmajuk et al., 1981) fits in the comparative analysis of contrast phenomena and contributes to our understanding of species differences in learning processes.

Experiments on discrimination learning have been also carried out in marsupials such as *Didelphis albiventris* (Papini, Mustaca, & Affanni, 1984), edentates such as *Chaetophractus villosus* (Mustaca, Papini, & Affanni, 1985; Papini, Mustaca, & Affanni, 1984, 1985), rats (Papini, 1984), and primates such as *Cebus paraguayanus* (Fachinelli & Valciukas, 1975). It is interesting to note that all the works on learning reviewed so far have been carried out on a comparative framework. I already mentioned Schmajuk's research on successive negative contrast in the toad, but also Papini et al. (1985) began a series of experiments that systematically compare differences in the acquisition of behavior chains in marsupial and placental mammals, and Fachinelli and Valciukas' (1975) work was also directed at comparing discrimination thresholds in monkey and man.

An increasing number of works are being published on social behavior. One of the most extensive and important contributions in this area is that of Avelino Barrio on the characteristics of the sexual song of anurans. Barrio studied not only the acoustic features of songs in several species but also used the songs to identify sympatric species (Barrio, 1964, 1966).

Semicaptivity and laboratory observations of social interactions have been reported in both rodents and edentates. Villafañe, Velázquez, Bonaventura, and Torres (1983a, 1983b) reported a series of studies in seminatural settings aimed at determining social interactions and resource exploitation in *Calomys musculinus* and *Akodon azarae*. Campagna, Papini, and Affanni (1984) studied several aspects of agonistic and social interactions of pairs of armadillos (*Chaetophractus villosus*) including topography of behavioral patterns, effects of weight on aggressive behavior, and effects of knowledge of the territory and of the opponent also on aggressive behavior.

Studies of social behavior in natural contexts are also being developed by several groups. In Northern Argentina, Rumiz and Zunino (1983) reported their results on troop composition of *Alouatta caraya,* and Piantanida, Puig, Nani, Gil, Rossi, Mazzucarelli, and Cavanna (in press) studied a variety of behavioral aspects in this species, including troop composition and vocalizations. Rathbun and Gache (1980) reported data on group composition in another primate, *Aotus trivirgatus.* In Southern Argentina, Campagna (1982a, 1982b) is working in an extensive study of social behavior of the Southern Sea Lion, *Otaria byronia,* in its natural breeding environment.

Important contributions to the study of insect behavior are the works published by Josué A. Nuñez and Jorge F. Genise. Nuñez (Fischbarg & Nuñez, 1970; Nuñez, 1966; Nuñez & Fischbarg, 1969), performing field experiments to determine the relationship between collected energy and costs of foraging, studied the foraging behavior of bees. Genise studied nest building, hunting, and transport of the prey to the nest in several species of hymenopterans (Genise, 1980, 1981b), the effects of environmental temperature on activity peaks of *Prionyx bifoveolatus* (Genise, 1981a), and what he called "discarding behavior" in *Rubrica nasuta,* carrying out field experiments (Genise, 1982).

General studies on the behavior of different species in natural environments have also been reported in birds (Daciuk, 1973, 1983; Erize, 1983; Fraga, 1983), marsupials (Cajal, 1981), rodents (Contreras, 1972), and cetaceans (Wursig, Wursig, & Mermoz, 1977). Juán C. López's in-progress observations on predatory behavior of orcas (*Orsinus orca*) must also be mentioned as an important contribution to the behavior of a poorly known species, particularly in its natural environment.

CONCLUSIONS: ARGENTINA AND THE STUDY OF ANIMAL BEHAVIOR

The field of animal behavior in Argentina is emerging and many important steps must be taken to develop it to a higher level. Research groups, societies, periodical meetings, specialized journals, libraries, etc. are important prerequisites for scientific activities in any discipline. These factors tend to increase communication between researchers and to show common interests and difficulties in the planning and carrying out of research projects.

This review clearly shows that Argentine researchers can contribute to the field of animal behavior in two important ways. First, they can develop and test theories concerning different behavioral phenomena. Second, they can (and usually do) use in their projects species of our local fauna that, because of this reason, are in many cases poorly known from the behavioral point of view. Although the first point is shared with all members of the international scientific community, the second is, to a large extent, dependent on our capability to detect the unique contribution we can effectively make to science by studying autochthonous species. In this regard, perhaps animal behavior should follow paleontology and emulate the tradition begun by Florentino and Carlos Ameghino. By emphasizing the study of local species and spreading research both in geological time and taxonomic groups, that tradition led to a true Argentine school in paleontology. An analogous emphasis in the behavioral aspects of local species at the present could lead to the development of an Argentine school of animal behavior. This will give us the opportunity for discovering new phenomena, testing theories on a different background, and sharing a common point of reference.

ACKNOWLEDGMENTS

The author wishes to thank J. M. Affanni, G. Hermitte, and A. E. Mustaca for their comments on the manuscript, and C. L. Azcuy for his comments on the Ameghinos.

REFERENCES

Affanni, J. M. (1972). Observations on the sleep of some South American marsupials and edentates. In M. H. Chase (Ed.), *The sleeping brain. Perspectives in the brain sciences* (Vol. 1). Los Angeles: University of California at Los Angeles Press.

Affanni, J. M., Papini, M. R., Filipello, A. M., & Mustaca, A. E. (1981). Efecto de la sección de un pedúnculo olfatorio sobre la retención de un aprendizaje de discriminación visual, sobre la actividad motriz y sobre el número de bolas fecales eliminadas, en el armadillo. *Revista Latinoamericana de Psicología, 13,* 281–291.

Alvarez López, E. (1934). *Félix de Azara.* Madrid: Aguilar.

Azara, F. de (1934). Antología. In E. Alvarez López (Ed.), *Félix de Azara.* Madrid: Aguilar.

Barbanza, J. (1944). *La psicología animal.* Buenos Aires: Atlántida.

Barrio, A. (1964). Especies crípticas del género Pleurodema que conviven en una misma área, identificadas por el canto nupcial (Anura, Leptodactylidae). *Physis, 24,* 471–489.

Barrio, A. (1966). Divergencia acústica entre el canto nupcial de *Leptodactylus acellatus* (Linne) y *L. chaquensis* Cei (Anura, Leptodactylidae). *Physis, 26,* 275–277.

Cajal, J. L. (1981). Estudios preliminares sobre el área de acción en marsupiales (Mammalia, Marsupialia). *Physis, 40,* 27–37.

Campagna, C. (1982a). *Observaciones sobre el comportamiento agresivo intraespecífico del lobo marino del sur Otaria byronia. I. Descripción de algunos patrones y su comparación con otras especies de la subfamilia Otariinae.* Paper presented at the Third Iberoamerican Meeting on Conservation and Zoology of Vertebrates, Buenos Aires.

Campagna, C. (1982b). *Observaciones sobre el comportamiento agresivo intraespecífico del lobo marino del sur Otaria byronia. II. Algunas variables ambientales correlacionadas con el despliegue de conductas territoriales por parte de los machos reproductores.* Paper presented at the Third Iberoamerican Meeting on Conservation and Zoology of Vertebrates, Buenos Aires.

Campagna, C., Papini, M. R., & Affanni, J. M. (1984). Observaciones sobre el comportamiento agresivo intraespecífico del armadillo *Chaetophractus villosus,* en condiciones de laboratorio. *Revista Latinoamericana de Psicología, 16,* 443–458.

Caviedes Codelia, E., Caviedes Vidal, E., & Alcalá, O. (1983). Body temperature regulation and behavior in rodents of *Ctenomys* genus. *Comunicaciones Biológicas, 1,* 484.

Colombo, J. A., & Segura, E. T. (1972). Effects of estradiol on brain electrogram of the female toad *Bufo arenarum* Hensel during the breeding season. *General and Comparative Endocrinology, 18,* 268–275.

Contreras, J. R. (1972). El home range en una población de *Oryzomys longicaudatus philippi* (Landbeck) (Rodentia, Cricetidae). *Physis, 31,* 353–361.

Daciuk, J. (1973). Notas faunísticas y bioecológicas de Península Valdés y Patagonia. XI. Etología y desarrollo de los pichones de cuaco o garza bruja (*Nycticorax nycticorax obscurus*), de una colonia estudiada en la Isla de los Pájaros (Golfo de San José, Prov. Chubut, Rep. Argentina). *Physis, 32,* 107–121.

Daciuk, J. (1983). Notas faunísticas y bioecológicas de Península Valdés y Patagonia. XXVI. Estudio etológico en el hábitat (comportamiento colonial, caliológico, sexológico y parental) de *Spheniscus magellanicus* (L. R. Forster, 1781) en Bahía Janssen, Punta Tombo y Punta Clara, Chubut, Argentina. *El Hornero,* 218–244.

Erize, F. (1983). Observaciones sobre el macá tobiano. *El Hornero,* 256–268.

Fachinelli, C. C., & Valciukas, J. A. (1975). Observaciones sobre la discriminación visual del mono *Cebus paraguayanus. Physis, 34,* 53–64.

Fischbarg, B. D., & Nuñez, J. A. (1970). Comportamiento de abejas recolectoras de néctar. *Physis, 30,* 105–111.

Fraga, R. M. (1983). Parasitismo de cría del renegrido, *Molothrus bonariensis,* sobre el chingolo, *Zonotrichia capensis:* Nuevas observaciones y conclusiones. *El Hornero,* 245–255.

Furlong, G. (1943). *Naturalistas argentinos durante la dominación hispánica.* Buenos Aires: Huarpes.

Gallardo, A. (1907). De cómo se forman los nuevos hormigueros de hormiga negra. *Revista del Jardín Zoológico de Buenos Aires, 3* (Epoca, II), 312–316.

García Samartino, L., Scaravilli, A. M., Affanni, J. M., & Cinto, R. O. (1974). Estudio cuantitativo de la vigilia y el sueño en *Chaetophractus villosus* (Mammalia, Dasypodidae). *Physis, 33,* 145–150.

Genise, J. F. (1980). Comportamiento de nidificación de *Prionyx bifoveolatus* (Tasch.) (Hymenoptera, Sphecidae). *Physis, 39,* 51–54.

Genise, J. F. (1981a). Influencia de factores meteorológicos en la actividad de *Prionyx bifoveolatus* (Tasch.) (Hymenoptera, Sphecidae). *Physis, 39,* 19–24.

Genise, J. F. (1981b). Observaciones sobre el comportamiento de nidificación de *Stictia arcuata* (Burmeister) (Hymenoptera, Sphecidae). *Physis, 40,* 15–17.

Genise, J. F. (1982). Comportamiento de desecho de presas en *Rubrica nasuta* (Christ) y revisión de esta actividad en Sphecidae (Insecta, Hymenoptera). *Physis, 40,* 101–109.

Horas, P. A. (1960). La enseñanza de la psicología en el período emancipador. *Revista de Educación, 5,* 26–43.

Ingenieros, J. (1919). *Principios de psicología.* (6th ed.). Buenos Aires: Rosso.

Jacob, C., & Onelli, C. (1913). *Atlas del cerebro de los mamíferos de la República Argentina.* Beunos Aires: Kraft.

Muñiz, F. J. (1916). El ñandú. In F. J. Muñiz, *Escritos científicos.* Buenos Aires: La Cultura Argentina.

Mustaca, A. E., Papini, M. R., & Affanni, J. M. (1985). Aprendizaje de probabilidad en el armadillo *Chaetophractus villosus. Interamerican Journal of Psychology, 19,* 45–56.

Nuñez, J. A. (1966). Quantitative Beziehungen zwischen den Eigenschaften von Futterquellen und dem Verhalten von Sammelbienen. *Zeitschrift für Vergleichende Physiologie, 53,* 142–164.

Onelli, C. (1909). Anécdotas de psicología zoológica. *Anales de Psicología, 1,* 314–340.

Papini, M. R. (1976). Datos para una historia de la psicología experimental argentina (hasta 1930). *Revista Latinoamericana de Psicología, 8,* 319–335.

Papini, M. R. (1984). Procedimiento para el estudio de la adquisición de cadenas de conductas en el laberinto. *Revista Latinoamericana de Psicología, 16,* 235–246.

Papini, M. R., Mustaca, A. E., & Affanni, J. M. (1984). Spatial learning in South American opossums and armadillos. *Journal of General Psychology, 111,* 45–55.

Papini, M. R., Mustaca, A. E., & Affanni, J. M. (1985). Discrimination learning in the armadillo (*Chaetophractus villosus*): A study of positional strategies. *Journal of General Psychology, 112,* 119–127.

Piantanida, M. S., Puig, N., Nani, F., Gil, A., Rossi, L., Mazzucarelli, S., & Cavanna, L. (in press). Introducción al estudio de la ecología y etología del mono aullador (*Alouatta caraya*) en condiciones naturales. *Revista del Museo de Ciencias Naturales Bernardino Rivadavia.*

Rathbun, G. B., & Gache, M. (1980). Ecological survey of the night monkey, *Aotus trivirgatus,* in Formosa Province, Argentina. *Primates, 21,* 211–219.

Rumiz, D., & Zunino, G. (1983). *Fisonomía del hábitat, densidad, área de acción y variaciones de la composición de tropas del mono aullador (Alouatta caraya) en el área de Rió Riachuelo (Corrientes).* Paper presented at the 11st Argentine Meeting of Ecology, Córdoba.

Sánchez Labrador, J. (1968). *Peces y aves del Paraguay Natural.* Buenos Aires: Compañía General Fabril Editora.

Schmajuk, N. A., & Segura, E. T. (1982). Behavioral regulation of water balance in the toad *Bufo arenarum. Herpetologica, 38,* 296–301.

Schmajuk, N. A., Segura, E. T., & Reboreda, J. C. (1980). Appetitive conditioning and discriminatory learning in toads. *Behavioral and Neural Biology, 28,* 392–397.

Schmajuk, N. A., Segura, E. T., & Ruidiaz, A. C. (1981). Reward downshift in the toad. *Behavioral and Neural Biology, 33,* 519–523.

Segura, E. T., de Juán, A. O. R., Colombo, J. A., & Kacelnik, A. (1971). The sexual clasp as a reticularly controlled behavior in the toad, *Bufo arenarum* Hensel. *Physiology and Behavior, 7,* 157–160.

Snowdon, C. T. (1983). Ethology, comparative psychology, and animal behavior. *Annual Review of Psychology, 34,* 63–94.

Villafañe, G., Velázquez, C., Bonaventura, S., & Torres, M. (1983a). *Comportamiento social y uso del hábitat de pequeños roedores en semicautividad.* I. Paper presented at the 11st. Argentine Meeting of Ecology, Córdoba.

Villafañe, G., Velázquez, C., Bonaventura, S., & Torres, M. (1983b). *Comportamiento social y uso del hábitat de pequeños roedores en semicautividad.* II. Paper presented at the 11st. Argentine Meeting of Ecology, Córdoba.

Wursig, M., Wursig, B., & Mermoz, J. F. (1977). Desplazamientos, comportamiento general y un varamiento de la marsopa espinosa *Phocoena spinipinnis,* en el Golfo San José (Chubut, Argentina). *Physis, 36,* 71–79.

12 Comparative Psychology in the United States: A Status Report

Everett J. Wyers
State University of New York at Stony Brook

Two contrasting ways of defining comparative psychology at a programatic level are presented. The present status and future directions of the discipline are then briefly discussed in a fashion interleaving practical and programatic concerns.

COMPARATIVE PSYCHOLOGY: SPECIFIED

Comparative Psychology can be defined as a discipline within Psychology. It can also be seen as a bounded region within the realm of knowledge. In that sense it is a region of knowledge to which anyone can contribute, regardless of background. As such, it is harder to define. The boundaries of Comparative Psychology become fuzzy. Simple delimiting criteria become difficult to apply systematically. One is forced then to distinguish between various forms of comparative psychological knowledge, among them those admissible within the canons of science.

In his recent assessment of the status of Comparative Psychology in the 20th century Dewsbury (1984) adopts the former view. Comparative Psychology is narrowly defined in a practical and disciplinary sense. Accordingly comparative psychological work is done only when certain problem subareas are investigated by certain people. "Pragmatically . . . most physiological psychology, most process-oriented learning, and some studies of motivation are excluded. . . . Comparative psychologists typically study either unusual species or behavioral patterns that fall outside related areas of animal psychology, or both" (page 6). People who do comparative psychological work preferably have advanced training in a Psychology Department, or other psychologically oriented research institution. Explicit comparisons may, or may not, be involved in the work. The discovery of principles of generality governing the control, development, adaptive significance, and evolution of behavior in all animals is the goal of the work.

Dewsbury has done an admirable job in providing a wealth of both practical and detailed factual information regarding the current status of comparative psychology in the United States from the historical point of view. Only certain supplemental and recent information can be provided here (see also Snowdon, 1983). What people who were trained in psychology departments are doing, and what is happening to them, is certainly vital information as to the status and future of comparative psychology as a professional entity and career activity in the United States, and Canada as well. In part, what follows is an effort to promulgate a point of view intended to enhance the status of Comparative Psychology at a practical level and convince psychologists in general of the value of Comparative Psychology to their enterprise.

COMPARATIVE PSYCHOLOGY: GENERALIZED

Psychology is an evolutionary discipline. The extent to which Darwinian (and earlier evolutionary influences) pervaded and altered its development is seldom recognized today. Today the assumptions and biases of evolutionary thinking (in general), are imbedded in the fabric of the discipline and forgotten by most of its practioners; of whatever persuasion. This is nowhere more evident than it is in physiological, motivational, learning, and cognitive psychology. Human behavior in its foundation, process, and function is regarded by most psychologists as essentially and regardless of environmental constraint during development as at least potentially adaptive. The behavior of "organisms" is adaptive and therefore malleable and capable of modification through application of the appropriate sorts of "environmental" contingencies; i.e., behavioral consequents. One implication is that behavior can be adjusted within the limits of biological nature without changing the general environmental context of modern life. Another is that human genetical evolution ceased with the development of language and culture. Few have had the temerity to suggest otherwise (but see, Staddon, 1981).

Through its evolutionary substrate, Psychology assumes all human behavior to be essentially adaptive in character. If behavior is judged to be maladaptive the fault is usually seen as lying in the environment; i.e., events during his or her development deviating from the "norm," sometimes in a "biological mistake," or nowadays occasionally, in both. In each case emphasis is on the course of environmental events and the adaptive significance of behavior is seen as best evaluated through its relatedness to similar behavioral phenomena in other animals (humans included); hence, the basis of virtually all psychological testing and the emphasis on animal models constrained in laboratory settings by parameters of human concern, and the readiness to generalize across species differences.

It can be argued that in Psychology comparison seeks explanation of function in the simplist terms possible. However, to restrict the search within parameters of human concern violates the essence of the comparative approach by obfuscating delineation of species differences in similar behavioral phenomena (Demarest, 1983). Simplicity of interpretation requires delineation of such differences and attention to the nature and concerns of the animal studied (human included) draws emphasis to them.

Gilbert Gottlieb (1979) viewed comparative psychology as follows:

> A comparative approach to psychology signifies an interest in the ways the human animal is the same as, and different from, other animals, and the ways in which other animals are similar to and different from each other in adapting to their surroundings. . . . Comparative psychology has always been explicitly interested in the question of psychological mediation (perception, cognition) as well as the overt mechanics or form of behavioral adjustments. (p. 147)

An interest in central mediation has too often been equated in psychological and biological quarters with a traditional and now outdated mentalism (Gottlieb, 1979), and even today

> with unfruitful questions concerning animal consciousness, even though psychologists such as Tolman (1932) and Brunswik (1952) have shown that accounts of central mediation can be firmly tied to environmental and behavioral referents. . . . This point of view—a hardnosed interest in psychological processes mediating between situation and behavior—is well exemplified in T. C. Schneirla's approach to the problems of comparative psychology. (p. 159)

Virtually all areas of study in Psychology are open to the comparative approach within Gottlieb's definition. What topic of concern in psychology is not open to interpretation in terms of central mediation? It takes a very "hardnosed" empiricist indeed, to do with only minimal reference to "central processes." Even traditional operant conditioners must assume a "drive" state to mediate occurrence of their "respondents" and "operants." So, this is so, but what is the need of an evolutionary approach? Why not ignore the "fine-grain" of psychology's long distant past and concentrate on the process and fundaments of behavior?

Therein lies the central problem for comparative psychologists (of whatever persuasion) today. If one is studying "process," by whatever means, what is the need to be concerned with "origins"? The answer of course, is reflected in the aforementioned: One cannot draw accurate generalizations without comparative study. Another is that whatever the mediational process may be, it did not arise by "special creation." It evolved; and no one, no matter what the predictive power generated by his, or her, model or physiological mechanism may be, can assert his or her understanding to be complete without comparative (evolutionary) study. To solve the "central problem" one must convince one's colleagues of this.

It is true, as Plotkin (1979) has said, that behavior is not related to an evolutionary approach in any simple manner. The logic of any experimental research attempting to assess that relation is both subtle and complex. This is so because behavior is both selected and selective. It leads the way in making possible "the transmutation of species." As a result it is difficult (at best) to establish a direct link between the behavior under study (in living animals) and evolution (e.g., reproductive success). The behavior may have been "selected for" and thus exist in its present form, or be in itself a "selective force" (e.g., for structural characteristics, developmental processes, or even other behavioral characteristics). In the past this dual selective aspect of behavior has been too often overlooked, or perhaps ignored.

It may well be that evolutionary theory (natural selection at the level of individual reproductive success) cannot serve as a predictive base for the behavior of individual animals (in social context or not). Plotkin (1979) stated that evolutionary theory may simply be a central explanatory concept "organizing what is already known into meaningful and coherent patterns. . . . helping the scientist to distinguish between significant and insignificant fact" (p. 58). Beer (1980) notes that: "not all questions about behavior, including questions about social behavior, are questions about evolution" (p. 56). One may add: Not all questions about behavior, including questions about social behavior, and questions about evolution, are questions about how and why an individual animal behaves the way its does, given its social and evolutionary origins, in the particular situation it finds itself in. It can be said that this, the question of individual difference (i.e., "what makes Sammy run"), is the basic motivating question for all of psychology. Not all questions concerning its answer are questions about evolutionary origins, but some of them necessarily are; and they must be answered. It may take another "Darwin" to digest and derive from the implacable flood of behavioral research we are today subject to, a suitable principle commensurate in its epistemological implications to natural selection, but we must give that potential "Darwin" his or her chance.

In the comparative psychological study of behavior the mediation of adaptive behavior, as functionally relevant to the survival and wellbeing of the individual animal, is the central concern. The "how" (the process) of individual behavior is one thing. The "why" (the function) of that behavior is another. Plotkin (1979) as others, in other contexts have said (e.g., Hodos, 1982), urges that these two concerns, so frequently disparate and following their own concerns, be combined in research design and/or approach. The present state of animal behavioral science indicates this may be difficult but is becoming more feasible. It may be that this, in a way, states the present orientation and future of comparative psychology.

It is not that every process researcher must learn all there is in modern evolutionary and biological concerns, or vice versa: that functional researchers bend to every dictum of current neurophysiological methodology. It is that the functionally oriented can profit by taking into account what is known about physiological process in their species and its relatives. It is that the process server can profit by considering the implications his or her results may have from an evolutionary point of view. The onus is no greater on one than the other. Each need ask only if the implications of his or her research might lead to results inconsistent or consistent with the central integrative concept of Darwinian insight, natural selection. If so, why not introduce a condition putting the implication to test?

Plotkin (1979) has emphasized the need for such combinative studies combining the study of process and function together within an evolutionary context. His interest was combinative studies, "which involve manipulation or measurement of brain function and which are cast within an evolutionary context, or evolutionary studies of behaviour which have utilized brain manipulation" (p. 55). Some such studies are being conducted. He reports (perhaps not to the surprise of all) that no such studies appeared in the *Animal Behaviour* (1977) and *Zeitschrift fur Teirpsychologie* (1976) journals. Two other journals, noted for their neuroscience emphasis, also provided surprising results: *Physiology and Behavior* (1977) published only one such combinative article (by Plotkin's criteria) out of 228 published papers, whereas the *Journal of Comparative and Physiological Psychology* (1977) published 14 such articles in a total of 128. (Apparently comparative physiological psychology lives!) Perhaps this last result is not surprising. Physiological psychology is over 100 years old and comparative in its origins. What is surprising is the suggestion that other neuroscience type journals are not receptive to such studies. (Perhaps Plotkin's analysis should be extended to a broader sample, but informal observations confirm the suggestion.)

Combinative studies of process and function are certainly grist for some future Darwin's mill, but is comparative psychology to be restricted to such studies, valuable as they may be? Almost certainly not! Almost any purely functional study (whether based on an animal model or a physiological one) that can be related to human behavior, is open to interpretation from a comparative viewpoint. Even recondite studies of animal learning must not go unsuspect. If reference can be made to cognitions and/or strategies relating to making a living in the real world, they can supply some grist. The expansion (breakdown?) of animal-learning theory involved consideration of "contextual" elements. The experimental demonstration of the importance of contingency versus contiguity, of correlation versus both contiguity and contingency, and of predictability (i.e., individual control), followed. Other recent developments of cognitive (mediational) flavor, such as the application of game theory to animal interactions and optimality theory to foraging behavior, stem from interest in the ecological analysis of animal behavior. The impact of still other topical areas of research, such as primate communication in laboratory and field, attachment behavior (imprinting) in various forms, and comparative endocrinological behavioral interactions, is equally important in fomenting the changes now taking place in comparative psychology. All such soft comparative psychological studies, which in some way make animal reference to the human condition, are grist for any future Darwin's mill.

The evolution of common solutions to common problems in spite of diverse backgrounds is today a part of comparative psychology's concerns (as it is of animal behavior study in general) not only because generalization from one species, or condition, to another provides the basis for later elucidation of differences (i.e., limitation and differentiation of the generalization), but also because it is now a fact of life. Snowdon (1983) reported *Animal Behaviour* in 1980 and 1981 published a total of 249 papers. Of these, 52 were by authors having clearly identifiable backgrounds and present affiliations in psychology. The point is that those 52 papers involved research on 31 different species. In the same period *Developmental Psychobiology* published 115 papers involving 26 different species (proportionally a greater diversity than exhibited by JCPP in the same period). The first six issues of the recently reborn *Journal of Comparative Psychology* included 60 papers involving 36 different species. Comparative psychologists, as well as others who study animal behavior, must acknowledge the variety of species being studied from a functional or process point of view without immediate reference to an evolutionary context. Such studies relate to differences in the varied capacities (and/or abilities) of animals as they in turn relate to the human condition and therefore, must be recognized as at least "grist for the mill." They offer an opportunity for development of combinative studies combining process and function within an evolutionary context.

Combinative studies may be of at least three sorts; those that emphasize similarity of process (homology?) in relation to similar function, those that emphasize disparity of process (analogy?) and similarity of function, and those that emphasize similarity of process and disparity of function. It does not seem necessary that the "communality of descent" criterion as resolving the issue of homology versus analogy need enter into all combinative studies, although such studies should not be neglected. The finding that blue jays, rhesus monkeys, and chimpanzees show positive transfer from single problem reversal learning to learning set problems, and pigeons, cats, and squirrel monkeys do not, poses interesting questions in an evolutionary context (see Kamil & Yoerg, 1982) as does the finding that marmosets show learning set performance without specific training (Menzel & Juno. 1984).

A sampling of other recent research is indicative of future developments to be expected in comparative psychological and other animal behavioral study (see also Snowdon, 1983; especially pages 73–76 on heritability). Colin Beer's work on the subtleties of communication in gulls (1976, 1982), Emil Menzel's on spatial communication in chimpanzees (1973, 1978), and Lewis Petrinovich and

Luis Baptista's work on song development in white crowned sparrows (1984), all call for revision of fundamental concepts in both ethological and communication theory. We can expect further efforts, such as those of David Premack (1978) and Robert Epstein (Epstein, Lanza, & Skinner, 1980), to differentiate concept formation in pigeons and apes. A resurgence of comparative psychological interst in learning capacities of invertebrate animals, complementing the studies of Kandel, his colleagues, and others interested in the biology of learning and memory, may be heralded by the work of Haralson, Groff, and Haralson (1975), Haralson and Haralson (in press) on sea anenome and that of Hennessey, Rucker, and McDiarmid (1979), on paramecia, in particular.

Including and in addition to research results, more ambitious efforts oriented toward a theoretical reconstruction of comparative psychology within an evolutionary context have been supplied by Herb Roitblatt (1982; representational memory), Fred Masterson and Mary Crawford (1982; defense motivation), Karen Hollis (1982; Pavlovian conditioning), and Timothy Johnston (1982; learning and evolution), Henry Plotkin and F. J. Odling-Smee (1979; learning and teleonomy), and George Collier (Collier, 1982; Collier-Rovee-Collier, 1981; motivation and foraging). Other similar efforts could be listed (see for example the Hulse, Fowler, & Honig, 1978 volume, and the Kamil & Sargent, 1981 volume).

Conclusion

From the point of view of comparative psychology in general, the preceding discussion and citations are only partially indicative of the status of that view of knowledge at present. The view presented (like that of Dewsbury, 1984) is partially objective (one of history) and partially one of advocacy. From a practical (professionally realistic) point of view there is no more important problem for comparative psychologists than to convince their colleagues in psychology of the central importance of studying behavior within an evolutionary context. At the local (academic departmental) level the availability of jobs for comparative psychologists continues to decline (as indicated in periodic surveys of job offerings in the APA Monitor and other relevant sources). However interest in animal behavior amongst undergraduate students and the general population appears not to have slackened in recent years (inclusion of comparative animal behavior study in the introductory course for majors has helped stimulate undergraduate interest at some institutions). Ecological concerns amongst the general public spread to an interest in animal behavior. There is increasing interest (both professional and general) in the need to place comparatively trained psychologists in zoos, aquariums, and other animal conservation settings (the existence of the journal *Zoo Biology*, edited by Terry Maple, attests to the need).

At the national level several signs point to the continued well-being of comparative psychology in general. The traditional APA archival *Journal of Comparative Psychology* reappeared in separate format in March, 1983, under the editorship of Jerry Hirsch (submissions exceeded expectation, additional pages were added in 1984 and 1985, many species have been represented, but fewer field research studies have been submitted than expected).

Comparative psychology is typically well represented in the APA Animal Care Committee (Fred King, J. P. Scott, Gordon Gallup, Don Dewsbury, Evalyn Segal, and Doreen Berman, are all present or past members). A comparative psychologist (Don Dewsbury) is associate editor of the APA book review journal *Contemporary Psychology*. More generally, the APA Division of Physiological and Comparative Psychology (Division 6) has maintained its membership and three comparative psychologists (Bill Mason, Ethel Tobach, and George Collier) have served as president in recent years.

Apart from the APA, psychologists involved in animal behavior research continue to hold approximately 22 to 25% of the membership in the Animal Behavior Society (1983). (In 1983 over 450 members.) Five of the six national ABS Meetings from 1979 through 1984 have been organized by psychologists and their departments. In addition psychologists continue to serve in executive roles in the ABS (e.g., Don Dewsbury, president, 1979).

More generally, Jack Demarest's Comparative Psychology Newsletter hit a responsive chord. Starting with the first, December 1980, issue spontaneous recipients rapidly mounted to over 600 (since a paid subscription has been required the number of recipients has hovered between 300 and 400). Even more generally, a number of edited books emphasizing comparative psychology have appeared in the last 5 years (Bornstein, 1980; Griffin, 1982; Hearst, 1979; Oakley & Plotkin, 1979; Rajecki, 1983). In addition psychologists continue to contribute to the serial volumes, *Advances in the Study of Behavior,* and *Perspectives in Ethology,* both necessarily monitored by researchers in comparative psychology (other edited serials in the last 5 years have included chapters written by comparatively oriented psychologists, but not with the consistency of the two noted).

REFERENCES

Baptista, L. F., & Petrinovich, L. (1984). Social interaction, sensitive phases and the song template hypothesis in the white-crowned sparrow. *Animal Behaviour, 32,* 172–181.

Beer, C. G. (1976). Some complexities in the communication behavior of gulls. In S. R. Harnad, H. D. Steklis, & J. Lancaster (Eds), *Origins and evolution of language and speech* (pp. 413–432). New York: New York Academy of Sciences.

Beer, C. G. (1980). Perspectives on animal behavior comparisons. In M. H. Bornstein (Ed.), *Comparative methods in psychology* (pp. 17–64). Hillsdale, NJ: Lawrence Erlbaum Associates.

Beer, C. G. (1982). Study of vertebrate communication: Its cognitive implications. In D. R. Griffin (Ed.), *Animal mind-human mind* (251–267). Berlin: Springer–Verlag.

Bornstein, M. H. (1980). (Ed.). *Comparative methods in psychology.* Hillsdale, NJ: Lawrence Erlbaum Associates.

Brunswik, E. (1952). The conceptual framework of psychology. *International Encyclopedia of Unified Science, 1*(10), 1–102.

Collier, G. H., & Rovee-Collier, C. K. (1981). A comparative analysis of optimal foraging behavior: Laboratory simulations. In A. C. Kamil & T. D. Sargent (Eds.), *Foraging behavior: Ecological, ethological, and psychological approaches* (pp. 39–76). New York: Garland STPM Press.

Collier, G. H. (1982). Determinants of choice. In D. J. Bernstein (Ed.), *Response structure and organization: Nebraska Symposium on Motivation* (Vol. 29, pp. 69–127). Lincoln: University of Nebraska Press.

Demarest, J. (1983). The ideas of change, progress, and continuity in the comparative psychology of learning. In D. W. Rajecki (Ed.), *Comparing behavior: Studying man studying animals* (pp. 143–180). Hillsdale, NJ: Lawrence Erlbaum Associates.

Dewsbury, D. A. (1984). *Comparative psychology in the twentieth century.* Stroudsburg: Hutchinson Ross.

Epstein, R. R., Lanza, R. P., & Skinner, B. F. (1980). Symbolic communication between two pigeons. (*Columba livia domestica*). *Science, 207,* 543–545.

Gottlieb, G. (1979). Comparative psychology and ethology. In E. Hearst (Ed.), *The first century of experimental psychology* (pp. 147–173). Hillsdale, NJ: Lawrence Erlbaum Associates.

Griffin, D. R. (1982). (Ed.). *Animal mind—human mind.* Berlin: Springer–Verlag.

Haralson, J. V., Groff, C. L., & Haralson, S. J. (1975). Classical conditioning in the sea anenome *Cribrina xanthogrammica. Physiology and Behavior, 15,* 455–460.

Haralson, J. V., & Haralson, S. J. (in press). Habituation and classical conditioning in the sea anemone, *anthopleura xanthogrammica. International Journal of Comparative Psychology.*

Hearst, E. (1979). (Ed.). *The first century of experimental psychology.* Hillsdale, NJ: Lawrence Erlbaum Associates.

Hennessey, T. M., Rucker, W. B., & McDiarmid, C. G. (1979). Classical conditioning in paramecia. *Animal Learning and Behavior, 7,* 417–423.

Hodos, W. (1982). Some perspectives on the evolution of intelligence and the brain. In D. R. Griffin (Ed.), *Animal mind—human mind* (pp. 33–55). Berlin: Springer–Verlag.

Hollis, K. L. (1982). Pavlovian conditioning of signal-centered action patterns and autonomic behavior: A biological analysis of function. In J. S. Rosenblatt, R. A. Hinde, C. Beer, & M. Busnel (Eds.), *Advances in the study of behavior,* (Vol. 12, pp. 1–64). New York: Academic Press.

Hulse, S. H., Fowler, H., & Honig, W. K. (1978). (Eds.). *Cognitive processes in animal behavior.* Hillsdale, NJ: Lawrence Erlbaum Associates.

Johnston, T. D. (1982). Selective costs and benefits in the evolution of learning. In J. S. Rosenblatt, R. A. Hinde, C. Beer, & M. Busnel (Eds.), *Advances in the study of behavior,* (Vol. 12, pp. 65–106). New York: Academic Press.

Kamil, A.C., & Sargent, T. D. (Eds.). (1981). *Foraging behavior: Ecological, ethological, and psychological approaches.* New York: Garland STPM Press.

Kamil, A. C., & Yoerg, S. I. (1982). Learning and foraging behavior. In P. P. G. Bateson & P. H. Klopfer (Eds.), *Perspectives in ethology,* (Vol. 5, pp. 325–364). New York: Plenum.

Masterson, F. A., & Crawford, M. (1982). The defense motivation system: A theory of avoidance behavior. *The Behavioral and Brain Sciences, 5,* 661–696.

Menzel, E. W. (1973). Chimpanzee spatial memory organization. *Science, 182,* 943–945.

Menzel, E. W. (1978). Cognitive mapping in chimpanzees. In S. H. Hulse, H. Fowler, & W. K. Honig, (Eds.), *Cognitive processes in animal behavior* (pp. 375–422). Hillsdale, NJ: Lawrence Erlbaum Associates.

Menzel, E. W., & Juno, C. (1984). Social foraging in marmoset monkeys and the question of intelligence. *Philosophical Transactions of the Royal Society: Series B, 308,* 145–158.

Oakley, D. A., & Plotkin, H. C. (1979). (Eds.). *Brain, behaviour and evolution.* London: Methuen.

Plotkin, H. C. (1979). Brain-behaviour studies and evolutionary biology. In D. A. Oakley & H. C. Plotkin (Eds.), *Brain behaviour and evolution* (pp. 52–77). London: Methuen.

Plotkin, H. C., & F. J. Odling-Smee (1979). In J. S. Rosenblatt, R. A. Hinde, C. Beer, & M.

Busnel (Eds.), *Advances in the study of behavior,* (Vol. 10, pp. 1–42). New York: Academic Press.

Premack, D. (1978). On the abstractness of human concepts: Why it would be difficult to talk to a pigeon. In S. H. Hulse, H. Fowler, & W. K. Honig, (Eds.), *Cognitive processes in animal behavior* (pp. 423–451). Hillsdale, NJ: Lawrence Erlbaum Associates.

Rajecki, D. W. (1983). *Comparing behavior: Studying man studying animals.* Hillsdale, NJ: Lawrence Erlbaum Associates.

Roitblatt, H. L. (1982). The meaning of representation in animal memory. *The Behavioral and Brain Sciences, 5,* 353–406.

Snowdon, C. T. (1983). Ethology, comparative psychology, and animal behavior. *Añual Review of Psychology, 34,* 63–94.

Staddon, J. E. R. (1981). On a possible relation between cultural transmission and genetical evolution. In P. P. G. Bateson & P. H. Klopfer (Eds.), *Perspectives in ethology* (Vol. 4, pp. 135–145). New York: Plenum.

Tolman, E. C. (1932). *Purposive behavior in animals and men.* New York: Century.

13 Historical Bases and Current Status of Comparative Psychology in Japan

Kiyoko Murofushi
Primate Research Institute, Kyoto University, Japan

THE CONTRIBUTION OF K. MASUDA TO THE FOUNDATION OF COMPARATIVE PSYCHOLOGY IN JAPAN

Masuda's interest in animal behavior began when he was an undergraduate student at the Department of Psychology at the University of Tokyo from 1905 to 1908. He was supervised by Yujiro Motora, the first professor of that Department. Although he intended to study the philosophy of cognition at first, he chose psychology as his major field in the University. This choice was motivated by the belief that psychology is fundamental for the study of cognitive function. Although how he got such an idea was not known, Kitaro Nishida, who was the teacher of logic and psychology in his high school and became a very famous philosopher in Japan, may have influenced him. It is known that Masuda visited Nishida to discuss his system in psychology a few years after completing his studies. Why this rather philosophical student began to carry out animal experiments is also a puzzle to me. Perhaps he was influenced by the movements toward animal experimentation in the United States or in Europe.

Masuda was the first psychologist in Japan who carried out experiments on animals in the laboratory. His subjects included protozoa, insects, fish, birds, rats, and human beings. He repeated several of Yerkes' experiments with different species and modified procedures to provide comparative data and to examine his own hypotheses. Masuda was interested, however, not only in animal behavior, but in theoretical issues concerning the comparative study of animal behavior. It was his belief that psychology, as a modern science, should base its conclusions on data obtained through experimentation. Warning against the anecdotal studies on animal behavior, which were very popular in those days, he emphasized that such facts could be useful only to researchers who had learned the methods of scientific observation and precise experimental control. As far as this point is concerned, he strongly supported the views of Lloyd Morgan and E. L. Thorndike. He is well known for his work on the establishment of methods of behavioral measurement. His 1926 publication of *Jikken Shinrigaku Josetsu* (*Introduction to Experimental Psychology*) preceded J. P. Guilford's *Psychometric Methods* by 10 years. *Shinrigaku Kenkyuho* (*Methodology for Psychological studies*) was published in 1931, which was the main part of his PhD thesis.

Masuda's creativity as a theorist is exemplified by some of the work described in his undergraduate thesis. The thesis, "Ishi Sayo no Hikaku Shinrigakuteki Kenkyu" (Comparative Psychology on the Function of the Will) was published in the *Journal of Philosophy* as eight separate papers in 1908 and 1909. Although extensive references were reviewed and logic of each was examined, his main arguments were based on his own experimental data with birds, as illustrated by the following material (1908).

He gave sparrows a small cage in which a dish of grain was placed (a kind of Thorndikian "problem box" adapted by Masuda for his work with sparrows). Because the door of this small cage was hooked, the sparrow had to unhook it directly or pull a string fastened to the hook in order to open the door. After the sparrow learned to enter the cage through the opened door and to eat the grain, the door was hooked. The experiment was run at a fixed time each day after 4 hours' food deprivation. The time required to reach the grain and the qualitative details of the sparrow's behavior were recorded.

He found gradual learning as well as a sudden sharp decrease in time required to reach the goal, the phenomenon referred to by Köhler (1921) as "insight." This is nicely illustrated by the performance of one of his subjects. The time to success was suddenly reduced on the 7th day after a gradual decrease in random movements. Although the time required to reach the food did not change much during the following 2 weeks, the target of the sparrow's responses shifted gradually from the door to the string or hook. When the orientation of the small cage was changed, the sparrow's responses were mostly directed toward the side of cage where the door had been previously found. There was no evidence that the bird associated the string or hook with access to the cage. When the cage was reorientated a third time, however, the bird immediately opened the cage by pulling the string. Further carefully designed tests revealed that, although the bird learned that pulling the string was associated with food, it did not "know" how the door was opened.

From data such as these, Masuda concluded as follows: Learning to open the door depends on trial and error. However, the abrupt improvement in performance frequently observed after a period of gradual change is not as expected by the mosaic associationism of Thorndike's theory (1898). The qualitative data on the bird's responses indicated some structural changes in the bird's perceptual world as suggested by Köhler. These data suggested that learning should be thought of as neither exclusively trial and error or exclusively insight. Rather it is a combination of the two. Masuda (1931), therefore, assumed a continuous process from trial and error to insight in which the probability of success by chance was gradually reduced. He suggested that insightful learning is attained through the trial and error.

According to Masuda in his thesis, comparative psychology, in a narrow sense, is animal psychology as exemplified by the study of the sparrow's behavior. But comparative psychology, in a wide sense, involves individual development as well as phylogenetic variation. His discussion of the comparative study of intelligence illustrates this latter view (1931). He suggested that there is a continuum of the ability to learn along which different species may be compared. There are several stages through which learning progresses from simple motor activity to what appears to be insightful behavior. Each stage must be defined by objective criteria. The abrupt improvement in performance, described as insight, could be evidence of entry into a new stage.

Another difficulty in the comparative study of behavior as pointed out by Masuda was concerned with measurement of general intelligence versus specific ability. For example, in his experiment (1915) goldfish learned black–white discriminations faster than the dancing mice did in Yerkes' (1907) experiment, whereas mice were superior to fish in maze learning. He pointed out that fish's visual ability is better than that of mice, although mice are more sensitive to the positional cues than are fish. Masuda warned that it is not possible to estimate general intelligence from the results of each test for special ability. To overcome these difficulties, his greatest concern was turned toward the theory of psychological measurements.

The importance of Masuda in early Japanese comparative psychology cannot be overemphasized. He clearly defined elementary problems in the comparative study of behavior, provided careful experimental data, and suggested important theoretical concepts.

ESTABLISHMENT OF THE JAPANESE SOCIETY FOR ANIMAL PSYCHOLOGY

In 1933, the Japanese Society for Animal Psychology was founded by a small group of young students in Zoology, and the chief professor at the Department of Zoology at the University of Tokyo, Naohide Tanitsu, was elected as the first president of that Society. About 50 persons joined for the first meeting of the Society in 1936, with the majority of people coming from the field of Zoology. The Society was composed of a group of people interested in the behavior of particular species of animals rather than the comparative study of animal behavior through systematic experimentation. Only gradually did the ideas advanced by Masuda become a part of Japanese animal psychology.

In 1936, *Animal Psychology,* the first book on animal behavior written by a Japanese psychologist, Ryo Kuroda, was published. The management of the Society of Animal Psychology was transferred to the Department of Psychology at the University of Tokyo in 1942. Two years later the first volume of *The Annual of Animal Psychology* was published as the periodical of the Society. Due to unfavorable conditions for research during the last period of the war, the publication of the second volume of this periodical was delayed until 1948.

The experimental approach to the study of animal behavior continued to develop slowly among the psychologists in Japan. At the Department of Psychology at the University of Tokyo, the first learning experiment using white rats was done during the 1930s, and the first experiment with monkeys was conducted in 1942. At Keio Gijuku University, studies of operant conditioning with pigeons were started in 1919. Most of these studies were concerned with problems of discrimination and were strongly influenced by Behaviorism from the United States. By 1970 learning experiments grew to be the main body of research with which the Society of Animal Psychology was concerned.

Figure 13.1 shows classes of animals used as subjects in the studies published in *The Annual of Animal Psychology.* The ordinate indicates the percentage of animals included in each class and the abscissa represents chronological years. Insects and birds, which were mostly used in the first volume, were quickly replaced by mammals in the early 1950s. Today most of research is being done with mammals. These figures originally appeared in T. Okano's paper, "*A Short History of the Japanese Society for Animal Psychology*" (1978). The data for the years 1976 to 1982 were added by the author. Figure 13.2 shows which species were included under the category, mammal, in Figure 13.1. From 1944 to the present, rats and mice continue to be the most frequent subjects of study. The use of monkeys increased particularly in 1975. Figure 13.2 does not reflect the full scope of this work, because many of these papers were published in *Primates.*

Figure 13.3 shows the classification of topics in the papers presented at the Meetings of the Japanese Society for Animal Psychology. Most papers before 1975 were divided into two areas, learning and physiological psychology. In adding recent data to Okano's figure it was necessary for the present author to introduce a new category. The category, called "animal behavior," in Figure 13.3, consists of studies that do not fall into any of the categories used by Okano. The new category of "animal behavior" includes feeding, social behavior, and perception. Many of these studies were done in natural or seminatural situations. Studies on animal behavior are now as prevalent as studies in the areas of learning or physiological psychology. This new interest in the study of animal behavior probably reflects an influence of ethology on one hand, and a development of primate research on the other.

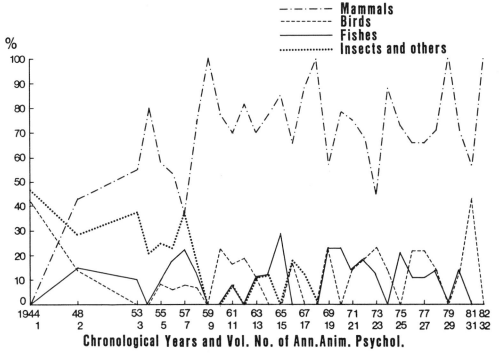

FIGURE 13.1. Classification of animals used in the studies published in *The Annual of Animal Psychology* Recent data were added to the original figure from Okano, T. (1978).

DEVELOPMENT OF PRIMATE RESEARCH AND RECENT NEW MOVEMENTS

The field study of nonhuman primates was begun in 1948 by Kinji Imanishi and his students at the Department of Zoology of Kyoto University. These field studies of Japanese monkeys differed from studies in other countries by the use of provisioned troops and individual identification. A few years later, a group of medical researchers of Tokyo University began to use monkeys as experimental subjects for medical research. Those two groups of researchers joined to establish the Japan Monkey Centre under the sponsorship by Meitetsu Railroad Company in 1956. At that time, a group of psychologists from Osaka University who were interested in ethological studies developed a field station at Katsuyama for the study of Japanese monkeys. The Japan Monkey Centre organized the Primate Research Society, which holds annual meeting. They also publish a journal, *Primates*. These activities, sponsored by the Japan Monkey Centre, greatly

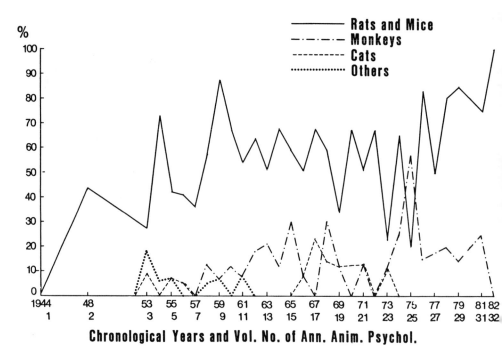

%

———— **Rats and Mice**
—·——·— **Monkeys**
---------- **Cats**
·················· **Others**

Chronological Years and Vol. No. of Ann. Anim. Psychol.

FIGURE 13.2. Species included in the mammals in the Fig. 13.1. Recent data were added to the original figure from T. Okano, (1978). The variability reflects the small number of articles on which these data are based.

promoted primate studies in the various research areas of Japan. Thus, in 1967, the primate Research Institute of Kyoto University was founded by the government. It serves as a center for researchers in primatology and, among other things, is providing basic data for comparative studies of animal behavior.

Papers presented at the Meeting of the Primate Research Society after the 1970s were classified into the five different areas. The percentage of papers included in each area is shown in Figure 13.4. The behavioral area continues to grow in importance. In terms of number of papers, behavioral research has become as important as the previously dominant areas of ecology and physiology.

Finally, the Japan Ethological Society was founded in 1982. At present only 3% of the current members are psychologists. On the other hand, only a small number of zoologists can be found in the Japanese Society for Animal Psychology. Probably, however, the interaction between researchers in ethology and animal psychology is deeper than suggested by these quantitative data.

At the beginning of this century Masuda looked toward animal psychology as

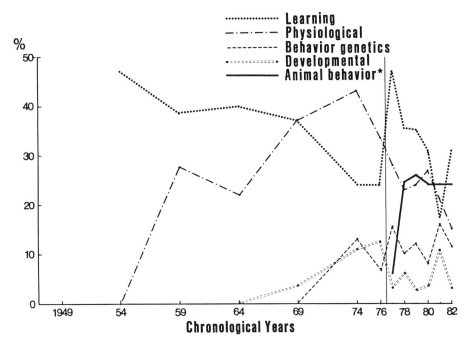

FIGURE 13.3. Topics in the papers presented at the Meeting of the Japanese Society for Animal Psychology (*Behavioral studies un-classified by above categories, including social behavior, feeding, and perception). Recent data were added to the original figure from Okano, T. (1978).

a means of solving problems concerning the nature and evolution of intelligence. These questions still are of concern to comparative psychologists as are the methodological problems with which be struggled. Although, at present, very little work is being done in psychology of Japan with animals other than mammals, comparative issues are of concern to Japanese animal psychologists. This is exemplified by recent work on foraging, species specific constraints on learning, and work on comparative and developmental issues in cognition.

SUMMARY

This chapter reviews briefly the historical bases and current status of comparative psychology in Japan. In the first part of the chapter, some early works by Koremochi Masuda (1883–1933), who is considered to be the pioneer of comparative psychology in Japan, were introduced. Next, the establishment of the Japanese Society for Animal Psychology and its development were described.

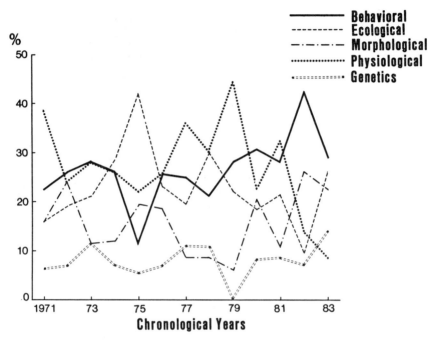

FIGURE 13.4. Topics in the papers presented at the Meeting of the Primate Research Society.

Then, in the third part of this chapter, new movements influenced by studies of primate behavior and current developments in Ethology were discussed. Those new trends might be an indication of renewal of interest in comparative psychology. It seems to me, however, that we are still groping toward the establishment of an appropriate methodology for the comparison of behaviors among different species—the task attempted by K. Masuda about 75 years ago at the starting point of comparative psychology in Japan.

ACKNOWLEDGMENT

I am grateful to Dr. T. Okano for his 1978 paper that furnished information on the fundation of the Japanese Society for Animal Psychology and the data presented in the second part of this chapter.

REFERENCES

Köhler, W. (1921). *Intelligenzprüfungen an Menschenaffen*. (2. Aufl.). Berlin: J. Springer.
Kuroda, R. (1936). *"Dobutsu Shinrigaku"* (*Animal Psychology*), Sansho-do.

Masuda, K. (1908). "Ishi Sayo no Hikaku Shinrigakuteki Kenkyu" (Comparative Psychology on the Function of the will), 1–4. *Tetsugaku Zasshi (Journal of Philosophy)*, *23*, 950–970; 1029–1070; 1139–1176; 1270–1302.

Masuda, K. (1909). "Ishi Sayo no Shinrigakuteki Kenkyu" (Comparative Psychology on the Function of the Will), 5–8. *op. cit. 24*, 36–60; 239–262; 352–374; 552–588.

Masuda, K. (1915). "Gyorui no Gakusyu no Jikken" (Experiments on the learning in fishes), 1–5, *Shinri Kenkyu* (Study of Psychology), *7*, 160–171; 336–343; 544–555; 771–778, *8*, 454–460.

Masuda, K. (1926). *"Jikken Shinrigaku Josetsu"* (*Introduction to Experimental Psychology*), Shibun-do.

Masuda, K. (1931). *"Shinrigaku Kenkyuho"* (*Methodology for Psychological studies*), Iwanami-koza, Kyoiku Kagaku, Vol. 2.

Okano, T. (1978). "Nihon Dobutsu Shinri Gakkai Shoshi" (A short History of the Japanese Society for Animal Psychology), *Reports of the Faculty of Liberal Arts, Shizuoka University*, (*Humanities*), No. 14, 141–151.

Thorndike, E. L. (1898). Animal intelligence. *Psychol. Review, Monograph Supplement;* Some experiments on animal intelligence. *Science, 7,* 818–826.

Yerkes, R. M. (1907). *The dancing mouse.*

14 THE COMPARATIVE PSYCHOLOGY OF A. N. LEONTYEV (U.S.S.R.)

Charles W. Tolman
University of Victoria, Canada

The status of comparative psychology as a discipline has been plagued with doubts and uncertainties for a very long time. These have often been brought to the surface by external attack, most seriously in recent years from sociobiology. This particular attack has been so serious in fact that some comparative psychologists have capitulated, proclaiming the final demise of their own discipline. Others are resisting or attempting to find a living accommodation with the source of the threat. A less dramatic response has been simply to give up the label of "comparative psychology" and proceed as before under some less committing rubric.

Of course no one is questioning the need to study animal behavior. The problem is rather whether there is a legitimate and distinct psychological need to study it. In my opinion it is the inability to give a clear and unequivocal answer to the question of psychological interest that has made comparative psychology so vulnerable to reductionist attacks.

At the heart of the difficulty is the absence in comparative psychology of a clear theoretical foundation, of any clear idea of what the similarities and differences among species will mean once they are discovered and described. Most important, the theory is lacking that can justify a uniquely psychological interest in the enterprise.

Successful theory in comparative psychology must fulfill at least two essential requirements. First, it will have to clarify in an empirically correct and logically coherent way the object of comparative psychological investigation. We expect that the object will be one that is unambiguously psychological and not one that begs for biological reduction. Second, adequate comparative psychological theory must include an account of its object's evolution. Comparative psychology has traditionally been weak in its understanding and use of evolutionary theory.

I am suggesting that the crisis in comparative psychology is a theoretical one, one that will require some fundamental changes in our thinking in order to attain a solution.

As an alternative approach to the tasks of comparative psychology, I would like here to present some highlights of the theoretical work of Alexei Nikolaevich Leontyev, which I believe meets the aforementioned requirements and goes a long way toward solving the theoretical problems comparative psychologists have struggled with over the years.

Leontyev was a student and colleague of L. S. Vygotsky in the late 1920s and 1930s. After Vygotsky's death, Leontyev became the principal theoretical contributor within the Vygotskian social-historical school. The position that emerged from his work, known as "activity theory," has become the dominant trend in Soviet psychology, and has, in the last 10 years, begun to exert a considerable influence in continental European—particularly German—psychology (e.g., Holzkamp, 1978; Schurig, 1976). At the time of his death in 1979, Leontyev was Dean of the Psychology Faculty at Moscow State University and a member of the USSR Academy of Pedagogical Sciences. Foreign honors included an honorary doctorate from the University of Paris in 1968 and an honorary membership in the Hungarian Academy of Sciences in 1973.

Leontyev's two main books have only recently been translated into English. By far the most important and influential of these is *Problems of the Development of the Mind* (1959, 1981). It is also this book that contains the material of greatest interest to comparative psychologists.

The concept of activity was put forward in opposition to the traditional focal concepts of mental process and behavior. Comparative psychologists will have little difficulty with the rejection of mental process, but the rejection of behavior requires closer attention. There are several lines of argument here. I mention only two. First, the concept of behavior is impossible to distinguish from mere movement or change. It is impossible to distinguish between the behavior of a liver and that of an organism. The concept of behavior is inherently reductionistic, recognizing no qualitative discontinuity between the firing of a neuron and discussing politics. According to Leontyev and his colleagues there is a qualitative distinctness of the activity of conscious living human beings that must be recognized.

A second line of argument is that the concept of behavior is too mechanical or abstract. It reflects an erroneous way of thinking—already criticized by John Dewey in 1896—which assumes an external influence leading directly to a response. What this ignores, according to both Dewey and Leontyev (1979), is "the process that *active* subjects use to form real connections with the world of objects" (p. 42). The problem is not solved by the introduction of motivation or other intervening variables because such accounts apply equally well to inanimate, i.e., obviously nonpsychic entities.

The only solution is to broaden our conception of what it is we are studying in psychology. This is what the concept of activity is intended to do. It moves us from the problematic mechanical mode of thought to a "systems" mode. Leontyev (1979) comments: Activity is "a system with its own structure, its own internal transformations, its own development" (p. 46). Activity includes behavior, but concretely within the "process that active subjects use to form real connections with the world of objects." As such it also includes the object of activity. It can be thought of, roughly, as a kind of dynamic envelope enclosing both subject and object. Leontyev (1979) refers to it as a "molar unit of life" (p. 46); see also Galperin, 1980).

The theory of activity is too complex to receive a comprehensive treatment here, but it is useful to mention its structural aspect, which is perhaps best illustrated by an example. A "beater" engaged in a primitive collective hunt is motivated by a need for food. Hunting is his activity that is directed at food. Food is the motive of the activity. But what he does in the hunt is frighten the animals, sending them toward other hunters who are waiting in ambush. The immediate goal of his actions does not coincide with the motive of his activity. Furthermore the particular operations he performs in achieving his goal may differ depending on the situation or conditions of the hunt.

We see here a three-leveled hierarchical structure in which the largest unit is the activity governed by its motive. This subsumes actions governed by distinct and separate goals, which in our example are shared socially. Each action then subsumes various operations, which are governed by specific conditions.

An important aspect of activity and its structural compents is reflection. An activity reflects its motive, an action reflects its goal, and an operation reflects the conditions of action. The concept of reflection, as we will see, becomes very important in the evolutionary account.

Before proceeding to that account, however, we must ask the question about what evolves. Much the same reasons advanced for rejecting behavior as the object of psychological investigation lead Leontyev also to reject the view that it is behavior that evolves. Behavior becomes more complex, more wide ranging in its adaptivity, etc., but this cannot be the result of the evolution of behavior as such, which would imply a highly problematic, and probably incorrect, direct relation between genes and behavior. Behavior is far too abstract, in the sense used previously, to have been the principal focus of the evolutionary process.

An alternative and almost traditional view in comparative psychology has been that it is intelligence that evolves—usually implying the rise of learning in opposition to instinct. This is also rejected by Leontyev (1981). He argues, in a manner that has become familiar in our own literature, that there is neither empirical nor theoretical "foundation for counter-posing, as different genetic stages of behaviour; (a) inherited behaviour, allegedly unalterable by external influences, and (b) behaviour built up in the course of an animal's individual development, in the course of its individual adaptation'' (p. 169). He cites experiments conducted by Blees (1919), himself, and his Soviet colleagues (between 1933 and 1943) which show that even the rigid phototropism of *Daphnia* is adaptively modifiable. With Pavlov, he claims that ''individual adaptation exists throughout the animal world.''

If it is not behavior as such, not intelligence, adaptability, or the like that evolves, then what? According to Leontyev it is the control and organization of activity. It is the process we spoke of earlier that evolves. Leontyev called it ''psyche'' or ''mind.'' This is best explained by looking at the evolutionary account itself.

There are two major stages, the psychic and the prepsychic. It is useful to look briefly at the prepsychic. Leontyev maintains that all material existence is characterized by reciprocal action or exchange of substances. Typical of this is the inorganic chemical reaction, e.g.,: $Zn + H_2SO_4 = ZnSO_4 + H_2$. Characteristic of such an inorganic interaction is that neither interacting substance is preserved in its original form. Either is preserved only by not interacting.

The transition to living, organic matter is the transition to a state of affairs in which one body, the organic one, is preserved in the interaction and depends on the interaction for its preservation. The interaction now takes the form of assimilation and metabolism by the organic body.

Both inorganic and organic interactions represent primitive forms of reflection. In each case one body or substance responds to the precise properties of the other. This is the case in the organic instance in which the organic body fulfills the role of subject to the object of the other. In order for the organic, living body to assimilate its object, it must reflect, i.e., respond appropriately to, the properties of the object. This stage of organic, prepsychic existence is designated by Leontyev as the stage of irritability.

The most primitive stage of psychic existence, which Leontyev calls the stage of elementary sensory psyche, evolves through a complication of irritability. This complication consists in the development of response to properties that are not those on which the the organism's life directly depends. Leontyev (1981) comments: Activity thus becomes ''governed, consequently, not by the affecting properties in themselves but rather by them in their relation[1] with other properties'' (p. 156). Daphnia respond to light, for example, not because they need light as such, but because light is related to substances that they do need and can assimilate.

Leontyev (1981) defines sensitivity, the identifying characteristic of this evolutionary stage, in the following way: ''sensitivity is genetically nothing other then irritability in relation to that kind of environmental influence that brings the

---

[1]But not relations as such as at the ''intellect'' stage.

organism into correlation with other influences, i.e., that orients it in the environment by performing a signalling function. The necessity for the rise of this form of irritability is that it mediates the organism's main vital processes that are now taking place in more complicated conditions of the environment'' (p. 42).

Once again reflection is stressed: The processes of sensitivity "must necessarily . . . conform to the objective properties of the environment and correctly reflect them in appropriate connections'' (p. 42).

At the stage of the elementary sensory psyche the animal's activity is governed by properties of things. The subsequent stage, which Leontyev calls the stage of perceptive psyche, arises out of complications that result in the reflection of things. This is associated with the development of an integrative nervous system, of the distance sense organs—particularly those of vision—, and of the organs of external movement.

The discrimination of things, associated with the formation of images, allows two very important developments. The first is the discrimination of the object of activity from its conditions. This, in turn, allows the development of the component of activity earlier referred to as operation. An animal will, for example, approach food in one way or another depending on conditions, e.g., presence or absence of a barrier. At the sensory stage a barrier becomes incorporated into the activity such that its removal does not immediately alter the approach behavior. Thus at the perceptual stage the animal is capable of developing a repertoire of fixed operations, which may be called habits, serving any particular activity.

The second important related development is the appearance of image memory. Both habits and image memory represent an advance in the mnemonic function made possible by the change from control of activity by properties to control of activity by things.

Again the reflective aspect must be stressed. The evolutionary advance is clearly one of increasing reflective capacity. The animal's activity becomes organized around more and more detailed, differentiated information in its environment. In a very real sense the movement in the evolutionary process is toward ever greater objectivity.

The third stage of the evolution of psyche is one Leontyev calls stage of animal intellect. It arises again through complication of characteristics present in the previous stage. It is best exemplified by the problem-solving behavior of Köhler's apes, which demonstrated ability, as Leontyev put it, to solve two-phase tasks (1981, p. 185). All Köhler's problems required the animals to do one thing (such as pick up a stick) in order to do another (such as obtain food). The activity is at all times organized around the food, but it now incorporates an action (at least in a primitive form) with a goal that is not naturally related to the food. To accomplish this, the animal's activity must be governed not only by properties and things, but by relations among things.

With this, the middle level of the structure of activity emerges. Activity is no longer structurally undifferentiated, nor is it restricted to differentiation consisting merely of different operations or modes of accomplishing its end. It is now a complex of distinct actions, all organized around the motive of activity and all subject to variations of operations depending on conditions but directed at specific distinct goals. An important characteristic of actions is that they attain a degree of independence such that they are detachable from particular activities and become available for others. This is evident when animals at this stage are placed in a new and puzzling situation. Instead of flying about at random like a chicken, an ape will appear to try different approaches to the problem. These approaches are of course detached actions developed within other activities.

It is obvious that with the evolution of a capacity to reflect relations of things, the animal is not only increasing its apprehension of objective reality, it is also substantially increasing its capacity to deal with that reality abstractly. This stage lays the foundation for human thought.

The fourth stage of the evolution of psyche is the stage of human consciousness. The principal characteristic of this stage is given by an extraordinary development of the capacity to abstract and deal with abstractions. In terms of the progressive order of what governs activity, we have moved from properties to things, to relations of things, and now to meanings of things requiring a high development of image memory, habit, etc.

This advance is best illustrated in collective labor. Here actions are socially exarticulated such that no single individual completes the entire series of actions making up an activity. Rather the actions are divided among different individuals, the unity of activity now being given only in social organization. It is this exarticulation of actions that allows not only the use of tools, but the preparation of tools for use at some indefinite time in the future. Leontyev (1981) stated:

> The separation of an action necessarily presupposes the possibility of the active subject's psychic reflection of the relation between the objective motive and the object of the action . . . but the relation underlying this link is no longer a natural one, but a social one. (p. 213)
>
> For a man to take on the function of a beater (in a primitive hunt) it is necessary for his actions to have a relation; that connects their result with the outcome of the collective activity; it is necessary for this relation to be subjectively reflected by him so that it becomes 'existent for him'; it is necessary in other words for the *sense* of his action to be revealed to him, to be comprehended by him. Consciousness of the sense of an action . . . comes about in the form of reflection of its object as a conscious goal. (pp. 212–213)

Leontyev proceeds from this basis to develop a comprehensive theory of the origin of thought and language. For our purposes here it is sufficient to see that he has laid the foundation for such a theory, a psychological theory, and that his foundation is an explicitly evolutionary, comparative one.

What are some of the implications of this theory for the discipline of comparative psychology? I mention two.

First, a variety of tasks is immediately apparent and can be expressed in questions such as the following:

1. What are the precise characteristics of sensitivity, perceptivity, and intellect?

2. What are the characteristics of the complications that lead from one stage to the next?

3. How are stages preserved, how do they overlap and interact within a particular species?

4. How are these capacities affected by conditions of ontogenetic development?

Numerous questions beyond these suggest themselves. Leontyev's work illustrates very well that a good evolutionary theory can be richly heuristic.

A second, and very important, implication is that a comparative psychology guided by such a theory would be unequivocally a psychology. Its motive—to borrow a term from the theory—is to elucidate the conscious human psyche. The processes and capacities that it studies are all stages and transitions in the evolutionary development of the human psyche. As such, there should be no confusion between its task and those of the biological disciplines. Not only would confusion be avoided, but so, too, would the threat of reductive cannibalization by sociobiology or any other discipline with imperialistic ambitions. The overall task of comparative psychology could in fact be described as discovering how human psyche evolves from, and is continuous with, more primitive biological processes, while simultaneously specifying how the more advanced processes are qualitatively discontinuous with the older, and thus understandable in terms of but not reducible to them.

The prospects of a comparative psychology guided by a theory such as Leontyev's seems to me very exciting indeed.

REFERENCES

Galperin, P. (1980). *Zu Grundfragen der Psychologie.* Berlin: Volk und Wissen.

Holzkamp, K. (1978). *Sinnliche Erkenntnis: Historischer Ursprung und gesellschaftliche Function der Wahrnehmung.* (4. Aufl.) Frankfurt/M.: Athenäum Verlag.

Leontyev, A. N. (1979). The problem of activity in psychology. In J. V. Wertsch (Ed.), *The concept of activity in sovet psychology.* Armonk, NY: Sharpe.

Leontyev, A. N. (1981). *Problems of the development of the mind.* Moscow: Progress.

Schurig, V. (1976). *Die Entstehung des Bewusstseins.* Frankfurt/M.: Campus Verlag.

15 Current Status of Comparative Psychology in Italy

G. Fiorito

Neurobiology Department, Stazione Zoologica, Naples, Italy

An analysis of the role of theory in determining the status of comparative psychology in Italy is a complicated task. Many aspects of the history of comparative psychology appear to be particular to Italy and to be derived from a tendency to resist debate. I now describe the situation briefly.

Above all, animal behavior has always been of interest to many people in Italy. However, the popular presentation of animal behavior is frequently inaccurate. In recent years, there has been a tendency toward a more precise presentation of research developed in Italy and elsewhere. This has improved the quality and quantity of interest in such topics. However, this interest is independent of the fact that there are very few training programs in animal behavior. In fact, there are only a few institutions in which courses in animal behavior are taught. In some institutions, where there are research groups in animal behavior, there are no courses in animal behavior.

Without a doubt, zoology courses include sections on animal behavior; however, in only a few cases are students introduced to theoretical issues in the study of animal behavior. The following data demonstrates the possibility that in Italy the fashion for ethology in teaching institutions hinders the possibility of awareness of current theoretical debates and thus affects our study of behavioral phenomena.

A questionnaire (Appendix A) was sent to the institutes (departments) of zoology, psychology, and general biology of 10 Italian universities. I received answers from 25% of the people at these institutions who where sent questionnaires. Of these, only 7% expressed an interest in the theory of research of comparative psychology. Table 15.1 shows the types of departments written to and the answers received. The responses to the questionnaire (Table 15.2) and

211

TABLE 15.1
Types of Departments Written to and Answers Received

Departments	Universities	Answers
Istituto di Zoologia	PISA	
Istituto di Biologia Generale	PISA	
Istituto di Zoologia	FIRENZE	
Istituto di Zoologia	MILANO	+
Istituto di Psicologia	MILANO	+
Istituto di Zoologia	NAPOLI	
Istituto di Biologia & Zoologia	MILANO	+
Istituto di Zoologia	ROMA	
Istituto di Psicologia	ROMA	
Istituto di Zoologia	PARMA	
Istituto di Psicologia	PARMA	+
Istituto di Zoologia	BOLOGNA	
Istituto di Zoologia	GENOVA	
Istituto di Zoologia Sistematica	TORINO	
Istituto di Zoologia	TORINO	+
Istituto Psicologia Sper.	TORINO	
Istituto di Psicologia	TORINO	
Istituto di Psicologia	PADOVA	
Istituto di Psicologia	NAPOLI	
Istituto Psicologia at Magistero	NAPOLI	
Istituto Biologia Animale	PADOVA	
Istituto di Psicobiologia CNR	ROMA	
Dipartimento di Ecologia	RENDE	+
Dipartimento Sc. Comportamento	RENDE	
Istituto Psicologia at Magistero	SALERNO	
Cattedra Psichiatria	ROMA	
Istituto di Psicologia	BOLOGNA	+
Istituto di Psicologia	VERONA	

Note: 28 questionnaires written and 7 answers received.

additional personal interviews with 10 persons representing institutions and departments that did not receive the original questionnaire create an impression that most of those queried lack information about comparative psychology.

Perhaps the following statements by Danilo Mainardi (1977), a foremost leader of ethology in Italy, best present the dominant thinking in Italy today: "the activity of Schneirla and his students developed an important balancing role between two different positions: European ethology and behaviorism in United States" (p. 22).

Does it appear that *comparative psychology* in Italy is a term resulting from the simple and musty addition of two categories, comparative method and classical psychology?

In some psychology courses, students are taught that comparative psychology is not very different from ethology. In other words, comparative psychology is considered the comparison of the behavior of different species, or ethology. After Hinde's mediation between comparative psychology and ethology, with the modern ethology, and moreover after the publication of Wilson's book (1975), the synthesis between those two schools appear to be essentially complete. But, is it also true for Italy?

In answer to the questionnaire and interviews, of the people who are interested in comparative psychology, seven identified themselves with ethology in England, four identified themselves with European neuroethology, and three with comparative psychology in the United States. Some of the people working in neuroethology identified themselves with English ethology rather than European neuroethology.

It is not a problem of labels or definitions, as some believe. One might ask why many books on ethology and sociobiology are translated in Italian. Wilson's book (1975), for example, was translated and published in Italy only 4 years after it appeared in the United States. On the other hand, few of the critics of ethology and sociobiology have been translated or published in Italy; neither have major contributions in comparative psychology. As a result, many researchers do not know the basic literature in comparative psychology.

I believe that aforementioned presents a problem for the scientific community in Italy. As many have indicated in their critiques of ethological and sociobiological approaches, the study of the evolution of behavior has great significance for society (Tobach, 1976). The debate about these theoretical issues should be stimulated in Italy and the new generation of students should be informed through courses, workshops, and literature.

TABLE 15.2
Responses to the Questionnaire

Answers Received From

Istituto di Zoologia—MILANO	lack information
Istituto di Psicologia—MILANO	interested
Istituto Biologia & Zoologia—MILANO	lack information
Istituto di Psicologia—PARMA	interested
Istituto di Zoologia—TORINO	no interest
Dipartimento di Ecologia—RENDE	CP=ethology
Istituto di Psicologia—BOLOGNA	no interest

Note: 28 questionnaires sent, 7 answers received, 2 answers of interest in Comparative Psychology.

REFERENCES

Mainardi, D. (1977). Intervista sull'etologia, Bari.

Tobach, E. (1976). Behavioral science and genetic destiny: Implications for education, therapy, and behavioral research. In E. Tobach & H. M. Proshansky (Eds.), *Genetic destiny* (pp. 142–158). New York: Academic Press.

Wilson, E. O. (1975). *Sociobiology. The new synthesis,* Cambridge.

APPENDIX A QUESTIONNAIRE

INTERNATIONAL SOCIETY FOR COMPARATIVE PSYCHOLOGY
Questionnaire August 25, 1983

Name:
Institution:
Institutional address:
Home address:
Institutional phone: Home phone:
. . . .
Research interests:

Theoretical interests:

How do you define Comparative Psychology?

Are your experimental and theoretical activities in Comparative
Psychology?   YES   NO

Please describe these briefly, whether your answer is Yes or No.

Does your University give courses in Comparative Psychology?
Does your University give courses in Ethology?
Do you know of other schools which give such courses? Please list.
Do you distinguish among Animal Behavior, Comparative Psychology and
Ethology?

Are you interested in joining the I.S.C.P.?

Date:

Thank you for your cooperation.

Graziano Fiorito
Operations Committee
International Society for Comparative Psychology
Stazione Zoologica, 80121 Napoli, Italy

16 Comparative Psychology in the Netherlands[1]

A. Nijssen
M. J. van Rijswijk
University of Amsterdam, The Netherlands

INTRODUCTION

Comparative psychology is the scientific discipline that deals with the evolution and development of behavior. Specifically, it attempts to answer questions about behavioral mechanisms and the ontogeny of individual behavior. It does this by comparing all animal species, including the human species.

The status of comparative psychology has become problematic in the last decade for many reasons, not the least of which is the emergence of sociobiology. Sociobiological premises are contradicted, in our view, by alternative hypotheses and data presented by comparative psychology. Some of the new topics in comparative psychology are:

1. The effect of social behavior on physiological function.

2. The role of coalitions and reconciliation in the aggressive behavior involved in dominance.

3. Linguistic and psycholinguistic approaches to animal communication.

There are many applications of comparative psychology to human well being. Snowdon recently (1983) surveyed areas in which the study of animal behavior has made important contributions.

---

[1]This article appeared in a slightly different form in "Universiteit en Hogeschool", XXIX, 329–333.

1. The variability of behavior. Documentation of the variability of behavior among animals is valuable for the understanding of human behavior and for attempts to alter it. As an example, Snowdon cites the differences in maternal behavior among certain species of monkeys that have given us testable hypotheses about human behavior.

2. Animal models can be used to study disturbances in human behavior; specifically, these can be used to investigate depression. This application is especially important when human experiments are not possible for ethical or technical reasons.

3. The application of ethological techniques in the study of human behavior; play and aggressive behavior in children; nonverbal communication among adults; social behavior within and between groups.

4. Protection and breeding of endangered species. In order to do this, it is important to know their behavior. (See, for instance, the behavioral studies of rhesus monkeys and chimpanzees in behalf of medical research at the Primate Center of the Organization for Applied Natural Science in Rijswijk, The Netherlands.)

5. Care of pets and the use of pets as "therapists" for people. Psychiatric patients who were given pets showed more nonverbal and verbal responses, first to the animals and later to staff and patients.

6. Work animals, for instance, watchdogs.

Although the applications and potential applications in many areas are quite impressive, comparative psychology in the Netherlands is threatened with extinction, just as in the U.S.A. According to a survey of the members of the American Psychological Association as to the status of comparative psychology, it seemed that comparative psychology was going through an identity crisis in the U.S.A. (Demarest, 1980). The source of the crisis was the lack of consistency in the various conceptualizations of comparative psychology. To evaluate the status of the field in our country a similar survey was conducted. As there is, however, only minimal interest for this field among psychologists in the Netherlands, it seemed more reasonably to conduct such a survey among all people studying animal behavior, rather than only those in comparative psychology. Thus, most of our respondents were trained in biology and differed in this respect from those of the Demarest survey who were all psychologists and members of the APA.

Almost all these investigators in the Netherlands are affiliated with at least one of the next three scientific communities: the Society for Comparative and Physiological Psychology of the Netherlands Psychonomic Foundation; the Ethology Division of the Foundation for Fundamental Biological Research (BION); the Brain and Behaviour Division of the Foundation for Medical Research (FUNGO). All three are subsidized by the Netherlands Organization for Advancement of Pure Research.

THE SURVEY AND ITS RESULTS

Of the 147 questionnaires sent out, 73, or 51% were returned and completely or almost completely answered, and 5 came back very incompletely answered. These 5 we used only to determine the profession of the respondents. The respondents were trained in the following disciplines: biology: 45; psychology: 18; medicine: 5; zootechnology and agricultural ethology: 4; biochemistry: 2; law: 1. One respondent came from a college of agriculture, and two did not list their training speciality.

The areas of research described were as follows: animal behavior; learning and motivation in animals; behavioral biology; behavioral genetics; neuropsychology; comparative psychology; physiological psychology; psychopharmacology; ethology; psychophysiology; behavioral physiology; neuroethology; ecoethology, and behavioral ecology.

Almost half of the biologists called themselves ethologists or researchers in animal behavior; 11 people listed their areas as physiological psychology, psychopharmacology, psychophysiology, behavioral physiology, and neuroethology. The remainder of the biologically trained researchers worked in the areas of learning and motivation in animals, behavioral biology, behavior genetics, and behavioral ecology. Of the 18 psychologists, 10 were more or less physiologically oriented and the other psychologists listed their areas as animal behavior, learning and motivation in animals, behavior genetics, and ethology. Only 2 psychologists called themselves comparative psychologists, the present writers not included. The four physicians listed behavioral biology, behavioral genetics, behavioral physiology or neuroethology. Those who completed their studies in the Agricultural University Wageningen mentioned ethology and animal behavior. The person who had studies law specified ethology as the field of work.

The survey also contained the following question:

Which of the following four descriptions of comparative psychology most closely agree with the respondent's? (The descriptions were taken from the following writers.)

1. Comparative psychologists investigate two fundamental questions: Which method has to be used to investigate how an animal behaves; and, how can we investigate consciousness (after Washburn, 1917).

2. Comparative psychology compares behavior that is demonstrated by different species, including humans. The main purpose is to reach or formulate general laws of behavior (after Beach, 1950).

3. Comparative psychology studies similarities and differences of adaptation to the environment and the behavioral organization of species of all phyletic levels, of individual acts and the integration of behavior within groups. The backbone of comparative psychology is the ontogeny of behavior (after Schneirla, 1966).

4. There are four fundamental areas in the study of behavior. There are problems of development; of immediate causation or mechanism; evolutionary history; and adaptive meaning (after Dewsbury, 1973).

The majority of the respondents preferred descriptions 2, 3, or 4, which, as a matter of fact, do not exclude each other. In 3 and 4, the comparative aspect comes to the fore; in 2, on the other hand, the search for nonspecies-specific behavior is evident.

We also asked the respondents to indicate whether they agreed with the following statements:

1. Comparative psychology and physiological psychology are two separate areas of research or two separate approaches.

The opinions expressed were quite diverse: 26 agreed, 33 not agreed, 14 had no opinion or did not answer this item. It appears to us that this is based on a conceptual confusion. In physiological psychology people study physiological processes, which are one of the categories of behavioral determinants, for their own sake; comparative psychology on the other hand, is concerned with all possible determinants, not only physiological ones.

2. Comparative psychology is important to psychology in general as well as to biology and medicine.

The majority of the respondents, whether they stressed evolutionary aspects or general laws of behavior, agreed strongly that comparative psychology was important to psychology in general, as well as to biology and medicine. It is remarkable that researchers other than psychologists had such a positive opinion about what psychologists could contribute to other scientific disciplines.

3. Comparative psychology should occupy a central position in the education of psychologists.

Thirty respondents agreed with this statement and 7 did not. In other words, most of the investigators of some aspect of animal behavior consider their own discipline important for the training of psychologists. We did not examine the curricula of the various training programs systematically, but the general impression is that there are very few instances in which comparative and physiological psychology are obligatory taught by a psychological faculty. The Subfaculty of Psychology of the University of Amsterdam has dropped physiology (3 credits) as a requirement for psychology students. In addition, even the modest request for support for research in comparative psychology are being scrapped now.

We asked the respondents to chose synonyms for comparative psychology in the following list (the number of choices is set in parentheses after the names; more than one choice was possible): animal behavior (19); behavioral biology (17); behavioral ecology (4); biopsychology (12); biosociology (6); ethology (9); psychobiology (13); sociobiology (3).

Seventeen of the respondents were of the opinion that none of these words could be considered synonyms. Remarkably few, only 9, considered comparative psychology and ethology synonyms.

CONCLUSIONS

The general conclusion is that comparative psychology is considered an important part of psychology and is considered important to biology and medicine as well. However, as in the United States, there does not seem to be a unanimous opinion about what comparative psychology is. There is a red thread, a thread of evolutionary context, however, running through all the opinions, no matter how they varied. From this base, comparative psychology can made a unique, characteristic contribution to investigations in many areas: origin of culture (the use of tools and the transfer of information); behavioral genetics; the origin of consciousness; the asymmetry of the brain; nonverbal communication and language; the function of sleep; learning in connection with brain function, etc.

Much of this investigation has, and would have, an interdisciplinary character. Comparative psychology contributes to the theoretical insights and practical applications that would result from such investigations. However, in the Netherlands today there are few psychologists working in the area of comparative psychology, and the few places in which they work are being threatened with extinction. It would be a real loss if their scientific endeavors were to disappear from the universities in the Netherlands.

Finally, we wish to put the results of this survey before a wider public than that of the practicing psychologist. They are important for all those who are interested in understanding how scientific investigations are administered and how decisions are made about education in the various scientific disciplines. Comparative psychological investigations as such are not clearly identified and are not well known; as a result they do not get their fair share of public support.

SUMMARY

This article is based on the results of a survey on comparative psychology conducted among investigators of animal psychology. Psychologists play a modest but important role in the study of animal behavior.

ACKNOWLEDGMENT

The authors thank Professor E. Tobach for her critical comments and Dr. G. Vroman for the translation of the Dutch text.

REFERENCES

Beach, F. A. (1950). The snark was a boojum. *American Psychologist, 5,* 115–124.
Demarest, J. (1980). The current status of comparative psychology in the American Psychological Association. *American Psychologist, 11,* 980–990.
Dewsbury, D. A. (1973). Comparative psychologists and their quest for uniformity. *Annals of the New York Academy of Sciences, 223,* 147–167.
Schneirla, T. C. (1966). Behavioral development and comparative psychology. *Quarterly Review of Biology, 41,* 283–302.
Snowdon, C. T. (1983). Ethology, comparative psychology, and animal behavior. *Annual Review of Psychology, 34,* 63–94.
Washburn, M. F. (1917). The animal mind. New York: Macmillan (First ed.: 1908).

17 Comparative Psychology in the United Kingdom

Robert A. Boakes
University of Sussex, England

19TH CENTURY BACKGROUND

The study of natural history had long been a strong tradition within British intellectual life well before the middle of the 19th century when debates over evolution made it a matter of interest to almost everyone. In addition to collecting fossils or plants, beetles or butterflies, the country clergymen or rich gentlemen who acquired a passion for the study of nature also recorded their observations of interesting examples of animal behavior. Such observations suddenly gained great theoretical significance in the context of Darwin's theories on the nature of instinctive behavior first appearing in the *Origin of Species* (1859), and then in the context of his arguments for mental continuity between animals and man in the *Descent of Man* (1871).

Comparative psychology in the United Kingdom began as a systematic study when Darwin and his followers looked for good examples of intelligent behavior on the part of animals in order to bolster their argument that the human mind was a product of the same evolutionary forces that produced an eye or a fin. This search was intended to refute the counterargument by Wallace, codiscoverer with Darwin of the principle of natural selection, that the human mind could not be explained by natural principles alone (see Boakes, 1984). Because the collection of appropriate specimens, whether geological or anatomical, had provided the main empirical basis for Darwin's theory of organic evolution, it was presumed to be the best way to understand mental evolution. Consequently, great importance and scientific respectability was attached to the casual reports on the habits and clever acts of pets, zoo captives, and other animals that have been popular in every age but not usually taken so seriously. The systematic presentation of such

223

evidence by Romanes in *Animal Intelligence* (1882) was directly encouraged by Darwin and marked the high point of this approach.

The British tradition in natural history also included the occasional ingenious experiment intended to settle some crucial point. Two notable examples in this tradition date from the 1870s. One study was that of Spalding (1873) who set out to test whether young birds are innately able to avoid obstacles, locate the source of auditory signals such as the sound of their mother, recognise predators, or fly; in the course of these experiments he stumbled upon the phenomenon of imprinting and published the first detailed account. The other impressive experimental study of behavior from this era was that of Lubbock whose account of the social insects in *Ants, Bees and Wasps* (1882) included reports of color discrimination training and maze learning.

By the 1890s it no longer seemed likely that any systematic survey of anecdotal evidence on animal intelligence would add much to the understanding of how the human mind had evolved. Another issue had come into prominence in evolutionary theory; this was the role of Lamarckian inheritance in the origin of instinctive behavior. Darwin had accepted both the natural selection of instincts and, as well as Lamarck and most other 19th century biologists, some genetic transmission of habits acquired during an individual's lifetime. By 1890 defenders of Darwin's dual theory of instinct, such as Romanes, were becoming embarassed by the lack of evidence in support of Lamarckian inheritance. In this instance the issue was not to be settled by naturalistic observations but only by careful experiment.

A key role in transforming comparative psychology in Britain from a branch of natural history to an experimental science was played by Lloyd Morgan. In his *Introduction to Comparative Psychology* (1894) he displayed a much more skeptical attitude towards anecdotal evidence than that of his former colleague, Romanes. This book introduced "Morgan's Canon," the special version of Occam's razor, which presumes that, as a result of the principles of natural selection, an animal's behavior is more likely to be a product of simple than of complex processes. In particular, he discussed the way that habitual skills could be gradually acquired by a process of trial-and-error with accidental success so that the end product might be the kind of intelligent performance that so impressed Romanes' correspondents. Two years later Morgan published a version of the lectures he had given in the United States on *Habit and Instinct* (1896). This book reviewed the evidence from animal behavior making Lamarckian inheritance unlikely in a way that led to a distinction between innate and learned behavior of the kind that has been maintained ever since by the majority of British and American psychologists.

Morgan's arguments were supported by experiments on early learning in chicks and other birds, as well as systematic observations of his pet dog. However, although—or, perhaps, because—he acquired an administrative position of great influence in his University College of Bristol, he did not establish a research tradition. At the turn of the century there was no institutional base in Britain for experimental work in comparative psychology. Whereas psychology laboratories were becoming numerous in the expanding university systems of North America, they hardly existed in the United Kingdom. At the same time departments of physiology or zoology in general had limited facilities and little interest in behavior. There was no British equivalent to the elaborate physiological laboratory in St. Petersburg where Pavlov was beginning his study of conditioning at this time.

Comparative psychology essentially disappeared from Britain for the first half of this century. The only laboratory study of animal behavior that stands out from this long era is that of Grindley, a student of Morgan who worked first in Bristol and then in the Psychological Laboratory at Cambridge. In extending Morgan's ideas of trial-and-error learning Grindley (1927) analysed the distinction between instrumental and Pavlovian conditioning and later obtained results on shaping head-turns in the guinea pig that anticipated Skinner's work on operant conditioning (Grindley, 1932).

THE MID-20TH CENTURY REVIVAL: 1949–1976

Psychology slowly became established in British universities during the early part of the 20th century. Departments of psychology were neither large nor numerous, but by the time of the Second World War the subject had at least an institutional footing in two of the largest and most influential English universities, Cambridge and London, and by 1947 at the third, Oxford. During the war almost all academic psychologists were employed on some kind of war-related work, notably on problems in perception and in the acquisition and performance of motor skills. By the late 1940s many British psychologists began to turn to other areas and to take interest in the new ideas on psychology coming from across the Atlantic and the developments in ethology that had taken place in continental Europe.

Ethology

A key event in British ethology was the arrival in Oxford in 1949 of Tinbergen, following almost 20 years of research on animal behavior in his native Holland (Thorpe, 1979). Two years later he published *The Study of Instinct* and his research group within Oxford's zoology department continued to study many of the topics covered by this influential book, including behavioral development in birds and behavioral ecology. At Cambridge, Thorpe had switched from insect physiology to ornithology and by 1943 had started his research on the relationship between learning and instinct in birds that included his pioneering studies of birdsong. In 1950 he set up a 4-acre "ornithological field station" at

Madingley, a few miles outside Cambridge, and this later became the Subdepartment of Animal Behaviour. The staff at the field station included Hinde, Matthews, and Marler.

Tinbergen's arrival in Oxford was by no means the only link with continental ethology. There were considerable personal contacts with ethologists in Holland, Germany, and Austria, which were maintained by regular international conferences from 1949 onwards. The greatest influence on British studies of animal behavior was Lorenz, and his key papers from the 1930s became widely read (Thorpe, 1979). The conflict between his theories of behavior and those of the American learning theorists, already familiar in Britain, plus his own research on imprinting (Lorenz, 1935), appears to have led to the huge interest in this topic in the late 1950s.

Learning Theory

An important sign of the revival of interest in animal behavior was the founding of a journal in 1953, the *British Journal of Animal Behaviour,* which a few years later was renamed simply, *Animal Behaviour.* It is significant that the first volume of this journal contained a paper by Hebb on "Heredity and environment in mammalian behaviour" (Hebb, 1953). Hebb's ideas on this question, his attempt to synthesize ideas from behaviorism and Gestalt psychology, and his deployment of animal data in analysing problems in human psychology, as in his *Organization of Behavior* (1949) were a major transatlantic influence on British psychology. The conceptual issues dividing Hullian learning theory (Hull, 1943; 1952) from its various opponents were of particular interest to a group of psychologists at Oxford. From 1953 Deutsch published a series of papers on maze learning in the rat that culminated in his *Structural Basis of Behaviour* of 1960. Such interests were transmitted from Oxford to Cambridge by A. J. Watson who supervised a series of PhD theses there on various aspects of learning theory.

When Deutsch left Oxford for California and physiological psychology, behavioral research within the psychology department was continued by Sutherland whose work on discrimination learning in the rat and the octopus concentrated mainly on the nature of perceptual processes in animals (e.g., Sutherland, 1957) and the role of attentional mechanisms in learning (e.g., Sutherland, 1959). Expansion of higher education in the United Kingdom during the late 1960s led both to the foundation of psychology departments within already established universities—for example, at the University of Birmingham—and to the inclusion of psychology within some of the new universities. The University of Sussex was the first of these new universities to be built and its School of Biological Sciences included an Experimental Psychology group from the beginning. Sutherland became its first psychology professor in 1965 and established animal psychology as one of the main research areas of the new laboratory. This was marked by an international conference at Sussex in 1967 on discrimination learning by animals (Gilbert & Sutherland, 1969), which was the first major meeting to be devoted to animal psychology in the United Kingdom.

After Sutherland's departure from Oxford, research there on animal learning was continued for a while by his former student, Mackintosh, until the latter left to go to Canada. Despite his absence overseas, Mackintosh continued to be a major influence in British psychology, partly through his joint book with Sutherland on attentional theories of discrimination learning (Sutherland & Mackintosh, 1971) and later through the draft chapters of his major work, *The Psychology of Animal Learning* (Mackintosh, 1974), which were circulated prior to his return to England and a chair at Sussex in 1973. The combination of Oxford discrimination learning with the Yale analysis of classical conditioning by Rescorla and Wagner, which became well known in Britain following their attendance at conferences at Sussex during the 1970s (Boakes & Halliday, 1972; Dickinson & Boakes, 1979), gave rise to a cognitive tradition in the study of associative learning, which has remained the mainstream of research on animal learning in the United Kingdom (Dickinson, 1980; Mackintosh, 1983).

Operant Conditioning

At least half of the contributors to the 1967 Sussex conference on discrimination learning were psychologists who had been greatly influenced by the work of Skinner. During the early 1950s Hurwitz had introduced operant conditioning methods into the United Kingdom (e.g., Hurwitz, 1953). A decade later there were sufficient people with an active interest in Skinner's approach to psychology for Hurwitz to found the Experimental Analysis of Behaviour Group in 1965. Since that date the regular meetings of this informal group have provided a forum for research on conditioning and animal psychology, whether Skinnerian in outlook or not.

Many of the first wave of British operant conditioners, including Hurwitz, emigrated to North America, leaving only a few universities in which an active research laboratory using such methods continued to flourish during the 1970s. These included: Exeter, where the operant laboratory founded by Reid initially concentrated on problems in discrimination learning, but more recently under Lea's direction has been mainly concerned with the relationship between reinforcement schedules and theories of foraging; Bangor in North Wales, where the laboratory has concentrated on the study of time-based schedules, initially under Harzem, and lately under Lowe, emphasizing comparative studies of conditioning in experiments employing both adult and very young humans; and Birmingham, where much of Blackman's research was in behavioral pharmacology, before he moved to Cardiff.

Primate Behavior and Physiological Psychology

The third major American tradition involving animal research to be transplanted to the United Kingdom during the 1950s, in company with learning theory and operant conditioning, was that strand of physiological psychology begun by Lashley. Weiskrantz set up a primate colony in Cambridge's psychology department in the late 1950s and started a research program whose main aim has been to study those parts of the monkey's brain involved in visual perception. A few years later this laboratory was transferred to Oxford when Weiskrantz became professor of psychology there. Although vision has remained the main topic of interest to Oxford psychologists working with monkeys, research there has also examined other kinds of psychological function including problem solving and complex learning and memory.

Except for Oxford, there has been little psychological research involving primates in England, but some in Scotland where monkeys have been maintained in the psychology departments of both Stirling and Edinburgh Universities. Monkey colonies primarily intended for more ethological research were maintained briefly at Bristol in the early 1960s and also at Madingley where the principle study was of mother–infant interactions in rhesus monkeys (e.g., Hinde, 1977).

Behavioral Ecology

The most recent distinctive research tradition in the study of animal behavior to take root in the United Kingdom had its origins in Hamilton's (1964) theoretical paper on kin selection and studies by Crook (1964) of social organization in the weaver bird. Although sharing common interests and approaches with American sociobiology (Wilson, 1975), this tradition has, to a large extent, been home grown. Its center has become Oxford's zoology department. In contrast to Tinbergen's interest in experimental analysis, development, and proximate explanations of behavior, this tradition has been very strongly driven by evolutionary theory and has concentrated almost exclusively on functional explanations. In 1973 Maynard-Smith at Sussex argued for the importance of games theory in understanding the evolution of behavioral mechanisms (Maynard-Smith & Price, 1973; also Maynard-Smith, 1976) and this was followed 3 years later by the most widely read book in this tradition, Dawkins' *The Selfish Gene,* which very powerfully placed the general study of behavior within current evolutionary theory. These theoretical ideas stimulated an expansion of empirical work on animal behavior, which has concentrated on kin selection, parenting, and foraging (Krebs & Davies, 1978; Lea, 1984).

This brief account of the revival of behavioral studies in the United Kingdom has been organized in terms of distinct research traditions partly for convenience of exposition. The disadvantages are that this leaves out the contributions of individuals who cannot be easily compartmentalized and that it may give an exaggerated view of the isolation of each tradition. On this latter point it must be emphasized that there was considerable cross fertilization of ideas. Thus, in the late 1950s the relationship between learning and instinct was of joint concern to psychologists and ethologists at Cambridge (e.g., Thorpe, 1956; Thorpe and Zangwill, 1961). At Oxford, MacFarland's studies of competition between motivational systems and interest in the application of control theory to the analysis of behavior began in the Psychology Department and continued when he became a member of the Zoology Department. The meetings of both the Experimental Analysis of Behaviour Group and of the Experimental Psychology Society provided regular opportunities for animal psychologists to exchange notes on research.

Finally, it is worth noting that there has been little comparative psychology in the strict sense of carrying out direct comparisons between the psychological abilities or mechanisms of different species. One of the few examples of this kind of research carried out by British psychologists is the octopus work already referred to. Another example has been the analysis of reversal learning, probability learning, and contrast phenomena by Mackintosh and his colleagues (e.g., Mackintosh, 1969; Mackintosh & Lord, 1973), that addressed the claims concerning phyletic differences in learning made by Bitterman (1965); however, much of this research was carried out in Canada. Despite the low incidence of comparative studies of this strict kind in Britain, a major survey of such research has recently been carried out by Macphail (1982) who documents in detail the failure to find systematic differences in learning ability across species and to make much sense of the relationship between brain and behavior by the use of comparative methods. In general, animal psychology in Britain has been comparative in the broad sense of trying to elucidate the nature of a particular psychological phenomenon by studying the behavior of just one or two species, and in most cases with only a distant aim of relating such findings to the understanding of the human mind.

THE CURRENT SCENE

As in many other countries, the general expansion of higher education in the 1960s supported a rapid growth of research in the United Kingdom. In particular, this period saw a considerable increase in the number and size of psychology departments that allowed the scientific developments described earlier to flourish. The energy crisis of 1974 put an end to expansion and heralded a series of financial cuts, culminating in special measures designed to reduce the number of university faculty positions during the 3-year period ending in 1984. Within psychology, comparative psychology was viewed as more expensive, of less practical relevance, and less attractive to undergraduates than other areas. Where new academic appointments have been made over the past few years, these have been primarily in developmental, social, or human cognitive psychology; of late there has been within the United Kingdom considerable interest in those aspects of cognition related to artificial intelligence and information technology.

The consequence for comparative psychology of these general developments in the past 10 years has been a gradual reduction in the number of doctoral students in animal research, fewer postdoctoral positions in the area, and almost no young scientist appointed to a tenured teaching post in a British university whose primary research area could be described as comparative psychology. The situation in zoology departments has not been very different, although there has probably been more sustained activity in behavioral research carried out by people employed on short-term research grants, particularly in the area of behavioral ecology. It is probable that the following survey covers a somewhat lower volume of research than in the previous 5 years.

To obtain a quantitative picture of the specific research interests of comparative psychologists in the United Kingdom, I surveyed typical journals, dating from 1980 through 1984, in which British psychologists publish their research. The only journal published in the United Kingdom to be included was the *Quarterly Journal of Experimental Psychology* (QJEP), which is the organ of the Experimental Psychology Society, an organization roughly equivalent to the Psychonomic Society in the United States, but with a membership of less than 500. In 1981 this journal divided into two separate parts, with Part B titled "Comparative and Physiological Psychology." As suggested by the following figures, this journal publishes the largest number of papers reporting research on comparative psychology carried out in the United Kingdom. Similarly, *Animal Behaviour,* the organ of the Association for the Study of Animal Behaviour, contains the largest number of papers on behavior from British zoology and ethology departments. However, this was not included in the present survey, because the majority of papers over the past few years have, at best, a very distant relationship to psychology and it was not obvious what coherent and easily employed criteria might be devised for deciding whether a particular paper in *Animal Behaviour* should be counted as one on comparative psychology. For similar reasons, the third British publication considered, the general science periodical *Nature,* was also not included in my survey.

A British psychologist deciding to publish abroad will almost certainly submit a paper to an American journal. Those included in the present survey were: the *Journal of the Experimental Analysis of Behavior* (JEAB), which is most frequantly chosen for research on reinforcement schedules; the *Journal of Experimental Psychology: Animal Behavior Processes,* (JEP), which at least during the period considered was preferred for research on associative learning; *Learning and Motivation* (L&M), in which British psychologists published on a range of topics somewhat wider than in JEP, including studies of spatial learning; *Animal Learning and Behavior* (AL&B), for shorter papers over as wide a range as QJEP; and finally the *Journal of Comparative Psychology* or *Journal of Comparative and Physiological Psychology* through 1982. The general science journal *Science* was not included, but few British psychologists publish in it. The aforementional list tends both to underestimate research on the ethological end of psychology and also that on the physiological end, which is published over a wide spread of neuroscience journals. Another bias is towards experimental rather than theoretical work; thus, for example, papers by Plotkin and Odling-Smee of London and Brunel Universities on the evolutionary context in which to consider mechanisms of learning did not come within this survey.

My search yielded a total of 110 papers. In order of frequency of papers reporting research from British laboratories the total was made up as follows: QJEP, 58; JEAB, 16; AL&B, 13; L&M, 8; JCP, 8; and JEP, 7. The distribution over journals is no doubt of far less interest to most readers that the distribution over topics and the remainder of this report describes this. For convenience of presentation papers were grouped into the following categories: Reinforcement schedules (24); Classical conditioning (24); Instrumental conditioning (18); Memory (11); Discrimination learning (10); Spatial learning (7); and Early learning/Developmental (7). This left nine papers uncategorized. The distinctions drawn between these categories should become apparent in the following descriptions of specific research issues.

Reinforcement Schedules.   A large proportion of the papers in this category were concerned with the behavior of rats on time-based schedules. Research of this kind involving a single response was reported by Wearden at Manchester, Keenan and Leslie at the New University of Ulster, and by Lowe at the University College of North Wales in Bangor. Another major concern has been the analysis of behavior when two time-based or other schedules are cocncurrently operating; the test of Herrnstein's matching law under such conditions has been pursued, for example, by Bradshaw and his colleagues also at the University of Manchester.

The latter have extended this research into the study of human schedule performance and found very close correspondence between rats and people in this respect. This has been challenged by Lowe and others at Bangor who find strong resemblance between human and nonhuman behavior on simple reinforcement schedules only if the humans are young infants; once language is acquired, they find children to be different from any other species in the patterns of responding they display.

A quite different approach to the study of schedules has been taken by Roper at the University of Sussex. He has reported a series of experiments on the inducement by reinforcement schedules of various kinds of independent activities, such as drinking, wheel running, and chewing, in rats and gerbils.

Classical Conditioning.   A very large part of British research on this topic has been devoted to the development, testing, and comparison of two major theories of associative learning, which differ largely in the functions they assign to attentional mechanisms: the theory of Mackintosh, previously at Sussex and now at Cambridge, and that of Hall and Pearce, at the Universities of York and Cardiff (see Dickinson, 1980; Mackintosh, 1983). Experimental studies of potentiation, blocking, posttrial surprise, latent inhibition, the role of orienting responses and of context conditioning, and other theroetically important phenomena have been undertaken by the authors of these theories and many others including, in particular, Dickinson at Cambridge. One of the latter's special interests has been inihibitory learning and this has also attracted studies by Mackintosh, E. Gaffan at the University of Reading, and Nieto at Sussex.

Another topic, which has also long been of interest to British learning theorists, is partial reinforcement. Much of the psychopharmacological research of Gray and his colleagues, previously at Oxford and now at London, has been concerned with the brain mechanisms underlying the effects of partial reinforcement and frustration. Recently Pearce and Kaye have supported a new attentional analysis of some effects of partial reinforcement.

One can study the behavioral consequences as well as enquire into the mechanisms and conditions responsible for the development of associations. The major British study of this kind has been the series of experiments on autoshaping in rats by Davey and Cleland at the City University, London that has emphasized the function of specific motivational systems in determining an animal's response to signals for food or water.

Davey has also extended the associative learning approach to the study of human classical conditioning using galvanic skin response measures. In a related development Dickinson has asked whether current learning theories can account for the way different contingencies alter subjects' judgments about the effectiveness of their actions when playing a video game.

Instrumental Conditioning.   A notable feature of recent learning research in the United Kingdom has been the application of principles gained from the study of classical conditioning to the analysis of instrumental conditioning. This was initiated by the work of Mackintosh on the overshadowing of response-reinforcer learning by stimulus relationships, an approach that has been applied to punishment by Goodall at Sussex, continued by Hall and reexamined by Lea, Tarpy, and Midgley at the University of Exeter. Another aspect to this approach has been taken in a series of experiments by Adams, Dickinson, and Nicholas at Cambridge on the effect on an instrumental response of changing the value of the reinforcing event after the response has been established.

An allied topic has been interactions between classical and instrumental conditioning, particularly in the case where classically conditioned stimuli are superimposed on a positively reinforced instrumental baseline. The conventional view that the effects of such superimposition are best understood in terms of response interactions has been challenged by Edgar, Hall, and Pearce at York, by Holman and Mackintosh at Sussex, and Lovibond at Cambridge. Each of these studies has described conditions in which a positive conditioned stimulus facilitates instrumental responding in a way that cannot easily be accounted for in terms of response additivity and has supported various associative or Konorskian alternative explanations.

Instrumental conditioning has also been approached from perspectives other than that of associative learning or the analysis of reinforcement schedules described earlier. The question of whether the law of effect is best considered as reflecting molecular contiguity processes has been examined in different ways by Evenden and Robbins at Cambridge and by Thomas at Birmingham. Thus, the latter has shown that the short-term consequences of a response are much more important in predicting subsequent performance than the overall response-reinforcement contingency.

Memory. It came as a surprise to me to discover the relatively large proportion of papers devoted to the study of memory in animals. These have encompassed a wide variety of methods and theoretical approaches. Colwill and Dickinson at Cambridge and Macphail and Mitchell at York have examined short-term memory in the pigeon, the former for the light it might throw on associative learning and the latter as part of a general investigation into functional localization in the avian brain. Thomas, together with Lieberman and other colleagues at the University of Stirling, has examined the ability of rats to recall previous events in order to understand the role of special "marking" events in enabling their subjects to learn discriminations despite long delays of reinforcement. Yet another approach to short-term memory has been taken by Robertson and Garrud at the University of St. Andrews in employing a latent inhibition procedure to look at memory for a flavor in the conditioning of flavor aversions.

Perhaps the most concentrated and original study of recognition memory is represented by D. Gaffan's studies at Oxford of both rats and rhesus monkeys. This work has been largely motivated by the aim of understanding the function of the septo-hippocampal-fornix systems; Gaffan has claimed that to understand the effects of fornix lesions in monkeys an important distinction must be made between their recognition of an object as familiar and recall of any voluntary action they have made previously in relation to the object.

Spatial Learning. Since Olton and Samuelson (1976) it has been common to distinguish an animal's memory for where it has been or where things are, i.e., spatial memory, from other forms of memory. And for the purposes of this survey it turned out to be appropriate to group experiments using Olton's approach with studies concerned with other aspects of spatial knowledge. One set of studies concerned with the behavior of rats on an Olton maze has been that of Einon at Durham, now at London University, in looking at variations in early experience, sex differences, and the effects of hippocampal lesions on the strategies her subjects employ in such a maze. Shettleworth and Krebs at Oxford used what, for psychologists, is an exotic species, the marsh tit, and a far more naturalistic setting than the eight-arm maze to examine the role of spatial memory in foraging.

The question of whether rats remember where reward has been, places they have visited, or simply display a form of spontaneous alternation by avoiding recently familiar places has been addressed in a striking series of experiments by E. Gaffan and Davies at Reading. Their results showed that it is inappropriate to describe a rat as displaying a "win-shift" strategy in an Olton maze, but rather they display strong spontaneous alternation slightly modified by "win-stay" behavior.

The different issue of whether animals reach locations by means of orienting with respect to individual landmarks or, more abstractly, by identifying locations by computing their relationship to distant cues has been studied by Morris at St. Andrews. He has used an ingenious approach that requires rats to swim to the location of a platform just beneath the surface of the opaque liquid (water with milk added) filling a tank. His subjects learn quickly to locate the platform in a manner that does not seem to rely on orientation with respect to particular landmarks.

Discrimination Learning.   This category includes a heterogeneous set of papers, many of which are concerned with identifying the behavioral effects of various kinds of lesion in rats and monkeys. A similar set of experiments has been carried out by Rawlins, Feldon, and Gray at Oxford to determine the effects of minor tranquilizers on discrimination learning in rats.

Research on this topic not concerned with the brain mechanisms involved has included the studies by Hall and Channell at York of preexposure to the stimuli and to context and the study by Anderson at Stirling of monkeys' responses to mirrors; he found that his subjects did not display the self-awareness reported for apes.

Early Learning/Developmental.   One study in this category has already been mentioned, that by Einon on early housing conditions and performance on Olton mazes. Others have examined undernourishment in infancy, as in the work by Stephens at Manchester, and the effects of sex hormones on the behavior of young animals, whether rats, as in Stevens' research at Nottingham or chicks, as in the research by Clifton and Andrew at Sussex. The early behavior of chicks has also been studied by Taylor and her colleagues at Leicester University.

CONCLUDING COMMENTS

Such a rapid skim over a wide range of disparate topics makes it pointless to draw any conclusions about the present state of comparative psychology in the United Kingdom. But it may be worth commenting that, despite the long absence of any such studies in the United Kingdom during the first half of this century, a surprisingly large amount of current research can be very directly related to the issues and approaches discussed by Morgan 90 years ago. Given this continuity, it is tempting to predict that for the next few decades research developments in British comparative psychology are likely to occur within the range of topics that comprise the present scene.

ACKNOWLEDGMENTS

I wish to thank Tim Roper, Nick Mackintosh, Geoff Hall and John Maynard-Smith for their help in preparing this chapter but should stress that the views it expresses are entirely my own.

REFERENCES

Bitterman, M. E. (1965). Phyletic differences in learning. *American Psychologist, 20,* 396–410.

Boakes, R. A. (1984). *From Darwin to behaviourism.* Cambridge: Cambridge University Press.

Boakes, R. A., & Halliday, M. S. (Eds.). (1972). *Inhibition and learning.* London: Academic Press.

Crook, J. H. (1964). The evolution of social organization and visual communication in the weaver bird (*Plocinae*). *Behavior Supplements, 10,* 1–78.

Darwin, C. (1859). *On the origin of species by means of natural selection.* London: Murray.

Darwin, C. (1871). *The descent of man and selection in relation to sex.* London: Murray.

Dawkins, R. (1976). *The selfish gene.* Oxford: Oxford University Press.

Deutsch, A. J. (1960). *The structural basis of behaviour.* Cambridge: Cambridge University Press.

Dickinson, A. (1980). *Contemporary animal learning theory.* Cambridge: Cambridge University Press.

Dickinson, A., & Boakes, R. A. (Eds.). (1979). *Mechanisms of learning and motivation.* Hillsdale, NJ: Lawrence Erlbaum Associates.

Gilbert, R. M., & Sutherland, N. S. (Eds.). (1969). *Animal discrimination learning.* London: Academic Press.

Grindley, G. C. (1927). The neural basis of purposive activity. *British Journal of Psychology, 18,* 168–188.

Grindley, G. C. (1932). The formation of a simple habit in guinea pigs. *British Journal of Psychology, 23,* 127–147.

Hamilton, W. D. (1964). The genetical theory of social behaviour. *Journal of Theoretical Biology, 7,* 1–16; 17–32.

Hebb, D. O. (1949). *The organization of behavior.* New York: John Wiley.

Hebb, D. O. (1953). Heredity and environment in mammalian behaviour. *British Journal of Animal Behaviour, 1,* 43–47.

Hinde, R. A. (1977). Mother–infant separation and the nature of inter-individual relationships: Experiments with rhesus monkeys. *Proceedings of the Royal Society of London B, 196,* 29–50.

Hull, C. L. (1943). *Principles of behavior.* New York: Appleton-Century-Crofts.

Hull, C. L. (1952). *A behavior system.* New Haven: Yale University Press.

Hurwitz, H. M. B. (1953). Response patterns in the rat. *British Journal of Animal Behaviour, 1,* 161–162.

Krebs, J. R., & Davies, N. B. (Eds.). (1978). *Behavioural ecology.* Oxford: Blackwell.

Lea, S. E. G. (1984). *Instinct, environment and behaviour.* London: Methuen.

Lorenz, K. (1935). Der kumpan in der umwelt des voegels. *Journal fuer Ornithologie, 83,* 137–214; 289–413.

Lubbock, J. (1882). *Ants, bees and wasps.* London: Kegan Paul, Trench, Truebner.

Mackintosh, N. J. (1969). Comparative studies of reversal and probability learning: Rats, birds, and fish. In R. M. Gilbert & N. S. Sutherland (Eds.), *Animal discrimination learning* (pp. 137–162; 175–185). London: Academic.

Mackintosh, N. J. (1974). *The psychology of animal learning.* London: Academic.

Mackintosh, N. J. (1983). *Conditioning and associative learning.* Oxford: Oxford University Press.

Mackintosh, N. J., & Lord, J. (1973). Simultaneous and successive contrast with delay of reward. *Animal Learning and Behavior, 1,* 283–286.

Macphail, E. M. (1982). *Brain and intelligence in vertebrates.* Oxford: Clarendon Press.

Maynard-Smith, J. (1976). Evolution and the theory of games. *American Scientist, 64,* 41–45.

Maynard-Smith, J., & Price, G. R. (1973). The logic of animal conflict. *Nature, 246,* 15–18.

Morgan, C. L. (1894). *An introduction to comparative psychology.* London: Scott.

Morgan, C. L. (1896). *Habit and instinct.* London: Edward Arnold.

Olton, D. S., & Samuelson, R. J. (1976). Remembrance of places passed: Spatial memory in rats. *Journal of Experimental Psychology: Animal Behavior Processes, 2,* 96–116.

Romanes, G. J. (1882). *Animal intelligence.* London: Kegan Paul, Trench.

Spalding, D. A. (1873). Instinct; with original observations on young animals. *Macmillans Magasine, 27,* 282–293. (Reprinted in the *British Journal of Animal Behaviour,* 1954, *2,* 1–11)

Sutherland, N. S. (1957). Visual discrimination of orientation and shape by *Octopus. Nature, 179,* 11–13.

Sutherland, N. S. (1959). Stimulus analysing mechanisms. *Proceedings of a symposium on the mechanization of thought processes* (Vol. 2, pp. 575–609). London: Her Majesty's Stationery Office.

Sutherland, N. S., & Mackintosh, N. J. (1971). *Mechanisms of animal discrimination learning.* London: Academic Press.

Thorpe, W. H. (1956). *Learning and instinct in animals.* London: Methuen.

Thorpe, W. H. (1979). *The origins and rise of ethology.* London: Heinemann Praeger.

Thorpe, W. H., & Zangwill, O. L. (Eds.). (1961). *Current problems in animal behaviour.* Cambridge: Cambridge University Press.

Wilson, E. O. (1975). *Sociobiology.* Cambridge, Mass: Harvard University Press.

Author Index

Subject Index

A

"Absolute" systems, 167
Actions, characteristics of, 208
Activity
    concept of, 204
    control and organization of, 206
    structure
        hierarchical, 205
        middle level of, 207–208
Adaptation, 26
Adaptive behavior, mediation of, 186
Anatomy, avian, 10
Anecdotal foundations, 131
Anecdotal school, 82–83
Animal behavior, new category of, 196
Argentina, study of animal behavior in, 173–
        174, 178–179
    historical perspective, 174–176
    recent developments, 176–178
Army testing program, 92, 95, 96, 97–98
Avian anatomy, 10
Avian behavior, 10–13
Avian taxonomy, 8–9

B

Behavior, 48–49, 50, 67t, 68t, 697, *See also*
        Animal behavior; Human behavior
    adaptive, 186
    avian, 10–13

comparison of, 219
    difficulties in, 195
    concept of, 204–205
    evolution of, 81–82
        Romanes' view, 82
    evolutionary theory and, 186
    instinctive, 27, 224
    offensive and defensive, 12
    primitive, 227–228
    social, 177–178
    variability of, 218
Behaviorism, nexus and origin of, 25–33
Bestiary, medieval, 8
Binet's test, 95
"Biological farm," 44
Biologist, influences, 128
Biology, systematic, 5
Bird calls, 12
Body
    separated from mind, Darwin's theory, 16–
        17
    surfaces, care of, 11

C

Captive animals, use in comparative psychol-
        ogy, 81–88
Casting, raptorial, 13
Change, 17
    Darwin's concept, 16
Chemotropism, 62t, 63t

243

DATE DUE